READERS' GUIDES TO ESSENTIAL CRITICISM SERIES

CONSULTANT EDITOR: NICOLAS TREDELL

Published

Thomas P. Adler	Tennessee Williams: *A Streetcar Named Desire/Cat on a Hot Tin Roof*
Pascale Aebischer	Jacobean Drama
Lucie Armitt	George Eliot: *Adam Bede/The Mill on the Floss/Middlemarch*
Simon Avery	Thomas Hardy: *The Mayor of Casterbridge/Jude the Obscure*
Paul Baines	Daniel Defoe: *Robinson Crusoe/Moll Flanders*
Brian Baker	Science Fiction
Annika Bautz	Jane Austen: *Sense and Sensibility/Pride and Prejudice/Emma*
Matthew Beedham	The Novels of Kazuo Ishiguro
Richard Beynon	D. H. Lawrence: *The Rainbow/Women in Love*
Peter Boxall	Samuel Beckett: *Waiting for Godot/Endgame*
Claire Brennan	The Poetry of Sylvia Plath
Susan Bruce	Shakespeare: *King Lear*
Sandie Byrne	Jane Austen: *Mansfield Park*
Sandie Byrne	The Poetry of Ted Hughes
Alison Chapman	Elizabeth Gaskell: *Mary Barton/North and South*
Peter Childs	The Fiction of Ian McEwan
Christine Clegg	Vladimir Nabokov: *Lolita*
Jay Corwin	Gabriel García Márquez
John Coyle	James Joyce: *Ulysses/A Portrait of the Artist as a Young Man*
Martin Coyle	Shakespeare: *Richard II*
Sarah Davison	Modernist Literatures
Sarah Dewar-Watson	Tragedy
Justin D. Edwards	Postcolonial Literature
Robert C. Evans	*Philip Larkin*
Michael Faherty	The Poetry of W. B. Yeats
Sarah Gamble	The Fiction of Angela Carter
Jodi-Anne George	*Beowulf*
Jodi-Anne George	Chaucer: The General Prologue to *The Canterbury Tales*
Jane Goldman	Virginia Woolf: *To the Lighthouse/The Waves*
Huw Griffiths	Shakespeare: *Hamlet*
Vanessa Guignery	The Fiction of Julian Barnes
Louisa Hadley	The Fiction of A. S. Byatt
Sarah Haggarty and Jon Mee	William Blake: *Songs of Innocence and Experience*
Geoffrey Harvey	Thomas Hardy: *Tess of the d'Urbervilles*
Paul Hendon	The Poetry of W. H. Auden
Terry Hodgson	The Plays of Tom Stoppard for Stage, Radio, TV and Film
William Hughes	Bram Stoker: *Dracula*
Stuart Hutchinson	Mark Twain: *Tom Sawyer/Huckleberry Finn*
Stuart Hutchinson	Edith Wharton: *The House of Mirth/The Custom of the Country*
Betty Jay	E. M. Forster: *A Passage to India*
Aaron Kelly	Twentieth-Century Irish Literature
Elmer Kennedy-Andrews	Nathaniel Hawthorne: *The Scarlet Letter*
Elmer Kennedy-Andrews	The Poetry of Seamus Heaney
Daniel Lea	George Orwell: *Animal Farm/Nineteen Eighty-Four*
Rachel Lister	Alice Walker: *The Color Purple*
Sara Lodge	Charlotte Brontë: *Jane Eyre*
Philippa Lyon	Twentieth-Century War Poetry
Merja Makinen	The Novels of Jeanette Winterson

Stephen Marino	Arthur Miller: *Death of a Salesman/The Crucible*
Britta Martens	The Poetry of Robert Browning
Matt McGuire	Contemporary Scottish Literature
Timothy Milnes	Wordsworth: *The Prelude*
Jago Morrison	The Fiction of Chinua Achebe
Merritt Moseley	The Fiction of Pat Barker
Pat Pinsent	Children's Literature
Carl Plasa	Toni Morrison: *Beloved*
Carl Plasa	Jean Rhys: *Wide Sargasso Sea*
Nicholas Potter	Shakespeare: *Antony and Cleopatra*
Nicholas Potter	Shakespeare: *Othello*
Nicholas Potter	Shakespeare's Late Plays: *Pericles/Cymbeline/The Winter's Tale/The Tempest*
Steven Price	The Plays, Screenplays and Films of David Mamet
Berthold Schoene-Harwood	Mary Shelley: *Frankenstein*
Nicholas Seager	The Rise of the Novel
Nick Selby	T. S. Eliot: *The Waste Land*
Nick Selby	Herman Melville: *Moby Dick*
Nick Selby	The Poetry of Walt Whitman
David Smale	Salman Rushdie: *Midnight's Children/The Satanic Verses*
Enit Steiner	Jane Austen: *Northanger Abbey/Persuasion*
Patsy Stoneman	Emily Brontë: *Wuthering Heights*
Susie Thomas	Hanif Kureishi
Nicolas Tredell	Joseph Conrad: *Heart of Darkness*
Nicolas Tredell	Charles Dickens: *Great Expectations*
Nicolas Tredell	William Faulkner: *The Sound and the Fury/As I Lay Dying*
Nicolas Tredell	F. Scott Fitzgerald: *The Great Gatsby*
Nicolas Tredell	Shakespeare: *A Midsummer Night's Dream*
Nicolas Tredell	Shakespeare: *Macbeth*
Nicolas Tredell	Shakespeare: The Tragedies
Nicolas Tredell	The Fiction of Martin Amis
David Wheatley	Contemporary British Poetry
Martin Willis	Literature and Science
Matthew Woodcock	Shakespeare: *Henry V*
Gillian Woods	Shakespeare: *Romeo and Juliet*
Angela Wright	Gothic Fiction
Michael Whitworth	Virginia Woolf: *Mrs Dalloway*

Forthcoming

Nick Bentley	Contemporary British Fiction
Kate Watson	Crime and Detective Fiction
Andrew Wylie and Catherine Rees	The Plays of Harold Pinter

Philip Larkin

ROBERT C. EVANS

Consultant Editor: NICOLAS TREDELL

BLOOMSBURY ACADEMIC
LONDON • NEW YORK • OXFORD • NEW DELHI • SYDNEY

BLOOMSBURY ACADEMIC
Bloomsbury Publishing Plc
50 Bedford Square, London, WC1B 3DP, UK
1385 Broadway, New York, NY 10018, USA
29 Earlsfort Terrace, Dublin 2, Ireland

BLOOMSBURY, BLOOMSBURY ACADEMIC and the Diana logo are trademarks of Bloomsbury Publishing Plc

First published in Great Britain 2017 by Palgrave
Reprinted by Bloomsbury Academic 2022

Copyright © Robert C. Evans 2017

Robert C. Evans has asserted his right under the Copyright, Designs and Patents Act, 1988, to be identified as Author of this work.

All rights reserved. No part of this publication may be reproduced or transmitted in any form or by any means, electronic or mechanical, including photocopying, recording, or any information storage or retrieval system, without prior permission in writing from the publishers.

Bloomsbury Publishing Plc does not have any control over, or responsibility for, any third-party websites referred to or in this book. All internet addresses given in this book were correct at the time of going to press. The author and publisher regret any inconvenience caused if addresses have changed or sites have ceased to exist, but can accept no responsibility for any such changes.

A catalogue record for this book is available from the British Library.

A catalog record for this book is available from the Library of Congress.

ISBN: HB: 978-1-137-51711-1
ISBN: PB: 978-1-137-51710-4

To find out more about our authors and books visit www.bloomsbury.com and sign up for our newsletters.

DEDICATION

As this book was being finished, we suddenly lost Taylor, one of our beloved dogs and one of the kindest, gentlest souls ever created. I have been very lucky to share so much of my life with such a loving, lovable creature. Ruth and I will miss him always.

CONTENTS

ACKNOWLEDGEMENTS   x

INTRODUCTION   1

Places Larkin's poetry in its biographical, cultural, and historical contexts, paying particular attention to his typical themes and stylistic traits and the specific characteristics of each of his major collections. Traces the trajectory of his career, from his early association with the new trend in mid-1950s poetry known as 'The Movement' to his eventual near-silence by the late 1970s. Discusses the controversies that arose after publication, in the early 1990s, of his selected letters and a major biography.

CHAPTER ONE   8

Larkin Arrives: The 1950s and 1960s

Discusses the rise of Larkin's reputation from the mid-1950s to the end of the 1960s – a rise fuelled by the publication of two of his most significant collections: *The Less Deceived* (1955) and *The Whitsun Weddings* (1964). Discusses commentary by (among many others) Richard Murphy, John Wain, Howard Sergeant, G. S. Fraser, William Stafford, Philip Gardner, and Keith Sagar.

CHAPTER TWO   28

Larkin Rises: The 1970s

Surveys the firm status Larkin achieved, during the 1970s, as perhaps the major English poet of his time. Discusses the impact of his last important collection, *High Windows* (1975), and the possible reasons for his eventual near-abandonment of poetry by the end of the decade. Analyses criticism by such writers as Anthony Thwaite, David Timms, Lolette Kuby, Hermann Peschmann, Bruce Martin, David Lodge, and David Cushman.

CHAPTER THREE 48

Larkin Triumphant: The 1980s

Comments on the irony that Larkin, now considered the most beloved of English poets, had by the early 1980s essentially ceased writing poems. Notes that after his death he was, if anything, even more revered than before, especially thanks to the 1988 appearance of his *Collected Poems*, which contained a number of previously unpublished and/or uncollected works. Commentary surveyed includes work by such authors as Grevel Lindop, Roger Elliott, Terry Whalen, Salem K. Hassan, G. Singh, Peter MacDonald Smith, and Janice Rossen.

CHAPTER FOUR 70

Larkin Under Siege: The 1990s

Recounts the controversy that arose in the early 1990s when Larkin's *Selected Letters* were published and were then soon followed by the publication of the first major biography. Both volumes revealed a Larkin who surprised and disappointed many readers because of his alleged racism, sexism, and apparent selfishness. Demonstrates that by the end of the decade, however, most critics had come to the conclusion that whatever his failings may have been as a person, he was still one of the best poets of his time. Commentators whose ideas are discussed include Stephen Watson, A. T. Tolley, Peter Snowdon, James Booth, Stephen Regan, Andrew Motion, Paul Volsik, and Andrew Swarbrick.

CHAPTER FIVE 94

Larkin Triumphant Once More: The 2000s

Explores the ways in which Larkin's reputation continued to recover from the blows it had suffered in the early 1990s. Critics now increasingly paid attention to the success of Larkin's poems as poems and to their thematic, stylistic, and technical complexities. Shows how Larkin was now often seen as ahead of his time in some of his basic philosophical attitudes and also discusses how some of his own explanations of his art were open to question. Critics whose views of Larkin are discussed include John Carey, Raphaël Ingelbien, Victoria Longino, Stephen Cooper, James Booth, Richard Bradford, Adrian Grafe, Tijana Stojković, Sisir Kumar Chatterjee, A. Banerjee, and John Osborne.

CHAPTER SIX 116
Newer Approaches to Larkin: The 2010s

Studies commentary from 2010 up to early 2016, showing the diversity of approaches that now existed to a writer increasingly seen, even more than before, as the major poet of his time. Analysts now tended to explore unexpected aspects of Larkin's works, such as his debts to Symbolism and Romanticism, the ways his writings might be seen as postmodern, and the ways his works lent themselves to analysis using recent critical theories, especially various kinds of particularly close (even deconstructive) reading. Analysts whose comments on Larkin are surveyed include Gillian Steinberg, M. W. Rowe, Peter Holbrook, Carol Atherton, John Osborne, James Booth, Ryan Hibbett, and István Rácz.

CONCLUSION 136

Discusses some reasons for Larkin's enduring popularity, providing an overview of his typical themes and stylistic traits and a survey of the development of his reputation. Offers suggestions about future directions for Larkin studies and the kinds of resources that might prove most helpful to readers in general and scholars in particular.

NOTES 142

SELECT BIBLIOGRAPHY 157

INDEX 164

ACKNOWLEDGEMENTS

I wish to thank Rachel Bridgewater and Nicolas Tredell for their encouragement and guidance. Nicolas in particular deserves thanks for his astonishingly quick replies to any queries and for his careful, thoughtful, and thorough attention to the manuscript. I am also deeply grateful to Karen Williams and Beth Parrish, intrepid interlibrary loan librarians at my university, who tracked down enormous numbers of articles with great speed and great grace under pressure.

Many thanks to Melissa Carden, my research assistant, and much love, as always, to my wife, Ruth.

INTRODUCTION

Philip Larkin is widely considered one of the very best English poets of the last 70 years. In fact, he is often mentioned as one of a handful of the best British poets of the twentieth century. And, more and more, he has come to be considered one of the finest writers of poetry *in the English language* during that same period. Although his first books of verse were largely ignored, the 1955 publication of *The Less Deceived* brought him growing attention and admiration. His stature as a much-loved but also highly respected poet was solidified in 1964 by the publication of his next collection, *The Whitsun Weddings*. This book sold remarkably well, indicating that Larkin was not a poet who appealed merely or mainly to academics or to the literary elite; instead, he was a poet who spoke movingly and memorably to numerous 'regular readers'. In 1974 he published his last collection, *High Windows*, which was again unusually popular and was greeted with great critical acclaim. By at least the mid-1970s and up until his death in 1985 (as well as thereafter), Larkin was widely regarded as not only the most respected but also the best-loved poet of his times. He was offered the post of Poet Laureate but declined, but in the last 20 years of his life (especially the last ten) he was showered with many other honours.

What caused the enormous popular and critical appeal of Larkin's verse? The simple answer is 'talent', or even 'genius'. Few poets know better than Larkin how to manipulate words, phrases, sounds, rhythms, and structures in ways that make them, in combination, unforgettable. A great poem by Larkin, once read, sticks in the mind and never leaves. But Larkin was (and is) also appealing because of the topics he addressed. These were the great themes explored by many previous poets before him, including love, death, loneliness, aspiration, disappointment, and mutability. Larkin, however, often gave these themes his own special twist. In his best works he wrote in ways that seemed to confront, honestly and directly, the lives and experiences of real people of his own day. But he did so with such genuine literary skill that his poems are likely to survive well beyond our era and speak to generations 'yet unborn'. Larkin is often accused of being a relentlessly 'dark' poet, one who is obsessed with ageing and death and disappointment. But Larkin is also often a very funny poet, as well as one who is rarely less than absolutely forthright and frank in describing life as it truly is, in all its complications and complexities. He writes well, but he also writes with unflinching candour and even bluntness. He understands human yearnings for consolation and peace, but he refuses simple consolations or easy pacifications. He is an immensely gifted writer with an astonishingly unblinkered vision – a fact that makes many of his poems (such as 'The Old Fools' or 'The Building' or 'Aubade') literally painful to read. His talent, however, also makes many of his works (such as 'Church Going', 'The Whitsun Weddings', or 'The Explosion') immensely beautiful.

Philip Arthur Larkin was born in Coventry, England, on 9 August 1922, the son of Sydney Larkin (1884–1948) and his wife Eva (1886–1977), who were also the parents by that time of a ten-year-old daughter named Catherine (or 'Kittie'). Biographers usually depict Sydney as a strong, forceful, if not overbearing character who exercised commanding authority over the people who worked for him in his role as Coventry City Treasurer.[1] Sydney Larkin was widely read in literature and encouraged his son to read widely, too. But the elder Larkin also admired the efficiency and perhaps even part of the ideology of Hitler's Germany during the 1930s and took Philip with him on visits there in 1936 and 1937. Larkin's mother, meanwhile, seems to have been a nervous, uncertain woman who was easily dominated by her husband. Biographers have argued that Philip inherited some of the complex traits of both his parents. Afflicted from childhood with a stammer that lasted into his early thirties, he developed an early passion for American jazz and a growing interest in, and talent for, writing. Several of his works – some of them surprisingly good – were published in the literary magazine of King Henry VIII School in Coventry, which he attended from 1930–40.

By September 1939, Britain was at war with Nazi Germany as part of the wider Second World War. Larkin, meanwhile, in 1940 entered St. John's College, Oxford University, where he pursued a degree in English Language and Literature. He made a number of close friendships, including one with Kingsley Amis, who would eventually (with Larkin's help) become an important novelist. In 1942, a physical exam determined that Larkin was unfit for military service (his eyesight was very poor). His love of jazz and literature dominated his time at Oxford, where he was part of a group of hard-drinking, facetious, but literary-minded undergraduates. During his time at college he continued to write poetry as well as prose fiction, including mock novels with lesbian overtones set in girls' schools, which were written (but not published until decades later) under the pseudonym 'Brunette Coleman'. The poetry of the great Irish bard William Butler Yeats was a major influence on Larkin's own poetry during this time – an influence he later claimed to regret. But Larkin was also at work on a serious novel, titled *Jill*. During the mid-to-late forties, he seems to have thought of himself first and foremost as an aspiring novelist.

But he also had a practical living to make. After being awarded a first-class degree (with honours) from Oxford in 1943, he returned to Coventry, lived with his parents while writing poems and continuing to work on *Jill*, and applied (unsuccessfully) for civil service jobs. By December he had secured a position as the town Librarian in Wellington, Shropshire, thus beginning (almost by accident) his long and highly successful career as one of the major librarians of his era. During 1944 he finished *Jill*, compiled a collection of poems titled *The North Ship*, and met Ruth Bowman, a young woman who was the first of his real romantic interests. The year 1945 saw the publication of *The North Ship* (which had little initial impact) as well as the completion of his second novel, *A Girl in Winter*.[2] In 1946, Larkin took a job as Assistant Librarian at University College, Leicester, where he met Monica Jones, the woman with whom he would be most closely involved (in complicated ways) for the rest of his life. During that same year, *Jill* appeared, and shortly thereafter, in 1947, *A Girl in Winter* was issued by Faber & Faber, one of England's major publishing houses.[3]

Larkin's growing success as a novelist was balanced by disappointment in placing his poetry. In 1948 a volume of his poems titled *In the Grip of Light* was rejected by all six of the major publishers to which it was submitted, and early in that same year Larkin's father died. Disappointed with this lack of enthusiasm for his poetry, and largely stymied in his work on further fiction, Larkin nevertheless began to prosper in his career as a librarian. In 1950 he took a job at Queen's University, Belfast, in Northern Ireland, where he stayed until 1955. There he made many friends and also became romantically involved with the young Winifred Arnott as well as with Patsy Strang, the wife of one of his closest colleagues. Patsy eventually became pregnant by Larkin but soon miscarried. Meanwhile, Larkin was continuing a long-distance relationship with Monica Jones. His love life, then as later, was highly complicated. Larkin had a strong sexual appetite but was (and remained) wary of marriage and of deep emotional entanglements. He wanted to devote his life, as much as possible, to his writing.

In 1951, he self-published a collection of verse titled *XX Poems*, but it quickly disappeared from view.[4] He continued writing, however, and, most crucially, began to develop the mature style for which he eventually became famous. He later claimed that he was saved from his earlier Yeatsian phrasing by discovering the poetry of Thomas Hardy, the great English poet with whom he had so much in common, not only in interests but in temperament. Although later critics have cautioned that the switch to Hardy was never as sudden or complete as Larkin let on, and although scholars have demonstrated many connections between his mature verse and the work of a wide variety of other writers, there seems little denying that Hardy had a major, and positive, impact on

Larkin's sense of the poet's job and how a poet should write. Rejecting both the ecstatic Romanticism of such writers as Dylan Thomas and the ultra-Modernism of such poets as Ezra Pound, Larkin increasingly turned to a kind of writing that seemed (by contrast) plain, straightforward, unvarnished, and accessible both in style and in subject matter. Suddenly, after decades of feeling that poets had become so much a part of the avant-garde that they had left 'regular readers' behind, increasing numbers of readers were discovering, in Larkin, a poet whom they could understand and who seemed to understand *them*.

The year 1955 was a great turning point in Larkin's life. In that year he accepted a position as Chief Librarian at the University of Hull, in north-eastern England – a place remote from literary London but a city that Larkin came (despite occasional grumbling) to love. He spent the rest of his life there, building (both literally and figuratively) one of the best academic libraries in the country. Over the next two decades he would preside over the construction of two stages of a massive library complex, greatly enhance the library's holdings, and see its staff swell as the number of students admitted to the university also greatly grew. Larkin sometimes complained about the need to work but was actually a very serious and successful professional. But his greatest accomplishments and recognitions – as a poet – were ushered in by the 1955 publication of a relatively short volume titled *The Less Deceived*.[5] Thanks to this book, by common agreement, the mature Philip Larkin first became widely known and broadly appreciated, partly because his phrasing seemed so refreshingly straightforward.

Yet Larkin was not alone in this new, stripped-down, less grandiloquent style of writing. In fact, he was quickly associated (not entirely by his own choosing) with a group of somewhat like-minded writers whom the press soon dubbed 'The Movement'. Many of these authors barely knew one another, and disputes about whether 'The Movement' actually existed in any real sense have occupied scholars for decades. It seems safe to say, however, that many of these poets and novelists (including such figures as Larkin's old friend Kingsley Amis and his new friend Robert Conquest, editor of an influential 1956 anthology of verse titled *New Lines*) did have much in common, and they were perceived as a part of a 'movement', if only briefly, when their work first began to attract wide attention. They were seen as bringing fresh voices and fresh perspectives to the literary scene, offering writing that was firmly rooted in the moods and experiences of their times and writing that seemed, above all, clear-sighted and honest.

Not everyone, of course, welcomed these new voices, and Larkin in particular came in for criticism from those who saw him as a traitor to the heritage of High Modernism (associated with Pound and T. S. Eliot) and as an author of diminished expectations who wrote poems that were willing to accept everyday life without trying to transform it or offer any larger, loftier vision. These critics attacked his style and his concern with traditional forms (including stanzas, rhyme, and metre) as retrograde, but they also often found his themes and his tone cramped, limited, gloomy, and self-pitying. They objected to his emphasis on ageing, death, disappointment, and other kinds of limitations, and they saw him as a spokesman not for a sophisticated international audience but for a kind of embarrassingly parochial 'Little Englandism' – middle-class in socio-economic status and low-brow in literary tastes.

Larkin, however, also had passionate advocates and defenders, and the more he wrote and published, the more assured his reputation became. In his mature period, he rarely composed quickly, and his surviving notebooks show how carefully and thoughtfully he revised, almost always waiting until he had achieved something truly worthwhile before venturing to publish. The appearance of his next major book, *High Windows*, in 1964 won him broad acclaim, unusually good sales, and, in 1965, the first of many subsequent major awards.[6] His early collection *The North Ship* was reissued, in 1966, with a typically self-deprecating introduction by Larkin himself,[7] and beginning in 1969 he received the first of what would eventually amount, over the years, to seven honorary doctoral degrees from various British universities, culminating in one from Oxford in 1984. But Larkin was not only writing poetry; he was also producing various essays and numerous reviews of books and of jazz. His collected music reviews were issued in 1970 as *All What Jazz*, a work whose introduction deliberately poked a finger in the eye of Modernism in all the arts, including music.[8]

Much the same kind of brazen impact was perceived, by many critics, when Oxford University Press, in 1973, published *The Oxford Book of Twentieth Century English Verse*, a controversial anthology edited by Larkin.[9] The fruit of several years of real labour, this work (an instant bestseller) gave him a chance to reassess, by inclusion and exclusion, the whole canon of modern English poetry. He stamped his own tastes on the book in ways that critics found either atrocious or attractive. In issuing both the volume on jazz and the Oxford anthology, Larkin knew he was risking a critical beating, but he was proud to stand up for aesthetic values that he sincerely admired, and he was also willing to make clear both his likes and dislikes. Later scholars have argued that Larkin in fact had more complicated tastes than either of these books implied, but by the mid-1970s he had become associated with anti-Modernism in more ways than one.

By this time, too, his politics seemed increasingly conservative and perhaps even right-wing. He saw England in the 1970s as a nation in decline, and he seemed to lament the perceived deterioration of traditional British values and ways of life. Never a religious believer, he nonetheless understood the attraction of spiritual ideals. But above all he became increasingly obsessed with ageing and death – especially his own. The 1974 appearance of *High Windows* (the last collection Larkin himself would oversee) was celebrated as the newest production of a poet who had, by this time, become a much-loved figure on the national and even international scene.[10] Larkin was seen as a quintessentially *English* writer, but by this time he was also increasingly seen abroad as one of the best writers of poetry in English. Some critics worried that by the time he had issued *High Windows* he had written himself into a corner from which he could not escape. In 1977 he published his last major poem ('Aubade') – a work so frank and unrelenting in confronting the inevitability and nothingness of death that Larkin seemed, to some, to have little alternative but to fall quiet and await his own demise.

And this, essentially, is what happened. He produced a few other poems after 'Aubade' (but none as great as that truly powerful masterwork), but more and more he came to feel that poetry had abandoned him. Rather than publishing just anything, though, he published almost nothing. His health declined, his depression deepened, and his love-life grew extraordinarily complicated (at one point he was simultaneously involved with three distinct, quite different kinds of women). He had long anticipated that he would die at age 63, the same age at which his father had passed away, and in December 1985 his worst fears came true. Terrified of death, he spoke his last words to an attending nurse in the middle of the night: 'I am going to the inevitable'.

The loss of Larkin was deeply painful for most people who cared about good poetry, especially in England but also abroad. As a poet Larkin had been relatively silent for years, but now he would be silent forever. He had in fact ensured part of that silence by begging that his remaining diaries be burned, and they were. But his will had been ambiguous about his surviving literary manuscripts, and eventually more and more of his previously unpublished writings found their way into print. A selection of previously unpublished or uncollected verse, for instance, appeared in the 1988 *Collected Poems*, edited by his friend and admirer Anthony Thwaite.[11] Despite complaints that Thwaite had reordered the poems so that they were printed, one by one, in chronological order (rather than as Larkin had arranged the already-published ones in the collections he had supervised), this book only seemed to solidify Larkin's standing as a major literary figure of his time. The 1980s ended with his reputation at perhaps its highest point ever.

But then, in 1992, Thwaite issued an edition of the *Selected Letters of Philip Larkin, 1940–1985*.[12] This book – huge but merely a sampling of the many, many letters Larkin had written to numerous correspondents – revealed a man whom many readers found, at least in parts, either disappointing or revolting. Even fervent admirers of Larkin were often saddened by the person who appeared in the letters. He had been strongly invested in pornography, which bothered some; but he also often seemed bitter, petty, manipulative, xenophobic, arguably sexist, and arguably racist. It was these latter two charges that caused many readers to turn away in disgust. Where it had once been common to praise Larkin unstintingly, he now came under bitter attack. And the situation was made even worse, in the eyes of many, by the 1993 publication of a huge biography by Andrew Motion, another of Larkin's friends. This book confirmed, for numerous readers, the disappointing findings suggested by the *Letters* and added many new details that made Larkin seem, to some, an unfortunately unsavoury figure.

Larkin did, however, have his defenders, especially among those who argued that he should be judged by the qualities of his writings rather than by flaws in his personality. And, as time wore on and more evidence appeared, even Larkin's life seemed more defensible. He had been much-loved, not only by his co-workers and literary colleagues but especially by the three different women who had been intimately involved with him in his later years. By the end of the 1990s, a Philip Larkin Society had been created and was flourishing. In 2005 and 2014, two new biographies (by Richard Bradford and James Booth, respectively) had appeared, and both presented Larkin more sympathetically than many thought Andrew Motion had. By this time, too, Larkin was increasingly recognised as a poet who, whatever his personal shortcomings, remained a great writer. He had devoted his life to his poetry, and now his poetry was giving him a kind of genuine life beyond death – the only sort of immortality, after all, that he had realistically hoped to achieve.

CHAPTER ONE

Larkin Arrives: The 1950s and 1960s

Much of the earliest commentary on Philip Larkin's poetry compared and contrasted his work with that of various predecessors and contemporaries. Early critics were especially interested in his similarities to – or differences from – important poets of the first half of the twentieth century. These included Hardy, Yeats, Eliot, Pound, Auden, and Dylan Thomas. Critics also often wanted to 'place' Larkin in relation to other writers emerging in the 1950s, including John Wain, Thom Gunn, Kingsley Amis, and Ted Hughes (to mention just a few). Larkin was often either praised or censured depending on critics' personal attitudes towards the kind of writing associated with a loose grouping of writers sometimes called 'The Movement'. Other issues explored by commentators in the 1950s and 1960s involved whether or not Larkin was 'developing' as a poet – that is, whether or not he was evolving in style, themes, and attitudes. Some critics argued that his vision was narrow, his tone monotonous, and his style repetitive. Others disagreed, arguing that all that mattered was his poetry's consistent excellence and the ways he honestly and even profoundly addressed genuine human concerns. Commentary during the late 1950s and throughout the 1960s tended to focus on two of his major collections – *The Less Deceived* (1955) and *The Whitsun Weddings* (1964). That second collection, in particular, helped win him an especially wide readership and helped earn him broad critical acclaim.

Larkin in the Mid- to Late-1950s

Anthony Hartley, writing in 1954, was one of the first critics who saw both Larkin and the 'Movement' as reacting against the kind of 'wild and whirling' Romanticism associated with Dylan Thomas and mystical flights of fancy. Instead these new authors attempted to write poetry that was calm rather than high-flown, colloquial rather than lofty, understated and ironic rather than excited and prophetic. (Hartley, however, was also one of the earliest of many critics to note that Larkin's range of tones and topics was wider than those of some other 'Movement' writers.)[1] Donald Davie spoke for many in characterising the 'Movement' poets as 'sceptical, robust, ironic, [and] prepared to be as comfortable as possible in a wicked, commercial, threatened world which doesn't look, anyway, as if it's going to be changed much by a couple of handfuls of young English writers'.[2] Some readers welcomed this new kind of writing; others disdained it. Larkin, as one its best representatives, was either celebrated or condemned accordingly.

Writing in 1955, Richard Murphy was one of the first critics to give Larkin himself sustained attention. He praised Larkin for writing (realistically and without moaning or protest) about the kinds of lives most people lived, although he did call Larkin's 'Mr. Bleaney' an example of a 'poetry of despair'. In an especially succinct summary of Larkin's typical tone and themes, Murphy asserted that:

> ■ Larkin is a poet who portrays things as they are with thorough accuracy. He does not try to change things, but express them. It is an austere satisfaction he gives. He writes, even in verse, in the bare idiom of his contemporaries, with conversational manners, and a deliberate dryness, to express a problem with flawless precision. But he surpasses his generation, now and then, in writing memorable lines and in depth of feeling. Behind the shrug of his shoulders is not a witticism, but actual suffering; behind his caustic comments or carefully noted situations lie experience and imagination.[3] □

Here, then, is a note already foreshadowed by Hartley and repeated in much subsequent criticism: Larkin not only resembles many 'Movement' writers but also surpasses them. He is both typical and distinct. Thus an anonymous reviewer for the important *Times Literary Supplement* asserted, also in 1955, that Larkin resembled his contemporaries in various ways but managed to avoid the unconvincing 'posture of cynical toughness' that hampered much of their writing. The reviewer argued that *The Less Deceived* 'should establish ... Larkin as a poet of quite exceptional importance; he has a mature vision and the power to render it variously, precisely and movingly'.[4] By mid-July 1956, a prominent profile of Larkin called him 'one of the most successful poets of his generation' and praised him not only for rejecting the 'formless mystifications of the last 20 years' but also for bringing English poetry back into touch with a 'middle-brow public'.[5]

Meanwhile, in the United States, Larkin was beginning, in 1956 and 1957, to receive similarly high praise, especially when compared to various English contemporaries.[6] John Holloway, interestingly, saw the rise of the middle-class 'Movement' writers as indicating, perhaps, the breakdown of the English class system. In any case, he found Larkin's verse more 'immediately endearing' than that of some other 'Movement' authors, and he was one of the first early commentators to single out Larkin's poem 'Church Going' for especially high praise.[7] Again and again, in subsequent criticism, this is the poem that would be spotlighted as evidence of Larkin's unusual poetic talent. Critics often discussed it in real detail and usually treated it without hesitation as an instant classic.

In a long and important article from 1957, John Wain set 'the Movement' within the larger context of 'The Immediate Situation' of English verse. Writing for an American readership, Wain (as usual) singled out Larkin for special commendation, arguing that if 'there is an *avant-garde* in English poetry, its chief document is Larkin's volume *The Less Deceived*'. He extolled Larkin's thoughtfulness, and he was one of the first critics to trace the poet's development – and improvement – from his first book to his latest. Wain found Larkin's earliest published poems small but fully finished and thought they reflected the influence of such earlier writers as Yeats, Housman, and even Hardy, with Hardy eventually overtaking the other two. Thus 'an ironic, rueful, self-parodying note crept in more and more, and to make room for this alongside the earlier qualities of tenderness and reflective melancholy, the texture of the verse was loosened, giving a more mobile and fluent effect'.[8]

Wain was one of the first of many critics to see time, history, and mutability as key themes of Larkin's verse. He noted the poet's strong focus on individual speakers who, nevertheless, often adopt a tone of reticence or impersonality:

> ■ Part of the paradoxical structure of a typical Larkin poem is this placing of the emphasis squarely on a central figure who then uses every device to evade and disperse it (by the use of 'we' for 'I', for instance, in the love poems). ... It is the exact opposite of the large personal claim that one feels in Romantic poetry.[9] □

Wain then explicated and defended 'Church Going', calling it an example of the 'bedrock honesty' often found in Larkin and sometimes missing even in Yeats, 'who could not always resist his fatal tendency to attitudinize'.[10] Larkin, in short, was now increasingly being seen not only as one of the best poets born in the 1920s but as one of the best poets writing in the twentieth century.

Not everyone, however, agreed. One especially persistently negative critic was Charles Tomlinson, an influential poet and literary commentator who faulted Larkin repeatedly. In a 1957 essay, for instance, he accused Larkin of xenophobia, distaste for Mozart (!), and lack of poetic ambition. He also found Larkin's tone timid, inauthentic, pessimistic, defeatist, and provincial, even suggesting (ironically) that French poets such as Laforgue had written Larkinesque poetry long before Larkin had, so that Larkin was either ignorant of these predecessors or secretly derivative.[11] Tomlinson spoke for various other commentators who considered Larkin less a striking new voice in English poetry than a self-pitying weak sister who appealed to the lowest common denominator in literary tastes. Howard Sergeant, attacking the 'Movement' poets in general in 1957, was equally dismissive:

> ■ Unfortunately, one finds that for many of these poets the much-vaunted toughness has become a pose, as phoney in its way as anything they have protested against; that purity of language more often than not means poverty of language; that their restraint hides a fear of exhibiting the least hint of personal feeling; that knowing glances and undergraduate sniggers make do for irony and wit; that concentration upon form is, in fact, concentration upon the same two or three forms and rhythms, repeated to the point of tedium.[12] □

Mostly, though, Larkin's reputation prospered throughout the late 1950s. Critics recognised his importance even if they expressed particular reservations about specific aspects of his achievement. A 1958 essay by Derek Brewer, for example, devoted extended attention to Larkin and (as was now becoming usual) reserved special praise for 'Church Going'. Brewer saw the poem as an especially significant reflection of a specific cultural moment, a moment when the English were beginning to feel ambivalent about their cultural traditions, partly because of changes in the class structure (specifically the rise of the middle class). The England Larkin depicted (Brewer claimed) seemed immediately familiar to his readers. Brewer, unlike some who faulted Larkin, saw him as free of sentimental self-pity and praised the way he combined intelligence and ironic perceptions with common speech and widely familiar topics. He admired Larkin's appreciation of human complexities, praising his poetry for its apparent simplicity of form and language but also for its genuine subtlety. Yet even Brewer suggested that Larkin, by seeking a wide audience, paradoxically ran the risk of seeming narrow and somewhat unadventurous.[13]

Similar ambivalence appeared in a 1958 article by the widely published American critic William Van O'Connor. He considered Larkin the most important 'Movement' poet and spent many pages not only discussing his fiction but also outlining his poetic development. He noted Larkin's emphasis on death (especially in the powerful concluding lines of 'Next, Please') and commented on his frequent ability to conclude his poems in a loftier tone than the one with which they began. This, in fact, became a frequent reason for praising 'Church Going', which was often seen by early critics as a perfect example of Larkin's skill in moving from the mundane to the mysterious. O'Connor praised this same process in 'Next, Please', but he concluded by suggesting that Larkin's preference for irony and neatness meant that his topics were often as limited as his tone, which O'Connor found generally lacking in enthusiasm.[14] Similar misgivings about the 'Movement' poets in general were also expressed by Geoffrey Moore, although he, like most critics by this point, admitted the virtues of the 'Movement' writers and conceded their real importance.[15]

Much the same approach was also taken by the important literary figure A. Alvarez, also in 1958. He praised the hard-won ease of Larkin's verse as well as its irony, skill, elegance, understatement, and high standards. He noted its tonal and thematic emphases on lost chances, reticence, sadness, and even, sometimes, mild indignation. He found Larkin's verse often self-critical as well as both loyal to, and ambivalent about, Britain's new welfare state. Similar ambivalence (Alvarez claimed) affected Larkin's presentation of his own hesitant persona, and Alvarez even found the speaker in the opening sections of 'Church Going' almost too self-consciously modest, as if affecting a lack of self-affectation. Sometimes (in other words) Alvarez felt that Larkin went out of his way to seem normal and down-to-earth, no different, really, from the middlebrow readers he sought to attract. Alvarez felt that Larkin was able to create real art out of his ambivalences, but he also concluded that Larkin revealed both what was strongest about the 'Movement' poets and also how they sometimes ultimately fell short of the best that poets and poetry could do.[16]

This, then, was how Larkin was frequently regarded as the 1950s ended: as an important figure, the best of his kind, but also as sometimes illustrating the shortcomings of the sort of verse he and the other 'Movement' poets wrote. Even commentators who merely dismissed some other 'Movement' writers rarely dismissed Larkin: they acknowledged his significance but hoped he would challenge himself to do even better. Typical, in this regard, is a balanced assessment issued in 1959 by G. S. Fraser, who defended Larkin while wishing he were even stronger:

> ■ Mr Christopher Logue, who dislikes the main trends of contemporary English poetry by younger writers, considers, for instance, the prestige of Mr Philip Larkin 'a disaster' (even a moral and political one) and describes his art as 'genteel bellyaching'. What is he getting at? I take Mr Larkin to be the most representative English poet of his generation .... But I will give Mr Logue this, that I feel a little worried about having to take Mr Larkin to

be this. There are strong positive elements in Larkin's poems, humorous insight, compassion, dry tenderness; but the strongest element seems deeper, and it is an honest negative element, an accepted defeat, an insistence that a reasonable man expects rather little from life.... More faith in life, and in risks[,] is what one would like, and not only in Larkin.[17] ☐

Far less even-handed was the American critic M. L. Rosenthal, who in 1959 fiercely indicted Larkin. He saw Larkin as glorying in an ostentatious self-loathing that was actually a petty plea for pity. Repeatedly (Rosenthal felt) Larkin presented himself as facing seemingly insuperable problems that most Americans could not take seriously – problems that were less real than products of the poet's stubborn timidity. It was as if (Rosenthal felt) Larkin or his speakers simply *refused* to be happy, although he did admit that some Larkin poems seemed less whiny and limp than genuinely sad. Even Rosenthal, for instance, found things to praise in 'Church Going', but in general he was (and remained) one of Larkin's sharpest early critics, thereby provoking an even sharper response from Alun Jones, who defended Larkin aggressively.[18] But there was, in Rosenthal's charges, a kind of contempt for Larkin that was less and less common by the late 1950s. And even the passion of Rosenthal's condemnation suggests that he realised Larkin's importance and felt the need to prevent him from becoming any more influential.

After all, Rosenthal was now very much a minority voice. Increasingly typical was the highly respectful treatment accorded Larkin in a 1959 article by C. B. Cox. Cox took Larkin's major significance for granted and praised his treatment of such key topics as alienation, uncertainty, the passage of time, disillusionment, and a genuine sense of dissatisfaction with oneself and one's era. Yet Cox considered Larkin's satire anything but smug, and he noted Larkin's willingness to be honestly self-critical. Even more, Cox commended Larkin not only for sometimes expressing joy, hope, and compassion but also for being able to find beauty even in the darkest subjects, such as death. He praised Larkin for writing unsentimentally about love and for controlling his melancholy rather than merely wallowing in it. Larkin (Cox felt) complexly explored important subjects, trying always to deal honestly with life's complications.[19]

As the 1950s ended, Larkin was increasingly considered his generation's major poet. Thus G. S. Fraser once more praised Larkin. He began by discussing the poet's often traditional stanza patterns and use of metre, yet also suggested that his verse was freer metrically than the writing of some of his contemporaries. Fraser noted Hardy's influence on Larkin's metre, commended the resemblances between some of his poems and fine short fiction, and extolled the way his poems often moved from seemingly prosaic details to a memorable climax, frequently clinched in a final well-phrased line. He studied the understated, unemphatic logic by which Larkin's poems often built up slowly to their final effect, arguing that they derived their impact from their success as coherent, subtle poems rather than by any direct, overt appeal to readers' emotions. Fraser contrasted this gradualism with the more immediate approach often used by Ezra Pound.[20]

Later in the same volume, Fraser returned to Larkin, suggesting that while a lack of moral substance hurt some poetry of the 1950s, this was not the case with 'Church Going', which (Fraser commented) was now widely read and studied. He noted that the poem moved from the commonplace and colloquial to lofty eloquence, and he suggested that something of the poem's power could be intuited simply from a bare summary of its plot. Fraser discussed the subtleties of the poem's specific phrasing, the way some phrases and then the whole poem became genuinely memorable, and the way this poem in particular posed a real challenge to anyone wanting to deny Larkin's importance.[21]

Larkin in the Early 1960s

By this point, then, individual works by Larkin were now receiving the kind of close, sustained attention accorded to works by undeniably major poets. And, even in American publications, Larkin was beginning to receive similarly respectful attention. A 1960 article by Derek Roper, for instance, explored the aesthetic principles of 'the Movement', the similarity between those principles and the underlying values of much earlier English writing, the stylistic development of Larkin's writing, and Larkin's predilection for melancholy topics emphasising the passage – and even the wasting – of time. Although Roper concluded that Larkin's poems were not uniformly successful (especially when they were too full of slang), he affirmed Larkin's real stature.[22]

Returning to Larkin once again in 1961, G. S. Fraser also returned to 'Church Going'. Writing (like Roper) for a primarily American audience, he compared the poem favourably to Wordsworth's 'Resolution and Independence', argued that it typified a kind of slow, steadily unfolding (and far from glib) strength found in much recent English poetry, and admired again the way it gradually built to its memorable climax. Discussing earlier works by Larkin, Fraser suggested that in their sometimes delicate lyricism they failed to fit the stereotypical pattern of allegedly tough-minded 'Movement' verse, and he regretted that Larkin, in various recent work, might have abandoned some of his earlier lyricism, perhaps in order to conform to 'Movement' precepts. In any case, Fraser's article showed once again that Larkin had a major advocate in the British literary establishment.[23] But various antagonists, of course, continued to find fault, as when Charles Tomlinson in 1961 briefly reprinted some of his earlier reservations concerning Larkin, this time in the widely read *Pelican Guide to English Literature*.[24] Tomlinson also took another quick swipe at Larkin in 1962, agreeing with M. L. Rosenthal that Larkin tended to wallow in self-pity over relatively minor problems. Larkin (Tomlinson suggested) owed his stature less to real merit than to the influence of an unnamed 'band of reputation makers' who were good at marketing defective products.[25]

Nevertheless, Larkin continued to win praise. Admittedly, Donald Davie, in 1962, briefly criticised this poet's tendency to stay in England, both literally and in his writing – a common complaint among critics who found him insular if not downright xenophobic.[26] Far more typical, however, was a 1962 article by Patricia Ball, who argued that the honesty and realism of the 'Movement' poets led them to value photography, which in turn inspired them to produce such unblinkered poems as Larkin's 'Lines on a Young Lady's Photograph Album'.[27] But it was John Press, also in 1962, who produced one of the best commentaries issued up to that point on Larkin's verse. He noted the acclaim this poet had received, quoted Larkin's statement that poetry was an art of preserving experiences, and suggested that Larkin enjoyed writing about the past because it was fixed in time and could not change. Press challenged the idea that Larkin's verse was too intellectual and emotionless, arguing instead that it often displayed sadness, kindness, and commiseration. He noted Larkin's tendency to emphasise pointless loss, and he extolled 'Church Going' as typical of Larkin at his best. He particularly praised that poem's varied tones, metrical skill, and range of emotions. He stressed that its speaker was not Larkin himself but rather a persona, although he regretted that Larkin's depiction of this character was not consistently credible, especially in the way the speaker moves from initial foolishness to final eloquence. Yet even in the course of praising Larkin in general and this poem in particular, Press offered some of the sharpest criticism the poem had yet received. He claimed Larkin treated the persona as an easily manipulated puppet. No sooner, however, did Press censure the poem than he returned to extolling it. He especially, of course, praised the concluding lines, where he thought the poet genuinely spoke for himself. Defending Larkin and similar writers from unjust criticism, Press nonetheless faulted them for being too self-aware and self-protective and for using irony to forestall anticipated criticism. He also accused them of sometimes seeming trite or too self-consciously clever. Later, however, he commended the careful, even rational designs of Larkin's best poems, but his last reference to Larkin expressed some regret that this writer seemed uninterested in being lyrical. All in all, Press's lengthy, substantive essay was an impressive attempt to do justice to Larkin without simply praising him uncritically.[28]

By this point in the development of Larkin's reputation, it could almost be expected that 'Church Going' would receive the lion's share of critics' attention. For some of them, it seemed grander, more substantial, and more serious than other Larkin poems. Nearly all commentators considered it important, and it became a central topic, once again, in a 1963 discussion between Anthony Thwaite and Jon Silkin. Thwaite argued that the poem developed organically, beginning with a mundane situation and then moving, gradually, to something more lofty. Silkin, on the other hand, found the poem altogether too predictable, depending on a carefully calculated final surprise and focusing too much on Larkin himself and his own desire to come to peace with Christianity. Neither Thwaite nor Silkin changed his mind, but their dialogue illustrated two things: that 'Church Going' was seen by almost everyone as a key text by Larkin, and that even at this point he still had his detractors.[29]

The Whitsun Weddings (1964)

In 1964, however, a major event – perhaps *the* major event – occurred in Larkin's career: he released a slim volume of new poems. Titled *The Whitsun Weddings* (after one of the volume's most appealing texts), this new book helped solidify Larkin's reputation as none of his previous books had done. *The Whitsun Weddings* was instantly seen as important even by those who found it less than wholly satisfying. As the years went by, this book would increasingly be seen as one of Larkin's most significant contributions to English poetry. At first, though, reactions were somewhat mixed.

An anonymous review for the *Times Literary Supplement* (*TLS*) set the tone for much other positive commentary. Surveying the development of Larkin's reputation in the 1950s and early 1960s, the reviewer predictably cited 'Church Going' as his major text and reported Kenneth Allott's opinion (published in an important anthology) that in England Larkin was 'the most exciting new poetic voice – with the possible exception of Dylan Thomas – since Auden'. The *TLS* reviewer then expressed a personal view, noting that *The Whitsun Weddings* contained 32 poems, 'of which ten are among Mr. Larkin's best and indeed among the best poems of our time'. The reviewer called them 'extraordinarily *finished* poems; no loose ends are left hanging about. Yet they are a long way from being trite and pat, for they have a deceptive openness too'. Although praising Larkin's distinctively 'apt and surprising language' and 'his precise and haunting images', the reviewer conceded that there was 'an occasional stock brashness in his less successful poems'.

Generally, though, the writer extolled Larkin for conveying 'a feeling of exact and searching honesty, a balanced poise between concreteness and abstraction'.

The *TLS* reviewer commented, however, not only on Larkin's style but also on his typical themes:

> ■ These poems are concerned with the impermanence of life, the loneliness of man, the sadness of age, the indulgence of memory, and the sense (and here one is reminded of Hardy, who is closest in spirit to Mr. Larkin) that life's meaninglessness and man's ignorance are in some obscurely moving way being *celebrated* by being recorded....What emerges from almost all these poems, even more strongly than from those in *The Less Deceived*, is a stoical acceptance of change, decay, diminution.[30] □

Ultimately, the reviewer defended Larkin against charges that his verse was constricted, stuffy, prim, or stark, arguing instead that his poems were comprehensive in their concerns, dealing with such matters as sympathy, brutality, comedy, affection, a focus on form, and a focus on dissipation. It would have been hard for Larkin or his publishers to wish for a better assessment, especially since it appeared in such a widely read and well-respected periodical.

Nearly as enthusiastic as the *TLS* review was a 1964 response by Philip Hobsbaum, who praised Larkin as England's most distinguished poet of the 1950s, especially thanks to his understated tone, his undeceived wisdom, and, especially, his powers of accurate perception. Hobsbaum thought Larkin had made the most important improvement in English verse since T. S. Eliot. He mentioned, for instance, the excitement he felt when reading some of the realistic details of the newest volume's title poem, and he suggested that Larkin's special talent lay exactly in such precision. He contended that this talent had never been given the praise it deserved, despite what he called all the generally adulatory commentary Larkin had received – adulation that he thought was beginning to abate. He argued that *The Whitsun Weddings* had been treated rather smugly by certain reviewers, particularly by competing poets who had not succeeded as Larkin had done. Hobsbaum himself found the new volume entirely appealing – better than just about every other collection of poetry produced by writers roughly contemporary with Larkin. He also considered *The Whitsun Weddings* a definite advance even on Larkin's preceding book, which had earned him his already high reputation. Admittedly (Hobsbaum conceded) there was not much new or different in the writing presented in this latest book, but neither had there been any regression. The new work struck Hobsbaum not as essentially different from its predecessor but as more profound. He praised Larkin's use of sprung rhythm, and he ended by emphasising this poet's revolutionary role in reviving the fortunes of English verse during the 1950s, a decade Hobsbaum considered a particularly low point in the history of the nation's poetry. He concluded by singling out two of Larkin's poems as definite masterworks: first, 'Church Going', and, now, 'The Whitsun Weddings'. Many subsequent critics have definitely agreed.[31]

Less entirely enthusiastic about the new book was a 1964 review by Ian Hamilton, who opened by noting that this collection had been heartily anticipated both by Larkin's admirers and by his antagonists. Hamilton found it even better than its predecessor, but he noted that when Larkin was criticised, he was faulted less for writing bad particular poems but for writing poetry that seemed, in general, limited, pessimistic, parochial, ineloquent, and relentlessly dejected, almost to the point of being ridiculously repetitive. Hamilton argued that Larkin's verse always ran the risk of seeming empty, bitter, and narcissistic, and he suggested that, in order to counter these impressions, Larkin sometimes adopted poses of smug, ironic condescension, as if to protect himself from the charge that he took anything seriously, himself included. Sometimes (Hamilton thought), Larkin would ultimately abandon his posing – as, for instance, in the final lines of 'Church Going'. And sometimes (he suggested) Larkin avoided such problems altogether, as in such poems as 'At Grass' and 'Next, Please'. Hamilton considered these and some others poems remarkably successful – unlike almost anything written by Larkin's contemporaries.

Hamilton found more of such successful poems in *The Whitsun Weddings* than in *The Less Deceived*. He thought the new book more generous (especially in treating other people) and less annoying (especially in presenting Larkin himself) than its predecessor. He particularly praised such poems as 'Mr Bleaney', 'Faith Healer', and 'The Whitsun Weddings' itself. He did fault Larkin for occasionally rhyming badly and for sometimes using a rather artificial syntax. But he ended with praise, seeing *The Whitsun Weddings* as displaying all the strengths and few of the weaknesses of *The Less Deceived*. He congratulated Larkin for skilfully broadening his subject matter and for seeming more genuine than in some of his earlier verse. Larkin (he suggested) might achieve even more if he kept moving in these sorts of directions. This was a review that gave with one hand what it took away with several others, but at least it ended on a note that was positive, if also somewhat patronising.[32]

Even more negative than Hamilton's review – but in many ways far more penetrating – was a long 1964 assessment of *The Whitsun Weddings* by Colin Falck. The sheer length of this piece suggests the attention Falck believed the new book deserved, even if his overall reaction was mostly critical. Falck began by repeating some of the by-now standard charges:

that Larkin's writing was too mundane, pessimistic, and uninspiring, especially in its cynicism about love; that his style was too abstract and plain; and that he apparently found it difficult to discover anything really beautiful or true or moving in life, so dark was his general attitude towards the alleged futility of existence. Only occasionally – as in 'The Whitsun Weddings' itself – did Larkin (Falck argued) resist his usual grim view of things. The best of the dark poems (Falck suggested) were the ones about Larkin himself, since they did not implicate other people or life in general in their pervasive despair. Poems about others tended to be either imprecise or maudlin, with 'Afternoons' being one admirable exception.

Especially interesting were Falck's comments on Larkin's typical style and structures. He found *The Whitsun Weddings* even more literal, more plain, and less metaphorical than *The Less Deceived*, although he argued that Larkin was often most effective when he permitted himself some metaphorical phrasing. Falck also maintained that whereas Larkin, in his earlier verse, had often constructed poems by emphasising a single controlling metaphor, he had now moved, in *The Whitsun Weddings*, to fairly plain depiction of realistic details that were ultimately followed by an evaluative comment. Even feelings were now mostly described rather than recreated or expressed, Falck thought: Larkin's poetry had become even more rational, even less tied to memorable images, than it had been already, and this trait helped explain Larkin's preference for predictable rhythms and regular stanzas. Since there was nothing very innovative in the poet's perceptions and phrasing, there was no great need for innovation in style and form. Falck's critical comments on Larkin were thus intriguing; rather than merely complaining about Larkin's style, he made some shrewd suggestions about its sources, nature, and effects. Especially fascinating was his suggestion that Larkin frequently tended to use adjectives in almost oxymoronic pairs. This kind of paradoxical phrasing was, Falck suggested, about as close as Larkin came to being metaphorical.

But Falck was ultimately less concerned with Larkin's style than with his overall tone and meanings. These, Falck thought, were potentially dangerous. They seemed to accept modern life as it was, displaying no urge to suggest anything better. Larkin's realism made him approachable, but his mild cynicism left him, and his readers, at a pointless impasse. Any ideals were dead and could only be viewed nostalgically, not lived. Larkin, according to Falck, gave readers no inspiring illuminations, even about love. The world he presented was tedious, disappointing, and small. His new book was even plainer than its predecessor, and perhaps the best alternative was to return to the kind of fierce emotionalism of D. H. Lawrence. That, at least, seemed true and full of life. The effect of Larkin, in contrast, was deadening.[33]

More affirmative in assessing Larkin was Francis Hope, who in 1964 thought that Larkin's new book confirmed his talent without deepening or broadening it. The new volume, he contended (including the title poem), only reinforced the sense of Larkin as a grim, cerebral, parochial, melancholy, and understated writer who occasionally tried to sound cruder than he could make convincing. As the review developed, however, Hope became more positive: he briefly compared Larkin to Housman and Horace before seeing him, finally, as authentic if also essentially dark.[34] But if Hope's praise seemed grudging, it was offset by the far more enthusiastic opinions of Anthony Thwaite. The third edition of his *Contemporary English Poetry* was issued in 1964 and extolled Larkin as the best poet of his generation. Among the 60 or so poems Larkin had published in *The Less Deceived* and *The Whitsun Weddings*, Thwaite found almost no missteps. He argued that Larkin had had relatively little impact on other writers because his own voice was so distinctive and hard to copy. But he praised the growing appreciation of Larkin's texts, himself finding them full of feeling, perceptiveness, discipline, and widely shared feelings without ever being merely mundane. He noted Larkin's tendency to begin a poem with a specific (perhaps even minor) set of circumstances and then to find meaning in the narrative he developed from them. He praised Larkin's resolute willingness to concede life's darker aspects, including disappointments, compromises, mutability, and ultimately death. But he also found passing moments of comedy and briefly positive assertions. He singled out 'Church Going' and 'The Whitsun Weddings' for special commendation, particularly for their appealing subtlety and grace.[35]

Even more substantial than Thwaite's praise was a long 1964 essay by John Wain devoted entirely to Larkin's work. Wain began by calling Larkin unusual: an author who actually owed his reputation to his talent for using words. He praised the poems for their vivid realism, their skilful metre and rhyme, and especially their clarity, precision, and general brevity. In some particularly interesting comments, he showed how Larkin's language was sometimes more suggestive than it might first appear, demonstrating a talent for finding words that could at first surprise but then seem utterly appropriate. He contrasted Larkin's work with various poems (such as ones by William Carlos Williams) that struck Wain as often prolix and shallow, and he even took a jab at Charles Tomlinson, Larkin's frequent antagonist. He praised Larkin's wit, calling it essential rather than ornamental, and suggested that Larkin's works required much more intelligent attentiveness from their readers than, say, the writings of the then-popular 'Beat' poets. Wain tackled head-on the critics who sniffed at Larkin's supposed negativity, and he even made a case for the seriousness of some of Larkin's seemingly 'light' satire. He argued that Larkin was actually an author with strong emotions, many of them centring on his love of England. Thwaite claimed that numerous English readers sensed and valued this aspect of Larkin's achievement, as in his poems reflecting English landscapes. To Wain, Larkin seemed far more complex than he was often given credit for being, and Wain frequently rooted his positive assessment of Larkin's writing in detailed examinations of particular poems, lines, phrases, and words. Rather than merely claiming that Larkin was a talented poet, Wain often demonstrated precisely why and how.[36]

By this point in the development of his career, Larkin was beginning to attract increasingly sustained attention. A 1964 article by Martin Dodsworth, for instance, compared and contrasted Larkin and Thom Gunn, especially in the ways they dealt with painful topics, arguing that, while Gunn approached such issues as violence and atrocities directly, Larkin tended to deal in understated ways with sadness, disappointment, loss, the pathos of hope, and the ways death touches almost everything. Dodsworth was most intriguing when claiming that Larkin's poems are often at war with themselves, as if Larkin felt a deep need to write but suspected that doing so ultimately made little difference and perhaps little sense.[37]

As 1964 shifted into 1965, Larkin received increasing notice on the other side of the Atlantic. An essay by William Dickey, for example, compared and contrasted him with a dozen other writers, including many Americans, concluding that Larkin was one of only three possessing a truly successful style. (The others were Robert Lowell and Theodore Roethke.) All three, Dickey argued, wrote convincingly, precisely, and concisely of things, persons, and relationships between the two. He especially admired Larkin's straightforwardness, not only in approach and phrasing but also in sentence structure, although he finally suggested that Larkin was somewhat narrow both thematically and stylistically. For these reasons, Dickey preferred Lowell to Larkin: Lowell's language, he thought, was richer, more suggestive, and more exciting than Larkin's, although finally he seemed to prefer Roethke best of all.[38]

Praise of Larkin was even more enthusiastic from other American writers in 1965, including a number of notable literary figures. Norman Holmes Pearson, for example, praised Larkin's lucidity, balance, simple sentence structure, and increasing compassion and assertiveness. He interestingly compared Larkin's style to Hemingway's but appreciated its greater humor.[39] Louise Bogan, a noted American poet, reviewing *The Whitsun Weddings*, especially admired Larkin's varied control of form and defended him against the charge that he was uniformly grim, suggesting instead that his poems often became unexpectedly gentle. She noted the ways British ideas of socio-economic class often underlay his writing, especially in the ultimately tender title poem. But Bogan also commented that Larkin was typically honest and sometimes even sardonic.[40] The fact that this very appreciative review appeared in the *New Yorker*, at that time America's pre-eminent literary magazine, would have helped call Larkin's work to the attention of an especially valuable readership.

William Stafford, another widely respected American poet, also celebrated *The Whitsun Weddings* quite enthusiastically in 1965. In a brief review packed with eloquent praise, he found Larkin's verse exciting because of his striking imagery and packed plots, so that, despite his often grim subject matter, readers were nonetheless invigorated as they moved through the poems line by line, partly because of the sheer vividness of the phrasing. In an especially concise summary of what had often been said about Larkin (but rarely said with such efficiency), Stafford wrote that

■ Philip Larkin, like a more reticent Betjeman, with less bounciness but much more trenchant views, loads into his rhymed, direct verses the felt evidence of present-day England, along with nostalgia about its past. That sense of bleakness, of emergency coupled with inertia, which marked his well-known poem *Church-Going* [sic] pervades this new volume. The effect is of straight communication about wintry prospects. He presents dull, dreadful, ordinary living. *Dockery and Son*, *The Whitsun Weddings*, *Mr. Bleaney* [sic] – these poems cling to the memory like a bad dream; they force horrors of realization about lonely, aging, superficial mankind.[41] □

This review, published prominently in *Poetry* magazine, would have been read by many people seriously interested in the art-form, whether as writers, readers, or both.

Having been extolled by Bogan in one of the country's best mass-circulation weeklies, and having been celebrated by Stafford in a leading 'little' magazine, Larkin was also highly commended by Louis Martz in *The Yale Review*, a major American academic journal. Martz agreed with others who contended that *The Less Deceived* and *The Whitsun Weddings* contained almost no poetic failures, and he suggested that a handful of Larkin's texts (including, inevitably, 'Church Going') would be read and studied for years or decades to come. He compared Larkin to the seventeenth-century poet Andrew Marvell (another poet from Hull and, unlike Larkin, a native of the city) both in style and in nuanced outlook, especially praising 'An Arundel Tomb' and citing Larkin's habit of shifting gears unexpectedly as a hallmark of his verse. Martz also noted the frequent subtlety of Larkin's rhymes or near-rhymes, and he praised Larkin as the best (but also as one of the few really successful) living English poet writing in the clever, intelligent, thoughtful style that Larkin epitomised. Larkin, in other words, was both representative and yet also one of a kind.[42]

The 1965 review of Larkin that probably earned him the widest possible American attention appeared in *Time Magazine*, at that point the nation's leading newsweekly. The mercifully anonymous writer of this badly written but positive review (which repeatedly referred to 'Poet Larkin') said nothing new, but this review was probably read by more Americans than anything else published about Larkin in the 1960s.[43] It probably helped sell more copies of *The Whitsun Weddings* in the United States than all the other American reviews combined, and then some. What more could Larkin have asked for? Well, one thing, perhaps: a long positive review in a major American intellectual weekly written by an admiring countryman. And that is what he got when Christopher Ricks extensively praised *The Whitsun Weddings* in the pages of *The New York Review of Books*. The title of the review – 'A True Poet' – pretty much said it all, but of course Ricks elaborated. He called Larkin the best current English poet, praised his honesty, and likened his poems, in their directness, to good letters or intimate talk. He compared Larkin favourably to Hardy and Wordsworth, celebrated the ease with which he moved from one section of a poem to the next, and praised his unfailingly successful conclusions.[44] One sometimes senses that Larkin, in 1965, was even more widely appreciated in the United States than in his own country.

Not everyone, of course, was so unreservedly supportive. A 1965 essay by Joseph L. Featherstone, published in the influential *New Republic*, described Larkin's style in typical ways, but Featherstone did interestingly note that some poems sounded like miniature essays, and in general he praised Larkin's understated but still significant artistry. He found *The Whitsun Weddings* darker than its predecessor, even noting a new emphasis on terror and dread, especially of death, as in 'The Ambulance'. Featherstone praised Larkin's ability to disturb and unsettle readers, but he, like other reviewers, sometimes thought that Larkin made mountains out of molehills and that Larkin's antipathies could sometimes seem predictable and routine.[45] Far more critical, however, was a rather contemptuous brief review by Harriet Zinnes, who found Larkin tedious and timid – a 'frightened bore', briefly fashionable, whose time would pass.[46] Likewise, J. M. Newton, in the English *Cambridge Quarterly* (1965), issued a vigorous attack. After admitting that Larkin's style was often appealingly clear and colloquial, Newton then went in for the kill. He called Larkin a writer who neither aspired to anything great nor inspired any elevated responses, so that his poetry was largely a waste of time. Newton thought Larkin a man of minimal talent who did little with his real but meagre gifts. He considered Larkin both limited and too self-consciously calculating, lacking the ability to think or write sublimely. He found Larkin's pessimism deadly, weak, and dour to the point of seeming distasteful. He even condemned the much-beloved (by others) 'Church Going', finding it both too clever and finally tedious. And, although he liked 'The Whitsun Weddings' better, he thought even that poem's speaker was at times too presumptuous in assuming to know the thoughts of the people he observed.[47]

The views of Zinnes and Newton, however, were untypically harsh. Even other critics who faulted Larkin were usually more temperate, as in the occasionally snide but ultimately ambivalent reactions of Frederick Grubb.[48] Most reviewers, even if they sometimes seemed disappointed with the narrowness of Larkin's range or faulted one poem or another, generally thought Larkin an appealing poet who was often more generous in depicting people than was sometimes assumed. Richard Kell, in a 1965 review, spoke for many in all these ways.[49] Especially typical of the reaction Larkin had now begun to receive was the appreciative 1965 close reading by Norman Page of a particularly memorable poem, 'Myxomatosis', which Page compared to works by Hardy in its grim acceptance of an indifferent universe. Increasingly, Larkin was not only being widely read but was being read with real attention to the details of his phrasing.[50]

Larkin's stature, in fact, had by this point become so significant that his very first book, *The North Ship* (1945) was reissued in 1966, not because he himself considered it very good but because his publishers knew it would interest his readers. An anonymous reviewer for the *TLS* found the book less derivatively Yeatsian than Larkin himself had self-disparagingly claimed; in fact, the reviewer welcomed the volume for offering foretastes of the kind of poet Larkin would eventually become.[51] Much the same tack was taken in a very brief 1966 notice of *The North Ship* by John Carey,[52] and a review by the poet Elizabeth Jennings was even more affirmative. She thought Larkin's significance in English verse was now certain.[53] Indeed, so solid did his status now seem that he had begun to be compared and contrasted favourably to various European writers, as in the 1966 version of J. M. Cohen's book *Poetry of This Age*, which briefly juxtaposed Larkin with the Spanish poet José Hierro.[54] Likewise, in another book from 1966, D. J. Enright highly extolled Larkin, even while expressing some mild misgivings about some of his slang and his general pessimism and occasional defeatism. Yet Enright noted, variously, the appeal of Larkin's self-mockery, his real kindness, and his muted idealism. He finally suggested that Larkin was so persistently talented that most readers found even his glumness appealing.[55] Similarly impressed was J. D. Hainsworth, who admired Larkin's candour about the limits of life and his era, his attempt to speak to and for a broader public, and the subtle optimism that lay beneath the obvious surface gloom.[56] Not everyone, of course, agreed: thus Peter Davison, in a 1966 essay, began by praising Larkin warmly (especially *The Whitsun Weddings*) but soon shifted into a lower gear. Larkin, he felt, dwelt too often on small, dark matters and would be a more appealing poet if he were less cramped and more compassionate.[57]

Larkin and the Late 1960s

One indication that Larkin's reputation was generally on the rise was the fairly long section on him in M. L. Rosenthal's 1967 book *The New Poets*. In 1959, Rosenthal had attacked Larkin so vigorously that he had provoked a long, spirited response in 1962 from Alun R. Jones. Jones had accused Rosenthal of being essentially ignorant of the English poetic scene in general and of Larkin in particular. Jones had extolled Larkin as the best English poet of the 1950s, as a crucial link with an earlier tradition of English poetry (represented especially by Hardy and Robert Graves), and as a superb craftsman and master of a detached, ironic tone. He had furthermore praised Larkin's objectivity, intelligence, urbanity, honesty, and rejection of easy affirmations. In contrast to Rosenthal, who had seen Larkin as weak-willed, maudlin, and self-indulgent, Jones had praised him for being just the opposite, especially commending his growing compassion.[58] Whether because of Jones's rebuke or because of a general change of heart, Rosenthal in 1967 was considerably more generous towards Larkin than he had been in 1959. In his new book, Rosenthal still faulted Larkin for allegedly being often timid, gloomy, superficial, insufficiently specific, too calculating, and embarrassingly clumsy in matters of structure, metre, and tone. But Rosenthal was also now willing to concede that Larkin's writing could sometimes be moving, witty, uncontrived, appealingly simple, attractively conversational, and even occasionally convincing despite its essential pessimism. Rosenthal rarely praised any of Larkin's poems without reservation, but the fact that he was now offering any praise at all was a definite change from his uniform hostility of nearly a decade earlier.[59]

Yet if Rosenthal was now willing to see Larkin's work as not entirely unsuccessful, Patrick Swinden, also in 1967, compared Larkin and Thom Gunn, not always to Larkin's advantage. Swinden did praise Larkin's capacity for subtlety, his use of himself as an often comic character in his own poems, his effective exploration of darkness and disappointment, his freedom from illusions (especially about love), and his ability to revivify common language. Swinden worried, however (like many critics before and since), that Larkin had painted himself into a kind of corner so that he was running the risk of repeating himself and thus perhaps of ceasing to write altogether. Gunn struck Swinden as the poet more likely to continue developing and writing, and time, of course, would eventually prove him correct. Larkin, by the late 1970s, would essentially descend into silence; Gunn would continue to write until his death in the early twenty-first century.[60]

As the 1960s drew to a close, commentary on Larkin became less extensive than in the immediate aftermath of the 1964 publication of *The Whitsun Weddings*. A 1968 article by Philip Gardner (published in the Canadian *Dalhousie Review*) suggested that Larkin was now attracting increasing attention throughout the English-speaking world, especially among serious readers of contemporary poetry.[61] Gardner noted that when *The Less Deceived* was published in 1955, Larkin was praised for being ironic, unsentimental, and formally conservative and also for rejecting poetic excess and focusing instead on ordinary people and ordinary life. He suggested that more recent reaction to Larkin had faulted him for his parochialism, distrust of emotional commitment, pessimism about time, and gloomy view of human aspirations. Gardner noted Larkin's regard for Hardy, his typical tone of disappointment and sadness, and the ways his early volume *The North Ship* was often typical of his later tone and themes even if it differed in its style. He suggested that one key difference between the earlier and later works was that the earlier pieces often lacked titles, making them seem less specifically tied to real experiences than the later poems.

Gardner commented that even when poems in *The North Ship* began by seeming romantic, their romanticism was often undercut by an emphasis on inevitable, usually negative change; rarely was the early Larkin able to embrace romanticism without qualifications. *The Less Deceived* was darker than that early volume, and *The Whitsun Weddings* was even darker still. Both of the more recent volumes dealt with themes of broad interest to all humans ('time, failure, love, death') and did so in realistic ways and in realistic contemporary contexts. Gardner thought it was such themes, rather than Larkin's tone, that helped explain his popularity, but he also defended Larkin against charges that his tone was too dark, pointing to prior examples of pessimism among great English poets. He especially emphasised Larkin's depth of feeling:

> ■ The basic point is that Larkin is an *emotional* poet: the irony of his tone may sometimes be the self-protection of a man who guiltily feels himself to be on the edge of life, but more often it is there to control strong feeling. Where irony is absent, as in 'Going', the strength of feeling is frighteningly apparent, but the presence of irony in other poems should not distract our attention from the emotion which is also there. Larkin is no disinterested observer, but a poet who feels that 'the man who creates' depends completely on 'the man who suffers': as an intelligent man he notices the ironic, the absurd, the amusing, and the plain dull, but fundamentally he responds to pathos, futility and the fear of death.[62] □

Gardner then discussed the complexities of the perhaps ambiguous title *'The Less Deceived'* as the designation for Larkin's first major volume of verse, suggesting that the title was not meant to seem self-congratulatory but ruefully honest. Commenting on various particular poems, he discussed their emotional complexities and the ways their ironies protected them from seeming sentimental or otherwise excessive. He closed by disagreeing with Charles Tomlinson, who had accused Larkin of being emotionally self-indulgent. For Gardner, just the opposite seemed the case.

A 1969 article by Peter Faulkner also, like Gardner's essay, praised Larkin for writing about contemporary life in convincing, accessible ways, noting that Larkin and various other authors of his generation disdained pretentiousness, grandiloquence, and unrealistic claims to knowledge. Larkin (according to Faulkner) *was* a man of feeling, but his feelings were often sad, sometimes tragic, but also frequently humorous and even full of compassion. Faulkner praised Larkin for the economy, quietness, specificity, and understatement of his phrasing as well as for dealing realistically with the sense of powerlessness many people often felt about their own lives. He ended by stressing Larkin's agnosticism as well as his perception of the frequent gap between the real and the ideal.[63] Faulkner's article suggested Larkin's real appeal to 'regular' readers, while another piece from 1969 – this one by Keith Sagar – implied that Larkin had now become part of the recognised canon of important twentieth-century poets. Sagar's essay appeared alongside articles on such other major recent writers as Hardy, Lawrence, Graves, Wilbur, and Lowell.[64] It focused especially on 'Church Going' and 'Wedding Wind', but Sagar also challenged claims that Larkin's range of tones and topics was limited. He concluded by offering strong general praise:

■ Larkin's stylistic achievement depends upon far more than technical mastery. The depth and subtlety of his response to language gives him access to the permanent realities of experience the language holds. As all true poets do, he makes words live; he makes us proud to share a language capable of such precision and splendour.[65] □

The new decade would see even more such praise, as the next chapter will show. As the 1960s ended, Larkin had become England's favourite living poet – a writer loved by a wide audience and respected by a growing number of literary critics and academics.

CHAPTER TWO

Larkin Rises: The 1970s

In the 1970s, Larkin criticism was marked by various key developments. The most important was the appearance of entire *books* on Larkin. No longer was commentary confined to periodical reviews and academic articles. Instead, publishers now began to see him as meriting full-length discussion, and some books – published as parts of ongoing series devoted to key authors – implied by their very existence that he was entering the contemporary literary canon. Critics in the 1970s also, by that time, had a tradition of previous criticism to extend, modify, or sometimes challenge. A real and ever-growing dialogue about Larkin was beginning, often involving the best critical minds of the period. Standard topics (such as his style, themes, tone, allusions, and 'development') continued to be discussed, but now there was a growing sense of Larkin as a highly (and increasingly) influential figure on the literary scene – one whose tastes (as in his selections for an important anthology of modern poetry published by Oxford University Press) might influence the tastes of many others. In the 1970s, too, Larkin was increasingly compared and contrasted with poets from other countries, including the United States and continental Europe.

Larkin in the Early 1970s

In 1970, Anthony Thwaite forthrightly called Larkin England's best living poet. Thwaite then spent almost 20 tightly printed pages explaining why. Despite Larkin's own claims, Thwaite found little trace of Auden (let alone Dylan Thomas) in *The North Ship*. And, even though that book did reveal, to Thwaite, the impact of Yeats, he nonetheless considered many of its poems more than mere imitations, especially in their technical skills. He noted the liberating effect that reading Hardy had had on Larkin's writing, especially in Larkin's realisation that poems might be fashioned from moments of mundane illumination, when everyday life revealed unsuspected insights. Thwaite called the early poem titled 'Wedding-Wind' Larkin's only truly joyous work, but he also cautioned that Larkin's more general emotional cautiousness should not automatically be seen as pessimistic. And, while he agreed with most critics that *The Whitsun Weddings* did not differ enormously from *The Less Deceived*, he nonetheless found more variety of tone, methods, and personae in Larkin's verse than was often realised. He likened the mood of much of Larkin's poetry to that of Matthew Arnold's 'Dover Beach', especially in its emphasis on the crucial themes of time and death. He found in Larkin an underlying attitude of stoic endurance: one simply had to face impermanence and then final extinction squarely, rather than trying to ignore or deny them, and he thought it unsurprising that the kind of jazz that appealed most to Larkin was the blues.

Commenting on Larkin's techniques, Thwaite suggested that, while many poems began with specificities and then moved towards final assessment and interpretation, sometimes the speaker's interpretation of facts was implied as the poems developed. Thwaite noted that Larkin's phrasing had recently become sometimes cruder than before, making him seem even more a *contemporary* poet. Echoing Christopher Ricks on Larkin's frequent use of negative prefixes (such as 'un'), Thwaite also noted Larkin's tendency to create complicated compounded adjectives by linking two descriptive words with a hyphen. Interestingly, he compared this kind of phrasing to the complex diction of Gerard Manley Hopkins, a poet Larkin respected, and Thwaite suggested that Larkin had achieved a poetic voice far more distinctive than the voices of some of his contemporaries. In other words, a poem by Larkin was immediately recognisable as one of his and no one else's. At the same time (Thwaite maintained), Larkin dealt with subjects – love, mutability, disappointment, time, and death – that were universally important. His distinctive voice explored archetypal themes.[1]

General readers interested in Larkin could not have asked for a clearer, more sympathetic introduction than Thwaite's. Meanwhile, academic readers would have welcomed a long scholarly essay by A. Kingsley Weatherhead published in 1971. Neither Thwaite nor Weatherhead said much that had not, by this time, already been said, but both – by writing about Larkin at such length – helped solidify and extend his reputation. Noting that in Larkin's first book the impact of Arnold and Donne (not only Yeats) was sometimes apparent, Weatherford also discussed the poet's often valuable present interest in seemingly dull, drab, ordinary topics taken from everyday life. He suggested that Larkin often structured poems by focusing on single, particular, concrete facts or things, using them as symbols for larger situations and circumstances. And even when the things emphasised were not symbolic, they were still often meaningful as fragments from an often fragmentary world. Weatherhead thought Larkin's poems often suggested an understated terror that was persuasive precisely because Larkin's tone often seemed so subdued, so clearly unrhetorical. He noted Larkin's tendency to use words implying carefully weighed assessments, such as 'almost', 'nearly', and so on. Thus the poet's phrasing, far from seeming inflated, instead usually seemed both exacting and measured.

Commenting further on Larkin's typical themes, symbols, and style, Weatherhead noted his typical stress on fate (often symbolised by railroad tracks) as well as on attractive – if ultimately elusive or illusory – alternatives to fate (often symbolised by the moon). Frequently, the desire to escape from fate was mocked or treated with irony, but the desire was nevertheless repeatedly acknowledged. Work could provide some kind of limited meaning to life, and traditions (often embodied, in Larkin's verse, in standard metres and forms) could also offer various satisfactions. Youth's illusions had little appeal for Larkin, and Weatherhead in fact suggested that the poet frequently explored life's middle years, when people had simply to live and cope with their earlier decisions. He praised Larkin for depicting England even more realistically than Auden had done, although he also noted that often, in a Larkin poem, a single word or phrase will shift the apparently ordinary language to a higher level, often helping to suggest not only a loftier tone but also a briefly happier point of view.[2]

Praise of Larkin also appeared in a 1972 book by Donald Davie, himself a significant poet. In *Thomas Hardy and British Poetry*, Davie situated Larkin squarely as one of Hardy's descendants. He also called Larkin the nation's unelected favourite poet, partly because his depictions of England seemed thoroughly convincing to many of his contemporaries, especially when Larkin described the loss of much of England's beauty due to the rise of suburbs and the still pervasive ugliness fostered by the industrial revolution. Davie considered Hardy more technically innovative than Larkin, and he ended by worrying that Larkin had mounted an even less effective resistance to the perhaps irresistible negative trends of modern culture than Hardy had. Mostly, though, he assessed Larkin very favourably.[3] So, too, did Dieter Welz in 1972, who argued that Larkin, far from glorying in pain, wrote so that he could better understand and explain it.[4]

In August 1972, Philip Larkin celebrated his fiftieth birthday. This key event may help to explain why the following year, 1973, was so important for Larkin scholarship and commentary. Perhaps the crucial development was the publication in 1973 of the first monograph devoted to the poet – David Timms's book titled *Philip Larkin*. Although both short and small in size, the book provoked real respect. It did everything an introductory book should do, especially by setting Larkin in his biographical, historical, and social contexts. Its chapters dealt with such topics as Larkin and 'The Movement', the two novels, the three collections of poetry, and the as-yet uncollected poems. Especially interesting were Timms's comments on Larkin's boyhood poems, which often involved a speaker angrily frustrated by the difficulties of performing some simple task. Timms also discusses Larkin's time at Oxford, the impact of various teachers there, Larkin's growing friendship with Kingsley Amis, his early jobs, the style and backgrounds of 'The Movement' poets, the flaws of some 'Movement' verse (such as its over-emphasis on poems about poetry), and the general formal excellence of Larkin's own 'Movement' poetry. Timms praised that poetry for not focusing on either Larkin or on poetry as subjects, and he noted how Larkin's works often resembled the blues both in tone and technique.[5]

Timms's chapter on *The North Ship* conceded (as had Larkin himself) that the poems did not stand up well as mature works but argued that they were interesting nonetheless. Timms did detect slight similarities to Dylan Thomas but thought the very slightness of the echoes indicated that Larkin, even as a young man, was already capable of poetic independence. Meanwhile, Timms heard many specific echoes of Yeats. He found the early poems often too abstract, derivative, predictable, self-pitying, and sentimental, but he considered some more original than others and noted that already the typical Larkin themes of time's passage and failures in love had begun appearing. Timms could detect then, even in this early volume, hints of Larkin's later development.[6]

Writing about *The Less Deceived*, Timms discussed such matters as Hardy's influence, Larkin's interest in describing and preserving reality, the roots of Larkin's poetry (like Hardy's and Betjeman's) in the poet's deeply felt experiences, and the poet's claim that in writing verse he valued content over form. Timms also listed some other poets Larkin admired (including Christina Rossetti, Robert Frost, Rudyard Kipling, A. E. Housman, William Barnes, and Wilfred Owen) and commented on Larkin's intent to appeal broadly by writing poetry that would be moving, memorable, clear, and pleasing. He noted Larkin's general distaste for Modernism in all the arts, and he defended Larkin against charges that he was anti-intellectual or simple to the point of being simplistic. Larkin (according to Timms) could write complexly while disdaining obscurity, and although the poet had strong opinions about art, he never erected them into a rigid system. His best poems (Timms thought) were rooted in concrete (often personal or archetypal) situations from which larger statements then grew, and if his poetry was not overtly political or social, his basic outlook on life could nonetheless be intuited. He had no need to openly condemn atrocities in order to show that he was sensitive and civilised. (Some critics had faulted Larkin for seeming to be apolitical.) Timms defended Larkin for not resembling other poets, such as the more obviously extroverted and emotional Ted Hughes,

Sylvia Plath, Robert Lowell, and John Berryman. Most significantly, perhaps, Timms rooted his defence of Larkin in insightful discussions of particular poems, including 'Church Going' but also many others. On this chapter's final page, Timms summed up what he thought *The Less Deceived* proved about Larkin. It showed, he argued, that

> ■ [Larkin] wrote movingly and memorably about aspects of life that were of great importance to his readers as well as to himself. He showed that he was a witty poet with immense verbal facility, capable of the most subtle modulations of tone, speaking a language vitalised by its relationship with the idiom we speak. He showed above all, to use his own phrases, that he was a poet 'capable of strong feeling' and 'of conveying strong feeling in poetry'.[7] □

In discussing Larkin's next collection, *The Whitsun Weddings*, Timms began by noting the widely positive but occasionally negative reactions the volume had received. To objections that the book showed little development over *The Less Deceived*, Timms responded that some poems in both books were written at around the same time. He then discussed such matters as the ways Larkin's language in the later book had become even more colloquial; the ways slang (sometimes crude) characterised its speakers rather than Larkin himself; and the ways the book's phrasing was often even more concrete and particular than that of its predecessor. The newest book (Timms noted) tended to focus more on people than the earlier one, and its tone was sometimes both more compassionate and more outwardly ironic than the tone of the preceding volume. Timms, while conceding that life, for Larkin, often seemed bleak and terrible, also drew attention to important differences between the poems' various characters (such as the stoic Mr. Bleaney) and the glum speakers who described them. Timms agreed with critics who considered Larkin often grim but argued that his grim poems were often very well written. And, besides (he also noted), Larkin's writings were not consistently dark, as 'The Whitsun Weddings' showed. Timms praised Larkin's poems for dealing honestly with love, for often concluding in memorable ways, for successfully employing iambic metre, for using subtly modulated rhythms to great effect, and for thoughtfully comparing and contrasting the real and the ideal.[8] Discussing Larkin's as-yet uncollected poems, Timms commented on such matters as the real breadth of the poet's range, his growing interest in satire and occasional poetry, his apparently conservative cultural and political views, but his continuing interest in the kinds of themes and style that had, by 1973, made him as famous as any poet could reasonably hope to be.[9]

One further indication of that steadily growing fame was the publication, in 1973–74, of a special 'Philip Larkin Issue' of *Phoenix*, a poetry magazine issued in England. This substantial volume brought together various previously published pieces, including essays by Alun R. Jones (1962), Christopher Ricks (1965), Philip Gardner (1968), Anthony Thwaite (1969), and David Timms (1973). Meanwhile, new essays by Thwaite, Edna Longley, George Hartley, Harry Chambers, and Frederick Grubb added to the issue's weight in every sense. Thwaite's brief new piece commented quickly on several as-yet uncollected poems, noting their similarities in style and theme to earlier pieces but also arguing for their specific successes in form, phrasing, and technique.[10] Longley's lengthy essay compared and contrasted Larkin with Yeats, Hardy, Hughes, and especially Edward Thomas, contending that more of Yeats survived in Larkin's later work than Larkin and others perceived but especially arguing for similarities between the writings of Larkin and Thomas. Those similarities (Longley thought), included a common commitment to England, a shared distrust of the modern and the foreign, and a similar interest in English landscapes, in the importance of finding a home, and in nostalgia, stoicism, and agnosticism. Longley also compared Larkin and Thomas in their skilled use of iambic metre, their broader than obvious range of themes and tones, and their major importance in the history of twentieth-century verse. Indeed, she thought Thomas even more open-minded and tolerant than Larkin, but it was obvious that she admired both poets greatly.[11]

George Hartley's essay argued that M. L. Rosenthal had praised Larkin's 'Dry Point' as his best poem while completely misunderstanding its precise (sexual) language, which Hartley then explicated in some detail.[12] Harry Chambers saw the speaker of 'Naturally the Foundation Will Bear Your Expenses' as a satiric target, not as the poet's spokesman.[13] Frederick Grubb surveyed and assessed (mostly favourably) some of Larkin's most recent works, defending him against specific allegations (especially from J. M. Newton) as well as against general grumbling.[14] All in all, the *Phoenix* special issue brought together some of the best examples of earlier commentary on Larkin while also adding various other solid pieces, with the Longley essay as perhaps the best of the newer contributions.

General Assessments and *High Windows* (1974)

The 1974 publication of Larkin's newest book – *High Windows* – unleashed another flood of commentary and praise. John Bayley's *TLS* review appeared on that prestigious paper's very first page and featured a large photo of Larkin sitting next to a substantial road sign displaying the word 'England' in huge letters.[15] Both the review's placement and the accompanying photo suggested Larkin's national eminence. Bayley's lengthy, somewhat rambling review was mostly positive, while a long biographical profile by Dan Jacobson in 1974 indicated that readers were now greatly interested not only in the poetry but in the poet.[16] But one of the best and most glowing assessments of Larkin ever published also appeared in 1974. This one, by Clive James, was far more substantive than Bayley's and remains an excellent discussion of Larkin's importance.[17]

James started by calling Larkin one of Europe's two best living poetic craftsmen (Eugenio Montale was the other), and then he began assessing *High Windows*. That book revealed (James thought) that Larkin had not so much developed since his last volume as he had deepened and become even more lucid, revealing once more that even hopelessness could be beautifully described. Far from finding Larkin predictably repetitious, James stressed the appealing uniqueness of each work. And, if Larkin's outlook on life admittedly seemed constricted, it was nonetheless always artfully expressed. James rebuked critics who found Larkin too narrow; they failed to appreciate (he thought) just how much artistic originality each particular poem embodied. Ultimately, for James, it was only the art that mattered. When Larkin used obscenity (according to James), those words characterised the speaker, not the poet: the poet did not always sanction how his speakers spoke or what they said (and, sometimes, neither did they). James argued that missed opportunities were among Larkin's major themes, that his poetry was far more packed with intense feeling than some critics realised, and that a new poem called 'The Building' was the best work in the new book. He noted the irony that while Larkin wrote poems about dying, the poems were themselves so vital that they would continue to live long after the poet and his readers were gone.

Almost as enthusiastic as James's review was another 1974 notice by Alan Brownjohn. Addressing the question of whether Larkin had 'developed', Brownjohn argued that *High Windows* showed that he had definitely done so, partly because the new book featured all the best aspects of Larkin's earlier work in a particularly comprehensive and well-balanced volume. He praised Larkin's command of various verse structures, his precise phrasing, and his new interest in the ways rituals and habits gave meaningful shape to life. He regretted Larkin's rare inclusion of overtly conservative political poems (poems Brownjohn considered either ineffective or unintentionally comic), and he worried that Larkin's poetry might ultimately make life seem more limited than it needed to be. But he ended by indicating that Larkin had nonetheless written many poems over his career that were literally unforgettable and that grew in significance as time passed.[18]

More ambivalent reactions to *High Windows* were offered (again in 1974) by William Bedford. He compared Larkin to the Anglo-Saxon poets who gloomily emphasised mutability, and he suggested that Larkin's latest book was even darker than its predecessors. Any hints of loveliness (he thought) seemed deliberately limited, but this emphasis on Larkin's negativity did not prevent Bedford from praising such grim poems as 'The Old Fools' and 'The Building' as among the poet's best. Bedford conceded that Larkin was free to write about any subject he wished, but he thought *High Windows* less successful than both *The Less Deceived* and *The Whitsun Weddings*, partly because the new book seemed more darkly, relentlessly monochromatic and also because its occasional use of cheap language struck him as flawed.[19]

Even harsher on *High Windows* was Humphrey Clucas, who in 1974 considered Larkin's latest volume a definite failure. He thought it far less likely to express compassion than Larkin's earlier works, but he also thought it lacking in life, poetically inept, and often crude and ordinary in its phrasing. Many poems struck Clucas as trivial, ridiculous, boring, unpersuasive, unmusical, clotted, metrically absurd, and strained in their attempted sexual humour. Rarely had Larkin been this roundly condemned.[20]

A 1974 academic article by James Naremore saw Larkin's poetry as an ongoing critique of the kind of metaphysical sublimity associated with Romantic literature (and, in a perverted form, with Modernism),[21] but this year's key academic event was the publication of Lolette Kuby's book *An Uncommon Poet for the Common Man: A Study of Philip Larkin's Poetry*.[22] Offering her volume mainly as a study of Larkin's themes, Kuby nonetheless also said much about his style. She began, in fact, by comparing and contrasting Larkin with the so-called 'Movement' poets. She then discussed stylistic issues, suggesting, variously, (1) resemblances between Larkin's concise phrasing and the 'plain style' tradition associated with Ben Jonson and the Augustan poets; (2) similarities between Larkin's verse and the colloquial phrasing of such nineteenth-century writers as Wordsworth, Browning, and Winthrop Mackworth Praed; and (3) both stylistic and philosophical similarities between Larkin and Hardy, especially in their evocative use of setting, restrained language, and pessimism. Interestingly, Kuby considered Larkin even more pessimistic than Hardy, partly because his era was darker and partly because his pessimism seemed less contrived and less predictable.[23]

Kuby then set Larkin within the contexts of later twentieth-century verse, distinguishing him particularly from the modernists and from Dylan Thomas. In an especially concise passage she wrote that

■ Larkin's poetry is not visionary, vatic, subjective, emotional, or wordy. It continues that strain of British poetry that emphasises thoughtfulness, plain language, moral consciousness, and reason. It is skeptical rather than optimistic; it sees the universe as physical process rather than sacred harmony; and it sees humanity as small, unheroic, selfish, anxious, pathetic, and conflicted. Its plainness of language and reasonableness of style reflect skepticism in a way that lyricism and poetic diction cannot. ... Rejection of a style that employs eloquence, exalted emotionalism, baroque diction is less a rejection of these rhetorical items *per se* than it is a recognition that they imply optimism and hope. They ring false to contemporary poetic sensibility. They seem an attempt to will into existence, or to shout into existence through sheer power of voice, universal harmony that does not exist.[24] □

Further discussing Larkin's typical phrasing and forms, she noted the ways he could sometimes move from the colloquial to the lofty when ending a poem, the ways he often used both standard, well-known structures and newer kinds of shapes, and the ways he usually employed iambic rhythms, traditional stanzas, and varied kinds of rhyme to achieve effects that nonetheless rarely seemed old-fashioned. Kuby distinguished Larkin's verse from the later, more complex writings of the older Auden (with his psychological lingo), noting Larkin's preference for common language and his avoidance of any personal, specialised vocabulary. He could (she thought) breathe new life into familiar phrasing, but he was democratic and ethical in his concern to write in ways most people could understand and in ways that were honestly plain rather than arcane or obscure. He was less concerned with communicating through imagery and symbolism than with finding a credible tone of voice, and, rather than emphasising sight to the exclusion of other senses (as many modern poets did), he instead appealed to the whole range of sensual knowledge.[25]

Focusing next mainly on Larkin's themes, Kuby commented on his tendency to explore such matters as the tension between the ideal and the real, the conflicts between nature's power and humanity's limitations, the ways nature uses humans for its own purposes, and the ways children often symbolise unbridled nature rather than admirably mature restraint. Intriguingly (and unlike some other students of Larkin), Kuby considered him quite suspicious of unconstrained nature, arguing that for him time was the most pervasive, frightening symbol of the purely natural. Kuby felt that while Larkin associated humans with minds, he linked nature with the ever-dissolving flesh, so that full mental awareness involved the pain of knowing one's own material impermanence. According to Kuby, Larkin saw society, like nature, as a source of impersonal, indifferent power – no more concerned with the individual's ideals and aspirations than nature is. Individuals were weak when facing both natural and social forces, and their weakness often made them selfish, lonely, and fearful – sometimes comic, sometimes tragic, sometimes both. But human weakness also made people, often, the object of the poet's compassion and fellow-feeling.[26]

Discussing Larkin's ideas about free will, Kuby argued that he doubted its existence but sometimes showed it being exercised, apparently, by loners who chose (or tried to choose) to resist domination by nature, society, or other people. Their choices, then, were mainly negative – rejections rather than affirmations, but rejections Larkin regarded as moral precisely because they sought to preserve or assert individual freedom, however limited. Yet Larkin was aware (Kuby contended) of the paradoxes this sort of freedom involved: he knew the ways such freedom might be merely illusory, and thus his speakers often mock themselves or are mocked by the poet. Choice in Larkin was further complicated, Kuby argued, because choosing one thing necessarily excluded choosing others, so that even choice could feel like constriction rather than liberty. Kuby typically tied her arguments to insightful discussions of individual poems, illuminating the paradoxes of Larkin's ideas by revealing the complexities of specific texts.[27]

Kuby's discussion of time in Larkin's verse emphasised that he saw time as humanity's essential antagonist, revealing the ultimate impotence of the human will. According to Kuby, Larkin emphasised the past and future (both out of reach) rather than the present (always quickly becoming the past). In all these senses, mutability is the essential human condition; no experience is permanent. Kuby considered Larkin a kind of Platonist for whom the ideal could never be real and for whom choices were always illusory since the thing desired could never be fully grasped. Disillusionment inevitably resulted from any desire, but humans could never, and *would* never, cease pursuing illusions (particularly in matters of love), because illusions were necessary to psychic survival. This essential psychological conflict in Larkin's speakers (their underlying realisation that everything is illusory, that nothing is stable, but their need to seek stability nonetheless) led (Kuby argued) to divided or complex voices in many of Larkin's poems: speakers were always in a kind of dialogue with themselves, never speaking with utter certainty or self-assurance. Part of the integrity of Larkin's speakers, for Kuby, resulted from the fact that those speakers, although often seeking truth, rarely found any truth that was finally stable, yet they nonetheless were willing to face the fact of this instability. In this respect, as in many others, Larkin (she thought) spoke for his era, an era in which most of the apparent certitudes of the past (such as religion) had begun to dissolve or had dissolved already.[28]

In an especially interesting chapter, Kuby argued that, although Larkin's language seemed clearer than that of many other modern poets, it always repaid rereading, seeming more complex on closer examination. She noted the various methods Larkin used to enrich common speech. These included puns, symbols, suggestive forms, implied comparisons, heavy use of logical conjunctions, and complicated, alternating tones of voice, so that the poems often conveyed the impression of a mind in the process of actual moment-by-moment thought. Intriguingly, Kuby noted that Larkin wrote in the colloquial style that had also become common in modern Anglo-American analytical philosophy. As in such philosophy, everything in Larkin's poetry and in his era was up for question and had to be tested empirically. And, as Larkin's writing had developed, it had become even more realistic and less obviously 'poetic' and 'Romantic' in the often negative senses of those terms. Comparing Larkin's earlier works with his later writings, Kuby found the latter more precise, more vernacular, less rhetorical, more personal, more self-mocking, and written more in the voice of older speakers, so that in all these ways the poet seemed, more and more, to be speaking even more than previously for himself rather than creating fictional alter egos.[29]

Kuby's 1974 book was, if anything, even more impressive than Timms's 1973 volume. Larkin had now begun to receive the sustained attention of intelligent academics who could see shrewdly and write clearly about both his style and his themes. Also in 1974, he received insightful attention in Calvin Bedient's book *Eight Contemporary Poets*. Bedient began by stressing Larkin's humour and explained Larkin's enormous popularity partly by arguing that this poet had shown his contemporaries that life was bearable and even, sometimes, comic. He considered Larkin a nihilist (like many other influential writers of his time), but he saw Larkin's nihilism as understated rather than melodramatic, wry rather than grimly overdone. Although not entirely uncritical, Bedient nevertheless praised Larkin's reticence, his simplicity, and his ability to combine seemingly opposite tones of voice in poetry that somehow seemed both traditional and absolutely his own.[30]

The next two years would see various new reviews of *High Windows*, the very last volume of Larkin's poetry (as it turned out) that Larkin himself would issue. Thus in a 1975 review in the influential *New York Review of Books*, Richard Murphy noted that Larkin was by now so popular in England that readers could often recite his verse from memory. Murphy attributed this popularity to his poetry's realism, vernacular simplicity, frequent movement from plain speech to final eloquence, and tendency to combine the comic and the serious, the light and the dark. Murphy argued that Larkin valued clarity of style and thought above mere novelty and that he usually resisted sounding didactic. But Murphy also warned that Larkin now ran the risk of stagnating in the phrasing and attitudes he had cultivated so well for so long. Ultimately, though, he praised Larkin's scepticism and traditional style, arguing that they contributed valuably both to contemporary poetry and to contemporary thinking.[31]

Further reviews of *High Windows* from 1975 offered similar praise. The most substantial was by George Hartley, Larkin's long-time acquaintance and one-time publisher. Hartley noted that although Larkin's eminence was now taken for granted, early comments about his verse had often been mixed or condescending. He himself extolled Larkin as one of England's best poets, singling out 'Church Going' for special praise. He found Larkin no more 'negative' than many other esteemed writers (such as Housman, Hardy, Eliot, or Edward Thomas), and he argued that Larkin's strong sense of humour distinguished him, in fact, from such other literary pessimists. Hartley commended the balance between plainness and lyricism found in *The High Windows*, suggested that Larkin had not so much developed as deepened, and explicated various poems. He thought Larkin's newest book darker and less hopeful than its predecessors (partly because Larkin himself was now older and closer to death), and he predicted that Larkin's future poetry would probably become even bleaker.[32]

Hartley's positive assessment was echoed by David C. Nimmo, who found *High Windows* sad but not sentimental, clear but exacting (especially in its demands on its readers' alertness), and more likely than previous Larkin volumes to emphasise constricted spaces and lack of movement. If Nimmo had any objection, it was to the new book's occasional vulgarity.[33] Meanwhile, Kerry McSweeney similarly praised the newest volume but emphasised its resemblances to Larkin's earlier works rather than stressing any differences.[34] Finally, William H. Pritchard praised the book enthusiastically, defending Larkin against various critics, finding his work at least as good as the writings of fashionable American poets, and singling out 'The Old Fools' and 'The Building' for special commendation. Pritchard thought some of Larkin's distinctive thematic traits resulted from his bachelorhood, and he likened Larkin both to Randall Jarrell and to Robert Frost.[35]

Equally impressed was J. R. Watson. He argued, also in 1975, that Larkin often moved from the mundane to the mystical; that he much resembled Robert Browning in using dramatic monologues and invented speakers; and, most importantly, that Larkin's real value lay in the ways he managed to suggest lingering sacred resonances in profane, everyday circumstances. 'Church Going', of course, helped support this claim, but Watson argued that Larkin was often, at root, a fundamentally religious poet – not for professing belief in any theological creed but for seeking (and sometimes finding) intimations of deeper meanings in mundane settings and occurrences.[36]

Another 1975 reviewer who praised Larkin was Stephen S. Hilliard, who commended *High Windows* for all the usual reasons (its forthright explorations of change and mortality, its emphasis on life's limits, its effective blending of the serious and the comic, its almost Elizabethan plainness of style, and its especially its integrity in facing darkness).[37] Far more interesting, however, was a review by Walford

Davies, who saw Larkin as a postmodern figure for having given up pretentious posturing. But Davies, even more intriguingly, praised Larkin's recent conservative political verse – verse that other critics disdained. He saw it as evidence of Larkin's interests in the larger world, just as he also perceived a growing interest by Larkin in nature. He found Larkin's verse frequently moving and even, sometimes, subtly tinged with symbolism.[38] Meanwhile, Edward Lucie-Smith, commenting on Larkin briefly, saw him as a perceptive nihilist who was popular because he depicted Britain as it really was and who dealt with its limits without much complaint. Interestingly, he compared Larkin briefly to Anne Sexton: both poets, he thought, emphasised alienation and impotence.[39]

Larkin in the Mid-1970s

Hermann Peschmann, also in 1975, helpfully reviewed Larkin's career.[40] He began by discussing (and disputing) various echoes heard by other critics in some of Larkin's apprentice verse and then suggested that the real problem of Larkin's earliest, Yeatsian poetry was that it seemed both contrived and derivative, inspired more by others' writings than by reality itself. The shift to realism coincided with Larkin's growing interest in Hardy, which led in turn to a growing interest in the writing favoured by 'The Movement', with its colloquial, hard-bitten phrasing and its lucid focus on contemporary life. Peschmann thought Larkin more compassionate than was often recognised, although he felt that by the time of *The Whitsun Weddings* the poet's language had also grown vernacular to the point of sometimes being awkwardly ribald. But it was in assessing *High Windows* in relation to Larkin's 'development' that Peschmann was most helpful:

> ■ This 'development' for the most part is in depth, not in opening up fresh areas of experience; confirmatory of earlier attitudes, not exploratory of new: a deepening of his controlled bitterness, disillusion, and pessimism, the very control testifying to their authenticity; and an extension of the area of his deep human compassion. The poems, whether single or in groups, link in turn with earlier poems, almost invariably to probe a theme or mood more profoundly... .the theme itself reverberates through the work, different facets of which are explored in different poems, demanding – though Larkin himself is the least didactic of poets – our assent to his disenchanted vision, to his minimal expectations from life.[41] □

Much of this had already been said by others, but rarely so succinctly.

Reviews of *High Windows* continued to appear in 1976. Steven David Lavine expressed admiration for the volume as a whole but misgivings about the right-wing politics and conservative social outlook some poems revealed.[42] Also in 1976, Robert B. Shaw began by noting Larkin's uniquely elevated reputation, suggested the ways his poems resembled small novels (by emphasising plot and character), but then complained about Larkin's agnosticism and his sometimes finicky phrasing. Shaw found Larkin's poetry somewhat repetitious when read in bulk, but he nevertheless praised *High Windows* for seeming ultimately more mature and less artificial than some of Larkin's earlier writing.[43]

Already by 1976, reactions to *High Windows* had begun to die down and critics now often returned to general overviews of Larkin's writing. Martin Scofield, for instance, in a long article in *The Massachusetts Review*, seemed mainly interested in introducing the poet to American readers. He stressed Larkin's high reputation in England and surveyed previous reactions to Larkin (especially the charges levelled by M. L. Rosenthal). Scofield defended Larkin against allegations that his poems were flawed for not confronting important political issues. He especially praised 'At Grass', expressed a preference for poems in which Larkin (or a speaker) was least visible, and noted differences in tone between Larkin and such respected American poets as James Dickey. He suggested that readers new to Larkin should begin not with *The North Ship* but with *The Whitsun Weddings*, singling out that volume's title poem as especially strong. Finally, Scofield (like others) argued that there were more sharp and gloomy poems in *High Windows* than in any of Larkin's preceding volumes.[44] Also in 1976, C. B. Cox – like Scofield apparently writing mainly with American readers in mind – explained that Larkin's poetry was not timid but deliberately anti-heroic, that his poems often intentionally avoided developing a single coherent tone, and that his sometimes puzzling use of personae reflected his purposefully anti-heroic stance.[45]

During that same year, John P. McIntyre published a brief but substantial essay full of specific points. He contended, for instance, that Larkin resembled the American poets Richard Wilbur and W. D. Snodgrass in being interested in everyday things, that he rejected nature and dreams as standard sources of poetic consolation, and that his poetry was actually more realistic than pessimistic. McIntyre argued that often a Larkin speaker will find something lacking in a particular circumstance he attempts to describe. According to McIntyre, Larkin resisted evading reality (whether through travel or other kinds of attempted transcendence), preferring instead to face life truly. McIntyre concluded that Larkin tended to write about the standard topics of innocence and experience, but in tones involving both romance and tragedy (but especially the latter) and in ways that distinguished inadequate fantasy from true (if brief) moments of genuine imagination.[46] Clearly McIntyre was one of Larkin's many admirers.

James Atlas, however, was far less sympathetic. In a 1977 essay for American readers, he noted Larkin's unusual popularity in Britain (even among people who did not normally read poetry), and then he suggested that Larkin's main themes were alienation and England itself. He praised certain poems, commended the haunting quality of some of Larkin's earliest lyrics, but thought that recently Larkin had become gloomier, less musical, more repetitive, more resigned to English decline and decay, less generous towards young people, and less convincing in his occasional use of slang and obscenity. Atlas found *High Windows* unfortunately limited at precisely the time when Larkin's stature seemed most assured.[47] Also commenting in 1977 on Larkin's American reception was Bernard Bergonzi, who suggested that Larkin was less read in the United States than in England partly because much of his phrasing, understatement, and gloom (and many of his cultural references) were so obviously home-grown. Bergonzi argued that a truly great poet could reach beyond native shores, but he concluded that Larkin, while quite a fine writer, was not truly great.[48]

Far more affirming than Bergonzi's essay was a 1977 piece by David Lodge, who set Larkin within the contexts of post-war literature, specifically outlining his relations with 'The Movement' in both style and attitudes. He suggested Larkin's relative disinterest in metaphorical and symbolic language but clearly emphasised his importance as one of England's greatest living writers.[49] Richard Swigg, meanwhile, offered a long, desultory essay placing Larkin within the larger contexts of twentieth-century poetry and generally condemning his alleged negativity and obsession with failure.[50] Far more helpful was a 1977 essay by John Press, written (like much else from this time) partly to introduce Larkin to an ever-growing American audience. Press dealt with such matters as allusions in *High Windows*, the literary intelligence reflected in *The North Ship*, the ways reading Hardy helped liberate Larkin from Yeats, and Larkin's long-standing idea that anything can be the subject of a successful poem as long as the subject genuinely moves the writer. Press also commented on such issues as Larkin's emphasis on suffering, sadness, and compassion; the Tennysonian tone of *The Less Deceived*; and the strong emphasis, in *High Windows*, on current conditions in England. Press then discussed Larkin's skilful use of rhyme, the compactness of some of his recent phrasing (bordering on obscurity), and a growing tendency to vulgarity. He ended by comparing Larkin once more to Tennyson, not only in his themes and tone but also in his immense public stature.

One further indication of that stature was the chapter devoted to Larkin in a 1977 book by John Wain, the poet's old friend and comrade.

By this time Wain had been elected to the Chair of Poetry at Oxford. His decision to lecture on Larkin was further evidence that these one-time 'Movement' rebels had both 'arrived'. Wain stressed Larkin's habitual focus on specific details, his tendency to use poems to broaden and deepen awareness, and his interest in people making choices, especially choices about how to live. This interest (Wain thought) would make Larkin a poet highly unsuitable to a dictatorial society whose citizens lacked free choice. Wain noted Larkin's concern with the impact of time and history on individual lives, his frequently subtle satire, and his refreshing freedom from left-wing political correctness (as it would later come to be called). He also complimented the breadth of Larkin's writing, not only in topics and themes but also in techniques, including stanza forms, metre, and sound effects. He noted Larkin's tendency to use certain images repeatedly (including water, brides, and especially trees), and he also – like many previous critics – praised Larkin for often moving from the mundane to the mysterious.[51] Little of this was very new, but Wain's new prominence surely helped Larkin win even more readers. The same might be said of further praise of Larkin in 1977 by Seamus Heaney, himself a poet of growing stature. Heaney mainly compared Larkin's poetry to that of the seventeenth-century Cavaliers and the post-Restoration Augustans, as well as to such early twentieth-century poets as Rupert Brooke and Edward Thomas.[52]

Larkin in the Late 1970s

1978 was a doubly important year for Larkin scholarship. One reason was the publication of an article by Roger Bowen that seems to have been one of the first to draw on unpublished archival notebooks now housed at the British Library. Bowen noted, for instance, the existence of an unfinished verse drama titled *Night in the Plague* as well as other unpublished work. Bowen also argued that Larkin, while frightened by the prospect of personal death, nonetheless had begun to imply, more and more, a belief that death was not the whole picture, at least for a constantly renewing nature.[53] Similarly, Kenneth Moon, also in 1978, commented on Larkin's tendency to distance or briefly lift himself from a confined perspective to an appealing (if temporary) larger one, often achieving a greater sense of intensity by momentarily employing striking imagery of nature.[54] Meanwhile, a 1978 essay by Norma Procopiow compared and contrasted Larkin and the American poet Frank O'Hara, commenting that their verse shared a sense of life's limits as well as a lack of anger, hopelessness, or lofty ideals. She argued that Larkin (unlike O'Hara) rarely wrote poems about composing poetry but that he resembled certain American poets in writing straightforwardly about himself, without much symbolic phrasing, or echoes of other writers, or mythic allusions. Procopiow found Larkin lacking in much sympathy for the people he described, suggesting instead that he found solace not in connections with others but in everyday routines. Her essay indicated, if nothing else, that Larkin was now increasingly widely read on both sides of the Atlantic.[55]

Much the same is revealed by the really major Larkin-related event of 1978: the publication of a book by Bruce Martin issued as part of an important series by Boston-based Twayne Publishers. Its appearance indicated that Larkin was now an increasingly common part of the US college curriculum.[56] Twayne books were widely available in American public and school libraries and were widely read by undergraduate and graduate students. Designed as relatively short, accessible, but still substantial introductions to the authors they featured, these books came as close as anything to indicating the accepted current shape of the literary 'canon'. Martin reviewed Larkin's career, his ideas about poetry, and the general settings and people featured in particular poems. He also examined Larkin's forms as well as his phrasing and methods. A chapter discussed his prose, his development, and his critical reception. Finally, a solid annotated bibliography briefly but helpfully surveyed the state of Larkin scholarship. Martin began by noting that Larkin's speakers often resembled the poet himself, that Larkin had loved reading from his days as a boy, that he had begun writing and publishing while still a youth, and that he had developed a strong early interest in jazz. He discussed Larkin's studies at war-time Oxford, his developing friendship with Kingsley Amis, his various other college friends and acquaintances, the influence on his early poetry of such writers as Vernon Watkins and W. B. Yeats, and his strong initial interest in writing novels.

Martin noted Larkin's distrust of theoretical prescriptions, his general disdain for Modernism in all the arts, his dislike for art that seemed too distant from actual human beings, and his attachment to the idea of form in general and to traditional forms in particular. For Larkin, the best poetry (Martin explained) should be generally accessible (not arcane or academic). It should be emotionally honest and stylistically clear and rooted in reason as well as feeling.[57] Larkin's poetry was popular (Martin maintained), partly because it was set in a recognisable, familiar environment. Larkin tended to write about large British towns, sometimes with countryside nearby, and his poems often featured travel within Britain (usually by train) as well as a broad cross-section of typical British people of different ages, classes, and cultural backgrounds. Like Hardy, Larkin wrote of a particular nation and its people but in ways accessible to anyone who could read English. He usually focused on individual speakers living in an increasingly secular world that was changing and darkening. The process of ageing, the threat of encroaching death, the tedium of work, the yearning for escape, and the uncertainties of love and other kinds of human relations – these were all (Martin noted) common themes of Larkin's verse. His characters, often bachelors, typically seemed distant from other people, and, like most persons, they were subject to time, attracted by illusions, and disappointed by mutability and the bleakness of living in a world apparently offering little hope of lasting satisfaction. Martin saw Larkin as sceptical about innocence, children, Romanticism, and any assumed beneficence in nature, which was lovely but largely indifferent to humans. The poet tried to face ordinary life with honest realism, but he was also capable of mocking his own weaknesses and treating others with compassion while still avoiding anything sentimental. His spokesmen were often outsiders, but in many poems he often remained preoccupied with love as an appealing (if frequently disappointing) ideal.[58]

Commenting on the designs and forms of Larkin's poems, Martin began by noting that the poet's very interest in form had sometimes been compared to that of great English poets of the post-Restoration period. Yet Larkin not only often employed traditional stanza patterns and rhyme schemes but also frequently created works exhibiting less obvious kinds of unity – unity of thought, feeling, implied argument, and ultimate development. His poems often began (Martin claimed) by confronting some problem which speakers then attempted to resolve, either successfully or in flawed ways that made the speakers themselves the subjects of the poet's irony. In such latter cases, the poems developed towards some reversal that undercut (by revealing) the speaker's own limitations of thought or feeling. Discussing many specific poems, Martin showed how the speakers often end feeling dissatisfied, either because of their own shortcomings, the shortcomings of the world in general, or some combination of the two. Sometimes the speakers seem to develop; sometimes they seem static; and often they engage in rationalisation or repetitive behaviour and end feeling regret. Not all Larkin's poems, however (according to Martin), focused on speakers. Sometimes they featured landscapes, places, events, or other people that became subjects of observation and meditation. And sometimes Larkin created argumentative poems (including his more topical or political verse) that were sometimes didactic or satiric. But, however Larkin chose to structure his various works, some kind of structure itself was, according to Larkin, central to his verse.[59]

Helpfully discussing Larkin's style, Martin explored the poet's tones, images, and use of metre. Typically (Martin wrote), Larkin's speakers (and the poet who could be intuited behind them) were everyday people with whom most readers could identify. Their words were often colloquial, vernacular, sometimes crude, and sometimes full of slang, implying a rejection of pretentious, artificial, academic, or arcane phrasing. Larkin's style was neither lofty nor low but usually somewhere in between, and his tone was often the subdued tone of actual conversation, employing realistically conversational language. Sometimes (often at the ends of poems), Larkin's diction would rise to a higher level, frequently through the use of some special or unusual phrasing, and sometimes he favoured words with negative prefixes (such as 'un' or 'dis') – and even occasionally doubled them – so that his phrasing would not seem too simplistic or positively assertive. He did use images, but not as frequently or symbolically as in much earlier poetry of the twentieth century. Compared to such verse, his writing could often seem prosaic and plain. He liked (Martin wrote) to use common clichés to keep his voice close to actual speech, but he also often employed resonant puns and other kinds of word-play. His use of imagery and metaphors seemed all the more significant because it was rarely overdone: when he did employ figurative language, it often carried real weight. Finally, his use of stanzas and metres tended to be simultaneously traditional and unpredictable. He avoided free verse (Martin claimed) because he doubted human freedom, but he rarely locked himself into rigid formal patterns, often running the sense of sentences beyond the endings of lines and even stanzas. Complex patterns tended to be associated with complex speakers or perspectives, and part of Larkin's power derived precisely from this kind of technical artistry.[60]

Martin's chapter on Larkin's prose described his novels in some detail and touched much more briefly on his criticism, in both cases suggesting the continuities between the writer of prose and the writer of verse. But it was in his next chapter, on Larkin's development, that Martin returned most fully to the poetry. He suggested how Larkin's first book, *The North Ship*, both differed from and resembled his later writing. It differed in being less realistic; it was similar in often focusing on single speakers aware of their alienation. Mostly, though, Martin found this early book sentimental and imprecise, featuring self-involved speakers who aroused little interest or sympathy. These early poems were also (Martin thought) too technically simple, with little of the intriguing syntax, metre, and stanza shapes Larkin would later employ. Such problems had largely disappeared, however, from *The Less Deceived*. Here the poems were more complicated in design and thought (but never confusing) and were also more likely to be set in cities and seem, in general, more convincingly realistic. As Larkin continued to develop (Martin thought), he had often grown less distant from his speakers; in his latest verse they were less likely to seem invented characters than actual alter egos. Nevertheless, Martin suggested, on the basis of such poems as 'The Card-Players', that Larkin might be developing in directions no one could have predicted from his earlier writings. Martin's concluding chapter briefly surveyed Larkin's critical fortunes up to the mid-1970s, noting how he had been attacked, why he had been praised, and why he had generally won the widespread respect he now enjoyed as an honest, realistic, accessible, and talented witness to a complicated, sometimes disappointing era.[61]

One of the last comments on Larkin from the 1970s came in a 1979 article by David Cushman.[62] He began by acknowledging Larkin's status as England's pre-eminent living poet but suggested that some American readers would find him out of step, in tone and form, with the confessional poetry then common in the United States. Cushman noted Larkin's emphasis on human limits and urban settings, but he also suggested the importance of Larkin's nature imagery, especially in the early, Yeatsian volume *The North Ship*, where that imagery struck Cushman as somewhat bookish and derivative. But he was much more impressed by *The Less Deceived*, calling it Larkin's representative volume, since his verse had changed little in later years. Cushman did, however, offer high praise for 'The Whitsun Weddings', seeing that work as ultimately one of Larkin's most positive poems and noting that its final affirmative vision is linked in many ways with images of nature. Cushman praised Larkin's generally precise phrasing, suggested that his best poems seemed unforced, and discussed the ways Larkin used nature imagery to explore two recurring topics – disappointment and mutability. He found the typical Larkin speaker a meditative loner and then described Larkin's typical presentation of nature:

> ■ Nature is a realm of pure beauty and pure being that humankind is unalterably prevented from reaching. We saw the newlyweds in 'The Whitsun Weddings' seeming to make contact with that realm, but that was only fleetingly in a visionary moment granted the poet. Ordinarily Larkin perceives nature as remote and powerful and somehow timeless, whereas human beings are drab and finite. Nature is beautiful in Larkin's poetry, [but] people rarely are. Larkin's natural images contain a powerful, latent sense of yearning. The pure world of 'unfenced existence' described in 'Here' is all the more painful for being both perceivable and unobtainable.[63] □

Later Cushman noted that Larkin usually associated freedom with the sun, particularly in *High Windows*. In general, Cushman's article foreshadowed a growing concern among critics with the role of nature in Larkin's verse – a concern that would become, as we shall see in the next chapter, especially prominent in commentary from the 1980s.

CHAPTER THREE

Larkin Triumphant: The 1980s

By the beginning of the 1980s, Larkin had become perhaps England's best-loved poet – the unofficial poet laureate of the nation even though he now felt that his inspiration had largely deserted him and that he would be producing few more, if any, significant poems. Throughout the 1980s, and especially after he passed away in late 1985, Larkin was increasingly celebrated. More and more essays and books appeared, and his premature death at age 63 was widely mourned. By 1988 a good edition collecting many of his best poems (poems already published, previously unpublished, and previously scattered) appeared, so that readers could now see his achievements more completely than ever before. Academic articles and scholarly monographs continued to be published, but they were now joined by an increasing number of collections of essays. By the 1980s, a Larkin critical industry was working full-time. He was now recognised, even more than before, as a key poetic voice of his era.

Larkin in the Early 80s

One of the earliest commentaries on Larkin to appear in the new decade was by Grevel Lindop, who in 1980 surveyed Larkin's poetry from the 1970s.[1] He focused especially on *High Windows*, seeing it as generally milder than much of Larkin's earlier work and as looking back, in some ways, to the kind of lyricism and symbolism (sometimes involving the four natural elements) often found in *The Less Deceived*. He emphasised the stress, in *High Windows*, on a wistful – occasionally *too* wistful – depiction of the past, but he also noted (without complaint) the satirical tone of some of the brief political poems and read 'This Be the Verse' (surely correctly) as itself partly a bit of satire on the speaker's curmudgeonly bitterness. Lindop even suggested that the influence of Yeatsian lyricism had begun to re-emerge in Larkin's latest book. But he reserved special praise for the very darkest of the newer poems:

> ■ Larkin's finest achievement of the 1970s ... has been a group of poems which eschew both symbolist experiment and the limitations of satire and social criticism. A small number of poems, in particular 'The Building', 'The Old Fools', and the uncollected 'Aubade', have confronted the things we can hardly bear to face – sickness, old age and death – with a degree of nervous honesty rare even in poetry and virtually unknown in common life. ... Poems like these, finding their terrible subjects at the heart of mundane daily experience and presenting them with an authority almost bardic and yet quite free from romantic trappings, form a substantial achievement, and one earned by the discipline of working, during previous decades, within the limited poetic of *The Less Deceived* and *The Whitsun Weddings*.[2] □

Lindop showed how such poems subtly implicated readers in the fates they so hauntingly described.

Another important commentary from 1980 was by Barbara Everett, who observed that Larkin was now considered, by many, not only the most talented living English poet but also one of the best in Europe. She noted, however, that some critics had found his latest book less lucid, more tangled in ambiguities, than earlier volumes. Everett traced this trait to the lingering influence of Modernism and symbolism, which he had tried to put aside but which affected his writing nonetheless. Everett contended that Larkin, in his latest collection, was far more influenced by French symbolist writers than many readers recognised.[3] Meanwhile, Mary Ford, also in 1980, intriguingly surveyed some of the best of Larkin's longer poems, such as 'Church Going', 'The Whitsun Weddings', and the recently published 'Aubade' – a poem almost immediately recognised as one of his best. These longer works (Ford maintained) usually followed a similar structure. They typically began with a description, then moved to intellectual pondering, then developed towards some emotional response, and then finally concluded with some sense of insight or even positive assertion. Ford compared them to seventeenth-century 'meditative' poems but also noted their debt to Thomas Hardy, especially in themes, forms, and basic attitudes. Ford explained why longer forms were needed to accomplish the poems' complex purposes, and she also noted the texts' frequent focus on shared routines. Finally, she suggested that the longer poems had darkened as Larkin's career had progressed, ending in the sometimes frightening works he had written most recently.[4]

The 1980s also began with the publication of a helpful new book: Simon Petch's *The Art of Philip Larkin* (1981).[5] Petch explained that he considered Larkin a great poet because of his talent for exploring common features of life in ways most people could understand but also in ways that did not seem superficial or supercilious. Petch was interested less in Larkin's themes than in *how* Larkin wrote, particularly by creating speakers who shaped readers' experiences of poems. Petch first surveyed previous (sometimes hostile) responses to Larkin's writing, then reviewed some of Larkin's own comments about his work, and then discussed such matters as the morality underlying Larkin's interest in the mundane, his reasons for disliking arcane Modernism in all the arts, his sympathy with eighteenth-century Augustan writing because of his desire to be accessible, and his similar sympathy with Hardy. Petch argued, however, that Larkin was still often more indebted to Yeats than he might like to admit, and he additionally agreed with critics who had suggested that Larkin's verse was more subtly intellectual (especially in its allusions) than many readers might suspect. Larkin's poetry was (Petch contended) more subtly artful than was often stressed, even suggesting that Larkin's skilful creation of particular speakers linked him more closely to Modernism than Larkin himself might want to concede. Petch asserted that many aspects of Larkin's art – including his use of rhyme, metre, imagery, recurring structures, *and* speakers – deserved much more attention. While conceding that occasionally Larkin's tone was indeed (as some had charged) too dark and even self-pitying, Petch nonetheless defended Larkin's realistic attention to life's limits and traps and to human self-deceptions, including illusions fostered by the imagination. As he proceeded, Petch helpfully reviewed (and cited) much previous Larkin criticism, engaging in real dialogue even with writers with whom he disagreed.[6]

Petch's chapter on Larkin's early work suggested, variously, that *The North Ship* is generally (but not always) too Romantic, superficial, stolid, placid, vague, and artificial in rhyme and metre to succeed very often. But Petch argued that Larkin's novels began to move his work in the more realistic, more archetypal directions that would later benefit his poetry, especially by exploring human transience. Turning next to *The Less Deceived*, Petch emphasised the book's general variety, its distinct treatments of varied kinds of deception (including self-deception), its occasional use of novelistic realism, and the often subtle ways Larkin prepared readers for unexpected conclusions, as in 'Next, Please'. Petch explored Larkin's effective use of metaphors, his crucial use of particular speakers, the important distinction that often exists between speaker and poet, and the benefits, to Larkin's poetry, of the ways he often distances himself from his speakers. Petch did not find all the poems in *The Less Deceived* uniformly successful. He thought the weakest the most didactic and least dramatic. But his comments on all the poems he discussed were anchored in close attention to specific details. Ultimately, Petch argued that in the best poems in *The Less Deceived*, the speakers seem intriguing characters rather than spokesmen for Larkin in any simple, unequivocal sense.[7]

Turning to *The Whitsun Weddings*, Petch again highlighted the importance of Larkin's tendency to use complex speakers, but he also commented on such matters as Larkin's changes in tense, the ways he uses different *kinds* of speakers, the ways he sometimes blends the symbolic with the colloquial, and the various ways he explores such recurring themes as alienation and the self. Here as previously, Petch paid close attention to such technical matters as rhyme, rhythm, enjambment, end-stopping, stanza form, and many others. He noted developments in Larkin's use of symbolism and imagery (including, for instance, imagery from advertisements), the ways Larkin sometimes employs form to subvert imagery, and the ways he explores not only such themes as loss, tedium, anxiety, fear, and loneliness but also (sometimes) human bonds. Petch ended by praising *The Whitsun Weddings* as wider-ranging than its predecessor, especially thematically.[8]

Petch's final chapter – on *High Windows* – surveyed many individual poems, helpfully concentrating on phrasing, form, rhythms, and design rather than simply on themes. He did, however, note such matters as the social emphases of many poems, their concern with death, the often realistic ways in which they presented nature, their frequent engagement with current events, their implied praise of English traditions, and their typical interest in such matters as alienation, self-consciousness, anxiety, and the particular personalities of specific speakers. Generally, however, Petch's volume helped call real and sustained attention not only to Larkin's characteristic themes but also to his precise use of particular words.

The appearance of two new books on Larkin in 1982 – one a brief monograph by Andrew Motion and the other an essay collection edited by Anthony Thwaite – helped mark the poet's sixtieth birthday. Motion's book commented, among other matters, on Larkin's debts to the modernists and symbolists; his nonetheless less frequent and more lucid use of symbols (when compared to Yeats); the ways his shift from Yeats to Hardy as models for his verse was relevant to larger tensions in English literary history; and the influence on his writing of other English poets besides Hardy, including Wordsworth, Tennyson, Housman, Thomas, and Auden. Motion then recounted Larkin's life, surveyed some of his artistic opinions (especially his emphases on stylistic clarity and everyday topics), and ultimately asserted that Larkin had never entirely abandoned his youthful interest in the kind of romanticism he associated with Yeats. Motion found, in Larkin's novels, some of the same concerns also expressed in the poetry, such as the tension between romantic yearnings and hard, dark facts, but he then spent the rest of the book discussing Larkin's verse. He challenged claims that Larkin was relentlessly pessimistic; noted his emphasis on individual quests for meaning; and stressed his interest in the positive effects of traditional social rituals, especially as alternatives to loneliness. Motion commented on Larkin's often wry depiction of love; his tendency to write poems that amounted to small debates between opposing ideas or ideals; and his recurring interests in such topics as time, mutability, free choice, and persistence and striving, even in the face of hard facts and dark fate. According to Motion, Larkin's poems were rarely satisfied simply with just one basic attitude or point of view; instead, they genuinely explored different possible ways of thinking and feeling, even if they often eventually opted for the darker perspective. Motion argued that Larkin never seemed *simply* or *entirely* dark; his poems were more dialogical than that, just as they also often involved a dialectic between realism and idealism as well as between the straightforward and the symbolic (as in 'The Whitsun Weddings').[9]

Anthony Thwaite was the editor of another book on Larkin in 1982 – this one a collection of essays designed to celebrate the poet's six decades of life.[10] Some essays were biographical, including reminiscences (often amusing, always interesting) by such friends as Noel Hughes, Kingsley Amis, Robert Conquest, Charles Monteith, B. C. Bloomfield, Douglas Dunn, Harry Chambers, Andrew Motion, Alan Bennett, and many others. Each essayist focused on a different aspect of Larkin's life or career, and the effect of reading the whole book was to realise just how many admiring friends this supposedly lonely, withdrawn man actually possessed. This volume also often illuminated just how genuinely *funny* Larkin could be, despite his reputation as a dour pessimist.

Finally, a further noteworthy publication from 1982 was another essay by Barbara Everett arguing that this poet was rarely as simple or literal as he himself (and others) often claimed. Everett thought his best writing was often both lucid *and* metaphorical, both down-to-earth *and* symbolic.[11] But not all critics praised his work. In 1983, Christopher Miller issued one of the longest, harshest indictments of Larkin ever published, dismissing him as a popular but ultimately very minor writer whose admirers revealed their own lack of taste and perception. Miller argued that some of Larkin's phrasing made little obvious or consistent sense; that his supposed 'compassion' was often rooted in condescension; that his alleged modesty revealed an underlying pride; that his poems were relentlessly and predictably pessimistic; and that his attempts to be moving often seemed calculated and unconvincing. Miller accused Larkin of both smugness and self-pity. He suggested that even the poet's occasionally good writing merely showed up the shallowness of his other work, and he especially accused Larkin of being a poet who, by rejecting any real attempts at loftiness himself, also discouraged attempted loftiness in others. Larkin, for Miller, was a bourgeois poet, a latter-day Georgian who resembled Edward Thomas while lacking that poet's talent. Larkin struck Miller (especially in his latest volume) as a bitter, vindictive, deceitful, and sneering poet whose recent work was perhaps even worse than anything he had written before.[12] Anyone seeking a compendium of the worst that could be thought and said about Larkin should consult Miller's essay. Placed beside this fierce denunciation, A. T. Tolley's 1984 article tracing the fortunes of Larkin's early manuscript poetry seemed by contrast genteel and academic, but it shared with most Larkin criticism from this period an assumption Miller could not abide: that Larkin was indeed one of the world's most important living poets, so that even juvenilia he had never published were worth discussing.[13]

Larkin by this point was also increasingly celebrated outside England. Thus a lengthy 1985 article by Michael Saladyga in *The American Poetry Review* (a publication actually read by many poets and writers) argued for Larkin's international importance. Among other things, Saladyga situated Larkin in relation to other living writers both at home and abroad; discussed his pre-eminent reputation in England; compared and contrasted (but mostly compared) him to Betjeman; and explored such issues as Larkin's use of personae, his interest in memory, and his relevance to other contemporary writers facing many similar sociological and cultural conditions.[14] Meanwhile, a lengthy scholarly (and somewhat theoretical essay) by John Reibetanz appeared in 1986 in the *University of Toronto Quarterly*. Reibetanz particularly discussed the relevance of Larkin's novels to his poetry (especially their relevance to issues of self, time, and knowledge of physical reality). For Reibetanz, the novels' protagonists were relevant not only to the speakers of Larkin's poems but also to their author, helping explain the simultaneous impulses of involvement and withdrawal often found in both. Larkin's turn from fiction indicated, for Reibetanz, a turn from other people to the self and a turn from the extended time of narrative fiction to the concentrated time of the lyric. Yet Reibetanz thought that Larkin also brought with him, into his poetry, a frequent narrative impulse (often expressed in long lines) that showed that he had not turned his back on storytelling completely.[15]

Even more theoretical than Reibetanz's article was a long 1985 book by Guido Latré titled *Locking Earth to the Sky: A Structuralist Approach to Philip Larkin's Poetry*. Latré began by extensively surveying important structuralist thinkers and theories, then offered a comprehensive overview of Larkin critics and criticism, and then eventually turned to his own detailed analysis of Larkin's verse in general and of many particular poems. He concluded that previous approaches to Larkin's work had been variously narrow, that Larkin's poetry often combined realism, metaphor, and symbolism (with much interaction among the three), and that his poems often in fact moved from realism through metaphorical writing and then to the symbolic mode. Latré found similar dynamism in the stances Larkin's speakers took towards the poems' subject matters: sometimes, he thought, those stances seemed distant, sometimes empathetic, but often shuttled between those options. Finally, and most interestingly, he suggested that Larkin's poetry often sought some kind of union between the real and ideal. Since such unions were rare, it was the *quest* for an elusive harmony, rather than its attainment, that characterised most of Larkin's poems.[16] Latré also found definite development in Larkin's career: he supposedly moved from an early, Yeatsian stage of '"romantic twilight"' to 'successive stages of respectively metaphoric revelations, disenchantment, symbolic revelations and dualism, to a stage of hope, doubt, and silence'.[17] Finally, Latré suggested that Larkin had far more in common with T. S. Eliot than was often perceived, especially in their shared rejection of the wasteland of contemporary existence and their shared yearning for satisfying alternatives.[18]

Larkin's Death and its Aftermath

By 1985, then, Larkin had become, in Latré's volume, the subject of the longest, most theoretically sophisticated book on him published so far. But of course the crucial event of 1985 for all admirers of Larkin was his death on 2 December. Appropriately enough, he passed away in the depths of winter and (as later biographies would reveal) also in the depths of depression and fear about his looming mortality. His last words – spoken to an attending nurse, the only other person present – were simply, 'I am going to the inevitable'.[19] Of course, a writer's literary afterlife can rarely be predicted and rarely seems inevitable. Many writers are attacked or forgotten after they die (only to be rediscovered, years later, if they are lucky). But Larkin's fortunes remained (at least into the early 1990s) remarkably strong. He continued to be, if anything, an even more beloved figure in the immediate aftermath of his death than he had been while alive. His passing was followed by even more recognition and celebration than he had received while he lived, not only in his own country but also abroad. Most commentators writing about his death assumed that a great poet had been lost.

Certainly this was the assumption underlying three brief pieces – by Donald Hall, Robert Richman, and X. J. Kennedy – published in February 1986. Hall especially praised Larkin's syntactical skill, comparing him in that regard to Robert Frost and Edward Thomas. He extolled the beauty of Larkin's verse and the real gratification it could give.[20] Richman saw Larkin as an increasingly dark representative of native English poetic traditions.[21] Finally, Kennedy celebrated his skilful use of form, rhythm, rhyme, and other sound effects.[22] Meanwhile, David Young, also in 1986, began by expressing reservations about the poet's sometimes excessive formalism, his frequent sentimentality, and his unfortunate commitment to an often unconvincing tough-guy persona. But these defects seemed quite minor (Young argued) when one realised how richly ambiguous and paradoxical the poetry often was – how far it was from being simple or simplistic, how riven it was with tensions and ambivalence, including an ambivalence involving the comic and the tragic.[23]

John Wain, Larkin's old friend, also published a long appreciative piece in 1986. Ironically, the essay began by suggesting that Larkin might never be as appealing to American readers as he was to the English, partly because the two literatures had grown somewhat distant and partly because Larkin often wrote in such a distinctively English idiom. But Wain definitely saw Larkin as a major English poet, one who had transformed how poetry could be written in England and one who had reconnected English verse with a broad readership. Wain considered Larkin an even more talented version of Betjeman, comparing him also to Pope as a poet who united real gifts of mind with utterly solid craftsmanship.[24] A briefer 1986 piece, by Philip Hobsbaum, contended that when Larkin wrote about England, he did so in ways that seemed full of life even when his subject matter seemed shabby.[25]

Of all the essays published in 1986, perhaps the most interesting and substantive was by John Wooley. Beginning with a detailed response to Larkin's poem 'Lines on a Young Lady's Photograph Album', Wooley then ranged more widely. He noted, for instance, Larkin's commitment to traditional British values and his misgivings about recent changes in British culture. But Wooley considered Larkin's satire of these changes sometimes unsubtle (occasionally attacking straw men) and therefore ineffective. He argued, nevertheless, that Larkin was occasionally a convincing polemicist and that often his best poems about Britain celebrated British traditions rather than merely satirising the nation's alleged decline. On the one hand, Wooley thought Larkin was sometimes too single-minded (as in some of the political poems or the darkest lyrics), but, on the other, he thought Larkin sometimes too ambivalent, as in the concluding stanza of 'An Arundel Tomb'. He compared Larkin to Austen, Johnson, and the Augustan writers in his basically traditional views, although he felt that Larkin's conservatism was more a matter of personality than of politics *per se*. In tracing Larkin's roots, Wooley also mentioned Browning and the moderns (who, like Larkin, liked to use personae), as well as Yeats and Hardy. He concluded that Larkin's best poems seemed most balanced, most open to diverse perspectives.[26]

In a somewhat technical analysis, also from 1986, Guido Latré argued that Larkin's style was so rich (despite its seeming simplicity) that it often defeated the best efforts of modern theorists to explain precisely how it achieved its particular effects. Latré concluded, however, that a constant shuttling back and forth between literalism and symbolism, between realism and metaphor, gave Larkin's phrasing its powerful impact.[27] Much the same point – it was becoming an increasingly common point to make – was argued in a 1986 essay by Roger Elliott. Trying to explain the popular appeal of Larkin's most famous poem, Elliott set himself a straightforward question:

> ■ What is it about *Church Going* that [so many] readers respond to? I would suggest two contradictory things: its casual informality, and its careful artificiality. The tone of the poem might be described as a brilliantly executed balancing act which avoids falling into the pit of mere inconsequential dullness on one side, or that of inflated pretentiousness on the other. It manages to be at the same time a man speaking to men, apparently without premeditation, in the flat tones of the mid-twentieth century, and a carefully structured piece of verbal artifice.[28] □

Ultimately, however, Elliott found the poem more than simply disappointing; he ended by condemning 'Church Going' as finally vacuous. He found it symptomatic of an era that could sometimes be sentimental about religion without really taking religion (or at least Christianity) very seriously at all. Elliott thought this poem (and, by implication, much of Larkin's other poetry) implied the era's spiritual emptiness. However, another essay from 1986 (by Mike Tierce) suggested that the poet, far from speaking for his age, had in fact increasingly come to speak mainly for himself. According to Tierce, Larkin's poetic output diminished and then ceased as he realised he had failed in a key objective. He had been unsuccessful in building, or holding, the interest of a broad mass of readers, the ideal audience for whom he had hoped to write. They, instead, now had many other ways to entertain themselves, especially thanks to pop culture. Larkin, according to Tierce, became dispirited and then finally silent as he realised that poetry no longer meant much to most of his contemporaries.[29]

Nevertheless, evidence of Larkin's own growing popularity proliferated. If anything, he became even more appealing to academics and regular readers after his death than he had been before it. One especially important example of this growing esteem was the 1986 publication of Terry Whalen's excellent book *Philip Larkin and English Poetry*. Based on various essays Whalen had recently published, this volume added substantially to Larkin scholarship. It did so not only because of its declared emphasis on close reading but also because it covered so many topics and themes. Whalen began by reviewing the different stages of Larkin's career, emphasising that Larkin had never completely lost contact with his early romantic, symbolist beginnings. He commented on such matters as the structures underlying Larkin's various books, the unappreciated breadth of his vision, and the varied English writers who seemed to have influenced his writing. Whalen next emphasised the variety of personae Larkin adopted in different poems as well as the various tones he often employed both within and between distinct texts. Larkin's tones (Whalen explained) could be alternately sardonic, melancholy, comic, and/or celebratory, sometimes even within the same work. He conceded that Larkin's occasionally bitter wit annoyed some readers, but he argued that the poet's sense of fun (including self-satire) made his frequent ventures into seriousness or celebration seem the responses of a complete human being. Whalen thought Larkin's humour (as in 'Church Going') was often put to serious uses, whether by mocking those who fell short of an ideal or protecting the speaker's own voice from sentimentality or pretence. Larkin's mockery (Whalen thought) did contribute to a typical sense of the speaker as distanced, but the irony often preceded some substantial, meaningful closing statement. Thus these twin impulses in Larkin's speakers – towards the comic and the serious – often worked in tandem, reinforcing and complicating one another. Larkin could often mock life and celebrate beauty in the same poem, and it could be a mistake to take some of Larkin's self-consciously clever speakers too seriously. Often poems would ultimately undercut such speakers' facile wit by moving to a finally serious point, and sometimes the speakers themselves would discover something more serious even in themselves by the time a poem concluded. Larkin's tones, Whalen persuasively argued, were rarely merely simple; they were almost always complex or ambivalent in one way or another. Thus his frequently melancholy tone often helped enrich or complicate his affirmations, and this process also worked in reverse, making Larkin a more dialogical poet than was often realised. His humour, for example, made him less grim than his master, Hardy, so that life to Larkin could sometimes seem tragic, sometimes funny, sometimes beautiful, and sometimes all at once. Part of the satisfaction of reading Larkin (Whalen maintained) was the pleasure derived from rethinking, from contemplating existence (and good poetry) as more complicated than it might first appear to be.[30]

Whalen's third chapter began by comparing Larkin to Samuel Johnson, especially in their mutual detachment and scepticism and in their shared emphasis on such themes as tedium, disappointment, work, mortality, unhappiness, the complexities of human psychology, and the 'vanity of human wishes'. All these interests contributed, to the work of both men, a strong sense of compassion for human suffering; both understood the strength of human folly and perceived life all the more clearly by viewing it from the perspective of inevitable death. Larkin, in particular, was at least as willing to mock himself as to mock others;

he realised that he shared with most humans a yearning for comforting illusions, and this realisation helped prevent him from merely disdaining folly in others. Larkin was, according to Whalen, temperamentally conservative much as Johnson was: he wanted to preserve the best of the past, realising how mutable life and everything in it could be and therefore how much the best was under constant threat. Thus it is not surprising to Whalen that Larkin shared with Johnson and other Augustans an interest in traditional forms (although always interwoven with a strong sense of colloquial phrasing and contemporary sentence structures). According to Whalen, many of Larkin's most characteristic traits of theme, style, and attitude seem less idiosyncratic if we see him as part of the same tradition as such writers as Johnson and such other, more recent English classicists as T. E. Hulme.[31]

Yet Larkin also (Whalen argued) had much in common with D. H. Lawrence, whom he early admired and whose love of beauty, the tangible world, and moments of awe (even religious awe) Larkin never entirely abandoned, especially in such works as 'The Explosion'. According to Whalen, Larkin shared with Lawrence an appreciation of nature's mysteries and vitality, which both poets often associated with the sun.[32] Larkin, like Lawrence, valued solitude, but he also (Whalen maintained) greatly admired many aspects of common life, including a strong sense of community with other persons and the social traditions that promoted such community, as in such poems as 'The Whitsun Weddings', 'Show Saturday', and 'To the Sea'. In their shared emphases on the actual details of lived existence and in the ways they valued moments of revelation, Lawrence and Larkin both (Whalen contended) had much in common with the early twentieth-century Imagist poets. This was especially true of the ways the Imagists emphasised sight as a crucial sense and the importance of vivid perceptions.[33] According to Whalen,

■ Larkin significantly emphasises a close connection between seeing, thinking, and feeling. In his view, each poem re-creates a real perception and moves it upward to transcend time in the qualified way that a work of art can.... The extent to which Larkin is a transcendent poet is both limited and liberating. He is an intuitive poet who refuses to turn his intuitions into myth or ideology, leaving the reader with a chronicle rather than a system of epiphanies.[34] □

Whalen resisted the temptation to link Larkin strongly to the Symbolists (as other critics had begun to do) precisely because he thought that in Larkin the impulse towards transcendence is always firmly grounded in what is real, common, and familiar. In this respect, Whalen found many similarities between Larkin and such other contemporary British writers as Ted Hughes, Thom Gunn, R. S. Thomas, Elizabeth Jennings, Charles Tomlinson, and Seamus Heaney, all of whom, to one degree or another, shared Larkin's keen interest in the minute details of life as it was really lived, not merely imagined.[35]

The publication of Whalen's fine book was just the latest indication of Larkin's growing reputation; another was the appearance of a guide for students, written by Andrew Swarbrick and also issued in 1986. Focusing on *The Less Deceived* and *The Whitsun Weddings*, Swarbrick stressed various characteristic features of Larkin's poems, including their clarity, accessibility, historical realism, focus on ordinary life, perceptions of natural beauty, stress on individual alienation, and interest in private yearnings and shared desires. Swarbrick noted that Larkin's typical themes included such matters as frustrated relationships, limited self-knowledge, and illusions and disillusionment, as well as the fact of mutability and the possibility of transcending it (if only briefly). Discussing Larkin's style, Swarbrick noted such matters as his inventive, flexible use of stanzas, his reliance on half-rhymes, his skilled use of rhythms that were perceptible but rarely rigid, and his similar flexibility in employing syntax: the structure of the sentence was rarely fixed by the structure of the stanza, thanks partly to frequent use of enjambment. Swarbrick commented on Larkin's typical focus on images from daily life, his occasional tendency to move from an everyday tone to more elevated language, and his general use of colloquial diction (sometimes to the point of employing slang or foul language). Swarbrick discussed Larkin's penchant for irony and satire, his frequent use of convincing dramatic monologues, his generally honest tone, and his speakers' frequent habit of engaging in a kind of dialectic or dialogue with themselves. He then offered detailed discussions of over 30 separate poems, concluding with a very helpful chapter surveying critical responses to Larkin's writing. Swarbrick here reported and then answered varied attacks on Larkin's verse, including charges that his poems were predictable, that he had failed to progress during his career, that his poems were too pessimistic, that they failed to engage with important issues of the day, and that his style was too conservative. Swarbrick's book packed much real substance into less than eighty pages: his brief volume conveyed most of the key concerns both of Larkin and of his many commentators.[36]

William Pritchard's 1987 article on Larkin amounted to yet another general appreciation aimed at American readers. It commented on such matters as the ways Larkin's voice inspired trust, the ways his poems often ended with small but important revelations, and the fact that few critics really disagreed about the basic meanings of most of Larkin's texts. Pritchard commented that the important American poets Randall Jarrell and Robert Lowell had both admired Larkin from as early as the 1950s, that Larkin often plays with (and off) his readers' own self-deceptions, and that (in Pritchard's opinion) *High Windows* was Larkin's best book and 'Aubade' one of his very finest poems. He commended Larkin's often intricate rhyme schemes as well as his craftsmanship in general, and he censured a recently published anthology of poetry for not giving Larkin higher praise.[37] Similarly positive in assessing Larkin was Angela Ball, also in 1987. Ball noted Larkin's affection for ceremonies and traditions as well as his variously balanced attention to beauty, seriousness, and significance (on the one hand) *and* to the mundane and the imperfect (on the other).[38]

Larkin in the Late 80s

By the late 1980s, then, interest in Larkin only continued to grow, manifesting itself both in the appearance of numerous academic articles and in the publication of various monographs and essay collections. One book, by the Iranian-born Salem K. Hassan, was titled *Philip Larkin and His Contemporaries* (1988). It opened by expressing interest in such matters as the design and phrasing of Larkin's works, the ways he used conventional structures to deal with ordinary life, the value of his detached perspective, and the ways his apparent gloom could actually be seen as evidence of a basically robust approach to life. Discussing *The North Ship*, Hassan explored a number of important themes, including fate, mutability, mortality, melancholy, disappointments, illusions, life's limits, unsatisfied yearnings, and failures in love.[39] Turning next to *The Less Deceived*, he focused on varied issues, including that collection's emphasis on time, death, the past, pessimism, and stoicism – all the familiar topics of Larkin commentary. Yet Hassan, while also predictably commending Larkin's lucid, vernacular, unsentimental, ironic, and often logical phrasing, did note the empathy and humour that began to appear in this new collection, and he also particularly praised Larkin's water imagery.[40]

Hassan's chapter on *The Whitsun Weddings* was his longest. Stressing once more such themes as destructive time, pervasive melancholy, disappointments in love, and a general sense of futility (inevitable issues in Larkin criticism), Hassan offered detailed readings of particular poems, paying very close attention to the choice of specific words and symbols while also suggesting Larkin's interest in such methods as description, discussion, and meditation. Hassan dealt with recurring image-patterns (including music and nature) and explored the connotations of many individual terms. Larkin's techniques were at least as important to Hassan as his topics, and particular poems (rather than broad generalisations) received the lion's share of attention. Much the same was true of his chapter on *High Windows*, although there he did address such matters as Larkin's use of paradox to express feeling as well as thought, his typical rejection of high-flown phrasing, his emphasis on movement in nature, and his frequent use of comedy and satire when treating serious issues. Generalising about Hassan's book is difficult because so much of it was valuably focused on individual words, lines, and even sounds.[41]

Later, however, Hassan offered chapters comparing and contrasting Larkin with a variety of other living English authors, including Thom Gunn, D. J. Enright, Kingsley Amis, and John Wain. In Gunn (but not in Larkin), Hassan found an emphasis on violence, vitality, the living past, and the lively present. In Enright (as well as in Larkin), he noted an interest in imaginative views of the mundane. Both Larkin *and* Amis (Hassan argued) were anti-Romantics interested in mutability and mortality. And whereas Hassan felt that Larkin and Wain were both unsentimental, he asserted that Larkin seemed more concerned with the past than Wain, whose main worries focused on the future. Hassan helpfully summed up his overall view of the five writers in several succinct sentences:

> ■ Apart from Larkin, all the rest accept the past and consider it as a vital period in the formation of one's life. However, they more or less share the same belief that life is contradictory. They also accept the view that life is tragic, yet they are driven by different impulses to carry on[:] ... Larkin by acceptance, Gunn by revolt, Enright and Amis by reconciliation and Wain by stoical resistance.[42] □

Hassan made his most distinctive contribution by relating Larkin to other major poets of his time, although many readers will also value the detailed studies he offered of many individual poems.[43]

Little in the first half of Hassan's book (except the specific analyses) was especially original, but the same was also increasingly true of more and more commentary on Larkin. Most critics by now agreed in their generally high assessment of him. Because they could not assume, however, that their readers had read much previous writing about him, they often repeated what had already been said before. Each new assessment, though, did tend to illuminate some new (if small) aspect of the poet's career or writings. Thus George Watson, in a mainly biographical 1988 essay, did interestingly relate Larkin's tone to the specific decades that had shaped his early life, especially the depression-era thirties, the war-time forties, and the constricted fifties. Watson suggested, for instance, that the limitations Larkin wrote about (and embraced) very much reflected the general post-war mood.[44]

Another 1988 article, by Barry Spurr, argued that Larkin's strong sense of detachment and isolation was hinted at even in his very earliest, most Yeatsian poetry, and Spurr also distinguished *The Less Deceived* from the later books by suggesting that the final collections were less equivocal and more decidedly gloomy than their path-breaking predecessor. Spurr considered *The Whitsun Weddings* better than *High Windows*: the latter struck him as too pervasively dark, especially in its determination to confront relentlessly the final fact of death.[45] Meanwhile, another essay from 1988, this one by G. Singh, went over much familiar ground, but it also offered an unusual comment about Larkin's similarities to T. S. Eliot:

> ■ Larkin was, at least in his later poetry, somehow closer to Eliot than to [Ezra] Pound and even Yeats – closer to Eliot both by way of temperament (shy, reserved, self-effacing as a man; and a master of poetically charged understatement, irony and paradox as a poet), and by way of his commanding style that is deliberately subdued, prosaic, and journalistic, and that fights shy of any display of too much lyric warmth or emotional intensity ....[46] □

Singh was one of many earlier critics who objected to Larkin's use of foul language (especially in 'This be the verse'), but in general his article took Larkin's stature and achievement for granted.[47]

Articles on Larkin began to flood forward in 1989, both as separate publications and as parts of essay collections. An essay by John Goodby, for example, dealt with such standard issues in Larkin's verse as isolation, detachment, loneliness, and his use of personae. Goodby's most interesting comments, however, concerned a possible connection between Larkin's own growing gloom and the breakdown of British political consensus in the 1960s and 1970s. The poet's darkening tone was (for Goodby) not simply a result of his private, personal ageing but also a reflection of an increasingly grim mood in British society in general.[48] Laurence Lerner, also in 1989, explored the familiar topic of Larkin's tendency to alternate (often in the same poem) between basic realism and brief transcendence, arguing that Larkin's typical inclusion of both traits gives added resonance to each. Larkin recognises (Lerner suggested) that humans do often yearn for seriousness and purpose and that they tend to invent almost any way to satisfy that yearning, including writing poetry.[49] Indeed, another 1989 essay (by M. W. Rowe) argued that the yearning for transcendence was so intense in Larkin himself that it often affected his typical imagery. Images of the sun, water, and space (Rowe contended) appeared repeatedly in Larkin's verse, often suggesting a combination of joy and of freedom from loneliness and constriction.[50]

Peter MacDonald Smith, also in 1989, may have been one of the first commentators to suggest that Larkin might be classified as 'postmodern' (although Smith readily conceded that this now-popular term was quite difficult to define). He noted, for instance, in Larkin's verse various traits often associated with postmodernism, including,

> ■ the prominence of the individual and the conversion of his life into art; the division between the poet and 'the poet' – that degree of detachment that leaves the reader unsure whether to curse or bless, to sympathise or to condemn; the reader's more general uncertainty whether to put faith in the poet, and then which attitude or course of action the poet is in sympathy with; the poet's own unease here, and the sense of one course of action cancelling out another, and neither being obviously for the best; the contraction, silence and nihilism:
> Get out as early as you can,
> And don't have any kids yourself.[51] □

This emphasis on radical uncertainty and scepticism sounds much like 'deconstruction' (postmodernism's close cousin, and another idea much in play during the 1980s and 1990s). But whatever term one wanted to use to label these interpretive conundrums, the mere fact that Smith found them in Larkin was symptomatic of the times. Earlier critics had often claimed that Larkin's meanings were so obvious that they needed almost no interpretation or explication. Smith, and increasing numbers of critics of his era, obviously disagreed. Also worth noting, however, was Smith's additional claim that Larkin's frequent, open depiction of himself *as* himself in so many of his poems was a strategy unparalleled in the history of English lyric verse.[52] Whether or not this claim could stand up to scrutiny was another matter (one thinks of Byron or Rochester, to name just two), but the assertion was certainly worth pondering.

Other essays from 1989 further contributed to the critical conversation. Thus Hugh Underhill found, in many of Larkin's poems, interacting impulses of affirmation and negation, especially in presenting nostalgia (which could seem appealing in Larkin's writing but which was rarely actually endorsed). Underhill likewise argued that Larkin expressed ambivalent views both of companionship and of rural existence, and in fact thought Louise MacNeice Larkin's most important predecessor as a poet primarily concerned with common life in urban settings.[53] Interestingly, Underhill briefly touched on a topic developed at great length in another essay from 1989, a particularly insightful piece by J. R. Watson. Watson explored Larkin's handling of clichés, arguing that his use of them was multifaceted. Sometimes they gave his poems the flavour of common, ordinary speech. Sometimes they suggested the ways most people typically feel and commonly think. Those feelings and thoughts could occasionally seem shallow or ridiculous but could also sometimes seem genuine and even moving. As an example of shallowness, Watson mentioned the academic clichés Larkin satirised in 'Naturally the Foundation Will Bear Your Expenses'; as an example of authentic, touching emotion, he cited the haunting use of italicised, formulaic language in 'The Explosion'. Watson's own phrasing was admirably lucid, and his insights were consistently suggestive.[54] Perhaps this was less true, however, of a 1989 essay by John Skinner. Skinner's piece may have been one of the first deliberately 'deconstructive' commentaries on Larkin. Beginning by highlighting the poet's affinities with Yeats and Wordsworth, the article ultimately suggested that Larkin's heavily autobiographical verse might finally be seen as mere self-subverting rhetorical play.[55]

1989 also saw the publication of three books on Larkin, including two essay collections. One – *Philip Larkin: The Poems*, edited by Linda Cookson and Bryan Loughrey – was particularly helpful. Designed for students but full of substantial articles, the Cookson–Loughrey volume began with a very fine essay by Andrew Gibson. He emphasised Larkin's concern with ordinary life, plain language, and the urge to appeal to a wide readership – an urge reflected in his frequent use of the pronoun 'we'. Yet Gibson noted that Larkin, despite claiming to be an anti-modernist Englishman, had in fact read widely in recent international literature and even sometimes alluded to foreign texts. Larkin, in other words, was for Gibson more complicated than Larkin sometimes wanted to seem, but this apparent simplicity was part of his appeal. Gibson noted Larkin's interest in moments of insight or revelation, in which the common could suddenly seem extraordinary. Larkin's perspective as a sensitive, perceptive outsider allowed him to view ordinary life in unexpected ways: he could appreciate and celebrate common life by using distinctive means and methods. Gibson argued, in fact, that Larkin was always interested in unusual perspectives, including perspectives not his own. For Gibson, there were multiple Larkins, often in dialogue inside single poems. Competing views were often juxtaposed within particular works, creating diverse effects. Larkin was especially attuned (Gibson claimed) both to moments of loss and to moments of liberty.[56]

Cedric Watts, in a brief essay on Larkin's love of jazz, discussed the poet's contempt for really modern jazz (a contempt Watts found unfortunate), although he noted that Larkin's published reviews of such jazz were actually often tolerant and open-minded. Most significantly, Watts saw Larkin's devotion to older forms of jazz (especially the highly accessible 'blues') as encouraging the kind of melancholy, unpretentious poetry he himself composed.[57] Another essay, by Michael Gearin-Tosh, reviewed Larkin's well-known interest in such topics as deprivation and love and the ways those two issues often appear in the same poems, while yet another article, by John Saunders, discussed various poems in light of Larkin's interest in such issues as the past, nostalgia, beauty, truth, and the complex relations among them all.[58] Meanwhile, Peter Hollindale's essay dealt with Larkin's tendency to see any present moment from a distanced perspective frequently involving reflection on the past and dread of the future. If Larkin often (according to Hollindale) viewed the present with scepticism and wariness, sometimes his vision was more positive and even affirmative, although he usually tried to guard against self-deceptive naïveté.[59]

Alan Gardiner's essay in the 1989 Cookson and Loughrey volume examined various specific poems while also commenting on Larkin's unpretentious, everyday speakers, his precise attention to social details, his gloomy attitudes towards contemporary life, and his identity as a specifically 'English' poet.[60] An essay by Harvey Hallsmith discussed Larkin's use of first-person personae who were often distanced versions of himself – personae whom he could mock in poems that often evolved from emphasising an 'I' to stressing a 'we', just as they also often evolved in tone from the ordinary and mundane to the serious and even profound.[61] In an especially fine essay, Roger Day examined evidence of Larkin's own basically agnostic or secular views of religion but thought his poems frequently revealed his intense interest in religious and spiritual subjects and his often awe-filled attitude towards the mere facts of existence and joy, however impermanent they might be.[62] Another excellent essay, by Ronald Draper, called attention to how variously Larkin often managed, by altering details of style and imagery, to raise the tone of his poems as they reached their conclusions, so that they frequently ended in far more affirmative or even celebratory ways than they had begun, especially when dealing with the rituals and traditions that often gave meaning to human life. The poems (Draper argued) often moved from simple descriptions of everyday details to complex yearnings for something loftier and more fulfilling.[63]

In an especially stimulating article, Graham Holderness compared and contrasted Larkin and Dylan Thomas, finding Larkin less adventurous, both in language and in fundamental aims and outlook, than his Welsh counterpart. Holderness argued that Larkin was content to take things (including language) as he found them rather than trying to transform or improve them, as Thomas often did. Larkin's typically English, typically empirical attitude towards life often made his poetry (according to Holderness) more superficial, less politically subversive (particularly in depicting women), and more conservative both in style and in thinking than the writing of figures such as Thomas, who were more challenging than Larkin in many different ways.[64] Rarely had an important critic recently assailed Larkin as forcefully as Holderness did, making his essay an article that anyone wanting to defend and celebrate Larkin needed to consider. The essay by Holderness was the final piece in a generally excellent collection.

Another 1989 collection of essays on Larkin was edited by Dale Salwak. It included biographical pieces by such figures as Kingsley Amis, Anthony Curtis, Edwin A. Dawes, Maeve M. Brennan, John White, Janice Rossen, Noel Hughes, and Hazel Holt, who discussed Larkin, variously, as a friend, student, librarian, lover of jazz, 'little Englander', and admirer of the novelist Barbara Pym. Meanwhile, the first two essays in the volume's critical section – pieces by William Pritchard and David Lodge – had already been published in 1987 and 1977, respectively.[65] A new essay, by J. R. Watson, discussed Larkin's distinctive, often complex 'voice', both as a man and a poet. Using italics for emphasis, Watson indicated the words Larkin stressed when reading some of his own poems aloud, but he also suggested that Larkin's poetic voice had changed from one volume to the next: each of his final three books (Watson argued) generally reflected the prevailing tone of the decade in which it was published, although Watson found the voice of *High Windows* particularly rich and various.[66]

John H. Augustine's essay in the Salwak volume suggested that Larkin's poetry showed a dialectical concern both with isolation and with social involvement, so that interest in one enhanced interest in the other.[67] An essay by Barbara Everett praised Larkin as a 'philistine' – that is, as a writer so committed to staying in touch with real readers, and so suspicious of 'arty', academic pretensions, that he knowingly risked the charge of writing in a way that was *too* common – a risk he was quite admirably (in Everett's opinion) willing to take.[68] In another essay, Bruce K. Martin suggested that Larkin, unlike most contemporary English poets, had a strong appeal to (and following among) American readers. Like Robert Frost (Martin argued), Larkin wrote in ways that readers almost everywhere found accessible, but he also wrote on topics of enduring interest, such as love, sex, time, mutability, and death. He wrote about the England of his own era in ways Americans could understand, adopting tones sometimes empirically detailed and sometimes intriguingly speculative, as the speaker imagined the thoughts, feelings, and lives of others. Larkin's poetry (Martin contended) expressed simultaneous impulses towards desire and doubt, knowledge and scepticism, and the interplay among all of these.[69] The Salwak volume ended with a small sheaf of memorial essays (some already published and discussed earlier in the present book), by Hilary Kilmarnock, John Bayley, X. J. Kennedy, and Donald Hall.[70]

Of the books published in 1989, perhaps the most important was Janice Rossen's *Philip Larkin: His Life's Work*. This was a full-scale monograph offering various significant– sometimes actually negative – assessments of Larkin as man and writer. Rossen opened by commenting on such matters as his habit of self-mockery, his ambivalent attitudes towards social involvement, the praise as well as the criticism he had received, and his sometimes hostile attitude towards critics and academics. Much of her emphasis was biographical; she traced Larkin's earliest years as a writer, discussed the well-known influences on his youthful verse, and speculated about the personal psychological impulses that may have prompted his initial writing, including fear of failure, general self-doubt and depression, and frustration with his attempts at writing novels. One especially valuable aspect of Rossen's volume was its use of evidence from Larkin's early notebooks and its discussion of the poet's revisions, as well as his strategies and possible motives both for writing, rewriting, selecting, and rejecting various versions of specific poems. Rossen generally saw the young Larkin as a highly conflicted person and author who sometimes dealt aggressively with his frustrations while also often turning them into art.[71]

Rossen next discussed the strong (and divergent) influences of Yeats and then Hardy on Larkin's early verse (the first writer romantically seeking union with nature, the second lamenting with irony his alienation from it). She noted Larkin's recurring tendency to place speakers inside of rooms, separated from nature but also highly aware of its existence outside. She especially explored his depiction of nature in *The North Ship*, where it frequently appeared as both cold and vigorous. Often unable to connect with nature, Larkin's early speakers frequently emphasised this fact; the typical speaker in the early poems remains distanced from nature but nevertheless very much aware of it. Sometimes (as in 'Church Going'), buildings became identified with nature, so that inside and outside merged. More often, however, Larkin's speakers remain separated from nature; real communion with it is (and always has been) impossible. The same is often true (Rossen argued) of the speakers' relations with other people; the speakers often observe and desire connections but rarely achieve them, just as they often embrace atheism or agnosticism but yearn for the comforts religion promises but can never truly provide. As Rossen depicted him, Larkin was fundamentally and variously torn: between yearning and frustration, sentiment and irony, and the desire for connectedness (on the one hand) and the brute facts of isolation and alienation (on the other).[72]

Rossen next explored the tendency of Larkin's speakers both to celebrate England and to keep their distance, both from the place itself and from actual English people. His poems about England (she argued) could be sometimes tender, sometimes hostile, sometimes nostalgic, sometimes fatalistic about England's decline, and they could even be occasionally petty. His presentations of actual English people could alternate between admiration and satire, so that the ambivalence Rossen noted in his attitudes towards nature carried over to his attitudes towards his nation and its people – a people he tended to describe in terms of class, gender, and/or age. Larkin's typical stance towards society, as towards most things (she argued) was detached; often his speakers observe and comment rather than fully participating in the social world they describe, even when they are celebrating aspects of that world (as in 'The Whitsun Weddings').[73]

Perhaps the most interesting section of Rossen's book was its discussion of Larkin's treatment of women, which she thought sometimes verged on misogyny (but which was, perhaps, part of a more general, deeper misanthropy). She felt Larkin's frequent hostility towards females was common among men of his generation, but she also tried to find explanations for it in his personal psychology, particularly his own insecurities in dealing with women, whom she thought he often depicted as powerful manipulators of relatively powerless men.[74] Rossen saw even Larkin's positive depictions of women as often inherently sexist and even violent, and in general she considered his views of women hostile and self-pitying:

> ■ For the most part, the very egocentrism, anger and frustration which Larkin articulates form the heart of his argument against women throughout his work. If life is painful, he insists on howling about it and on not allowing any dilution of his pain. ... From one point of view, the only way to counter feminine sexual allure as power is by means of retaliation and violence. Nonetheless, these outbursts are in part a rhetorical device designed to mock and satirise what was, to Larkin and others of his generation, a real dilemma; and to some extent he seems to have solved the problem by devoting himself to writing and insisting on its superior importance ....[75] □

Rossen often depicted Larkin as an angry man and saw his anger as rooted in a pre-emptive impulse to ward off attacks. She emphasised his alleged bitterness towards anyone who might challenge him or even disagree with his opinions, and she considered his anti-intellectual public persona a self-defensive pose. She noted how his passion for jazz had helped shape his attitudes towards his own writing: in both cases he valued art that was accessible and moving rather than arcane and academic. He sometimes used coarse language (Rossen thought) not only for literary effect but also because his views were indeed often coarse and angry, and one fact that especially angered him was death, which both frightened him and filled him with fury.[76] If there was one major keynote to Rossen's book, it was her stress on Larkin's indignation.

Rossen's book was fairly unusual, in the 1980s, in presenting a dark, even antagonistic view of Larkin. She was especially troubled by his depictions of women, and she made it clear that she found his personality variously flawed. This kind of scepticism had not been common in most previous criticism from the 1980s. But, as the next chapter will show, all that would change in the first half of the ensuing decade.

CHAPTER FOUR

Larkin Under Siege: The 1990s

By the beginning of the 1990s, Larkin's literary and public stature was firm and secure. Many now considered him *the* most significant English poet since the 1950s. The 1988 publication of his *Collected Poems* (edited by Anthony Thwaite) had only enhanced his reputation and added numerous previously unpublished texts to his *oeuvre*. His texts were now studied with more and more focus on their precise technical details, and he even began to attract the attention of literary theorists and to figure in debates about different kinds of literary theory. An important survey of previous Larkin criticism appeared, indicating that there was now enough to make a survey needed and worthwhile. In the early 1990s, more texts by and about Larkin – including selected letters and a forthcoming biography – seemed only likely to solidify his standing. In the event, however, just the opposite happened: the letters and biography (published in 1992 and 1993, respectively) revealed aspects of Larkin that badly damaged his reputation as a man and even as a poet. By the mid-1990s it seemed legitimate to wonder if his standing would ever recover.

Larkin in the Early 1990s

As 1990 began, however, his position seemed unassailable. Tom Paulin, admittedly, was already expressing misgivings about Larkin's right-wing politics and traditional cultural views. Paulin provocatively suggested that Larkin's real focus, despite his poetry's apparently personal emphases, was England's loss of worldly, material power. Paulin argued that, although Larkin's poems might superficially seem to explore the depressing limits of individual lives, their chief subtext was loss of English glory. He considered Larkin a cultural Thatcherite and actual misogynist whose attitudes were anything but enlightened or progressive.[1]

Mostly, though, commentary on Larkin in 1990 ignored his politics and took his poetry's worth for granted. Robert Faggen, for instance, ended a review of the *Collected Poems* by firmly asserting the poetry's importance.[2] Patrick Garland similarly assumed Larkin's significance, noting in passing his gift for musical phrasing.[3] James Richardson praised Larkin's tendency to publish only his best work, his willingness to explore the realities of day-to-day life, and his lack of illusions about himself or people in general.[4] Katha Pollitt heartily extolled his verse, citing its cleverness, lucidity, colloquial phrasing, and faithful reflections of everyday existence. She noted his humour, his consistency in theme and style, and his habit of qualifying potentially positive visions, but affirmed the appealing presence of those visions nonetheless. For Pollitt, part of Larkin's attraction lay precisely in his hesitations, second-guessings, and complexities of tones and attitudes. She compared his themes to Housman's, commended the accessibility of his topics and style, noted the ways he confronted alienation, and suggested that he was (paradoxically) so appealing partly because his vision *was* so dark.[5]

Peter Filkins, reviewing Thwaite's edition in 1990, praised Larkin's unpretentiousness, his striving for coherence and lucidity, his melancholy stoicism, and his avoidance of merely private, confessional topics and techniques. He commended Larkin for creating a distanced sense of awe; noted the sequential early influences of Auden, Yeats, and Hardy; applauded Larkin's progress from a youthful simple darkness to a later dark humour; and appreciated the way Larkin faced reality unflinchingly. He commented on Larkin's relatively silent final decade, noted his poetry's diminishing humour, and suggested that disappointments in love remained a key poetic theme. Like most commentators from 1990 (Paulin excepted), Filkins was obviously admiring.[6]

In an interesting 1990 'biographical' essay, Tim Trengove-Jones noted that Larkin's poems often drew strongly on his life even though he presented himself as intensely private. Trengove-Jones observed that from his boyhood into his early thirties, Larkin had severely stammered – an affliction that encouraged expression through writing rather than speech, but one that also shaped his preferences for privacy, his aversion to foreign travel and foreign languages, as well as his love of plain English – a love that linked him with a broad readership.[7]

Another especially interesting 1990 article was published by William Harmon. Intriguingly, Harmon questioned the common assumption that Yeats and Hardy had obviously influenced Larkin's poetry, although he did note that both Hardy and Larkin emphasised real experience as the basis of strong poems and that both had used the unusual terza-rima sonnet form. Harmon's article, in fact, extensively discussed Larkin's use of form, rhyme, metre, line-endings, and other techniques. He argued that Larkin often moved from an everyday experience to a thoughtful meditation, complexly interweaving affirmation and scepticism. Harmon also traced changes in Larkin's style, including a movement away from the heavy alliteration found in some early work to a later effective use of foul language. Yet Harmon also noted Larkin's enduring consistencies, such as his general (rather than specific) references to places as well as his formal inventiveness, especially in rhyme and metre. Harmon had produced one of the very best discussions ever of Larkin's techniques.[8]

Similarly worthwhile was a 1990 essay by Stephen Watson.[9] He commended Larkin for writing unpretentiously about everyday life, for developing a distinctive style and poetic persona that inspired readers' trust, and for memorably exploring such important topics as death, links between sexual disappointment and anger, and various other key concerns:

> ■ Larkin's other preoccupations [include] the gap between pleasure and reality principles, and the illusions that flourish between; the fear of personal failure; the *tristesse* [sadness] of sex, especially for a certain type of awkward, rather unhappy person; the conflict between love (always seen as culminating in marriage) and work (i.e. poetry); love's incompetents; and, everywhere, the irresolute and infirm in spirit. ... He was often at his most masterly in registering how certain central dreads, always kept slightly to the side of one's life, could encroach on the consciousness, returning with all the gathering, chilling force that the return of the repressed commonly possesses.[10] □

According to Watson, Larkin appealed partly because he habitually explored metaphysical questions (especially concerning the meaning of life) that he knew he could neither resolve nor ignore. His poetry implied the limits of individual lives – limits to which he responded sometimes gently, sometimes angrily, and often compassionately. He yearned, like a Romantic, both for solid meanings and for spiritual transcendence but lacked a Romantic's confidence that either could be attained. His poems, therefore, are often tinged with sadness, partly because they imply a diminished public role both for poetry and the poet himself in the twentieth century. Larkin (according to Watson) viewed poetry's traditional stature and place as under siege, partly thanks to newer kinds of academic critics. They sceptically questioned all the old alleged verities, including truth, beauty, goodness, artistic pleasure, and even the possibilities of such ideals as real meaning, genuine communication, and deeply emotional responses to life and art. Poetry, in short, had been deconstructed, but Larkin did his best (Watson thought) to fight a defiant rear-guard action, defending literature's value from sceptical assault. Even his best efforts, however, might not suffice. Watson thought the outlook for poets in general, and especially for poets like Larkin, seemed dark.

Watson's pessimism, however, may have been premature. By 1991, Larkin's popularity (even among academics) continued to grow. That year saw, for instance, the publication of two student guides. One, by David Punter, examined the poet's life and times, discussed many specific poems, and then commented more generally on his themes, form, style, imagery, and symbolism. Punter repeated many standard claims, emphasising (for instance) Larkin's economical phrasing, skill in using standard forms, focus on everyday life and lives, and interest in the social ceremonies that give limited meanings to human existence. Punter noted Larkin's stress on disappointment (rather than anger), his pervasive irony, his concern with family relationships, and his habit of presenting carefully balanced feelings rather than emotional extremes. He thought Larkin's verse reflected Hardy's plain-spokenness, the influence of vernacular speech, a rejection of preaching, and a refusal of easy answers. Larkin often wrote (Punter claimed) about persons affected by strong, unsettling external forces. His trapped people are often sad and lonely; they fear death but sometimes also desire it. His poems usually rhyme, often complexly, and often employ complex stanzas. Larkin was best (Punter suggested) when using pentameter lines and lengthy stanzas, and his phrasing was less routinely vernacular than was sometimes assumed.[11] Similarly helpful was another 1991 introduction, this one by Graham Handley, although it focused almost exclusively on individual poems rather than offering the kind of general commentary Punter provided.[12]

1991 also saw the publication of an especially impressive monograph. Written by A. T. Tolley and titled *My Proper Ground*, this relatively neglected book greatly benefitted from the recent availability of Larkin's manuscripts. It thoroughly reviewed the poet's life and writings, offering an overview both deeply sympathetic and sometimes critical when criticism seemed justified. It explored Larkin's style, forms, and themes, closely examining many poems. Tolley's opening chapter was especially important in discussing early influences. He mentioned Hardy (of course) but also discussed in detail the impact of Auden and various Audenesque poets of the 1930s, including Spender, MacNeice, Isherwood, and many others. Tolley showed that Auden's influence was eventually supplanted by that of Yeats, but he also argued that Larkin never escaped Auden's impact and that it strongly affected the writing that eventually made Larkin famous. Tolley then discussed Larkin's early novels, noting *A Girl in Winter*'s formal sophistication and the ways both it and *Jill* anticipated the poetry both in techniques and in themes. An ensuing chapter explored how Larkin moved away, in his poetry, from Yeats's visionary style to a kind of writing more firmly rooted in realism and mundane existence.

As Tolley steadily traced Larkin's stylistic development, he invariably pointed to specific poems, showing precisely how and why particular works (or even phrases) marked new stages in Larkin's achievement. But he also connected Larkin's evolution to specific historical changes, such as the rapid rise and fall of 'the Movement', the growth of empiricism in post-war British philosophy, and the ways 'the Movement' was both conservative and iconoclastic. Tolley also revealed his detailed familiarity with the evolution of Larkin's own writing:

> ■ The poems from 1954 and 1955 introduce something quite new in Larkin's poetry. The speaker is not the neutral, authorial voice presenting an experience or making a statement about it, as in 'At Grass' or 'Deceptions'. In 'Reasons for Attendance', 'Mr. Bleaney', and 'Church Going', the speaker – quasi-autobiographical – is dramatised through the details of the poem, and in all these poems there is an element of ironic self-deflation. More startling at the time they appeared was the association of this irony with certain attitudes that seemed to contradict conventional pieties [about work, family, religion, etc.] Most noticeable to readers of the early fifties would have been the fact that the poems stay with these attitudes, rather than seeking some redeeming mode of transcending them.[13] □

Tolley claimed, in short, that it was Larkin's pervasive *irony* – his willingness to think and say the unexpected in ways that could seem both comical and serious – that made his poetry seem distinctive while also linking it with work by other 'Movement' writers, such as the novel *Lucky Jim* (1954) by his friend Kingsley Amis. As Tolley moved patiently through the Larkin canon, one could see exactly how (and even in some cases why) the poet developed as he did. Tolley showed how Larkin's books were reviewed and anthologised, the degrees to which his poems resembled works by his contemporaries and the crucial role 'the Movement', but also how Larkin soon moved beyond any such grouping.

Tolley's familiarity with the ways particular poems evolved allowed him to comment precisely on their specific stylistic and thematic features. He showed, for instance, how 'The Whitsun Weddings' both did and did not resemble poetry by John Betjeman (whom Larkin admired) as well as how that poem was both unusual (in being less ironic) and also typically Larkinesque. Tolley commented on Larkin's common formal patterns (such as movement from placid normality to developing disturbance and then to a changed perspective, as in 'Dockery and Son'). He showed how such patterns reflected the influence of such earlier poets as Yeats. He likewise demonstrated how, later in *The Whitsun Weddings*, Larkin distanced himself from his speakers, creating observers (as in 'Faith Healing') rather than obvious stand-ins for the poet himself. Tolley admirably combined helpful generalisations about Larkin's career with equally helpful close readings of numerous particular poems. He gave readers a good sense of what had already been said about Larkin as well as a clear view of Tolley's own assessments. His willingness to confront potential flaws in Larkin's work (such as the possibly confused tones of 'Naturally the Foundation Will Bear Your Expenses' and other satires) was another strength of his book.

Like many critics, Tolley regarded *The Whitsun Weddings* as Larkin's highpoint – the book in which his style seemed most assured, his response to the world and other people most perceptive and even generous, and his objectivity most pronounced. In contrast, he found *High Windows* somewhat less impressive, including the title poem itself. He did praise 'The Explosion', reading it and other texts in consistently perceptive ways and detecting a new emphasis on symbolist phrasing in the latest volume. His intimate familiarity with Larkin's whole canon allowed him to insightfully compare and contrast poems from different periods, as when relating 'The Old Fools' to previous works. In two passages he nicely summarised his reactions to all three of Larkin's most important books:

> ■ *High Windows* ... as a whole is assertive rather than explanatory, in comparison with earlier [volumes]. The play of questioning wit in *The Less Deceived* had been succeeded by a firm and resonant assurance in *The Whitsun Weddings*; which, if it involved a simplification of idiom in this respect, went along with a broadening and sensitivity of response. One feels that at times the poems in *High Windows* are the work of someone who has too much made up his mind about things. ... Indeed, *High Windows* seems to show an emotional hardening. It is not merely that death is a more central and pressing concern than in *The Less Deceived* or *The Whitsun Weddings*, or that it is more directly confronted than in the two earlier books. There is a change of tone. The unconsoled look at life becomes the unconsoled look at death; and the sense of things is starker, even when death is not the theme.[14] □

When *High Windows* appeared, Larkin had only ten more years to live, during which time he produced (by Tolley's count) only 17 more poems – only a few of which, in Tolley's opinion (and by general consensus), equalled his earlier work.

Tolley's chapter on Larkin's love of jazz did much to relate the poet's tastes in music to his tastes in literature, showing how his early interests in informal, unpretentious music helped anticipate his later poetry. Likewise, Tolley's chapter on Larkin's literary likes and dislikes helped explain why, despite his general disdain for Modernism, he still shared certain interests with some Modernist poets. These included especially a preference for irony and a willingness to deal (as in Eliot's *The Waste*

Land) with some uglier aspects of existence. Later, he valuably discussed Larkin's editing of *The Oxford Book of Modern Poetry*, in which Larkin recovered the writings of many previously ignored poets whose work anticipated his own. This chapter helpfully explored Larkin's relations not only with his literary forbears but also with various contemporaries as well, including especially Auden, Betjeman, Barbara Pym, and Stevie Smith.

Tolley later dealt with Larkin's processes of composition (as revealed in his surviving notebooks) – processes that in the mature poetry involved emphases on storytelling, deliberative thought, overt statement, and specific, mundane details. Larkin's speakers usually functioned as observers and commentators, and when Larkin himself read his poems aloud (Tolley claimed) he tried to bring out their straightforward, conversational tones, preferring understated emotion to anything lofty or prophetic-sounding. Tolley's penultimate chapter reviewed Larkin's formal and stylistic traits, including the poems' clear, straightforward diction and commonplace imagery. Both traits implied that reality was comprehensible, however unpleasant or disappointing it might often seem. Larkin's poems often invite us (Tolley argued) to long for imagined satisfactions that the poems ultimately qualify or deny, and sometimes the poems are damaged (in Tolley's opinion) by compulsive negativity, especially in the ways they present their speakers. Yet Larkin had attained a modern popularity equalled only by Housman and Betjeman, perhaps in part *because* of his speakers' implied humility and their refusal of easy optimism. Both in his life and in his art (Tolley concluded) Larkin was never as uncomplicated as he wanted to seem: he owed more to Modernism, for instance, than he pretended, and he was more culturally sophisticated than he tried to appear. Originally a literary rebel, he eventually became a member of the literary establishment – a transition that went hand in hand with a hardening of his opinions and a growing coarseness in his diction.

Tolley's book seemed an impressively focused study of Larkin when juxtaposed with another book from 1991: Hans Osterwalder's *British Poetry between the Movement and Modernism: Anthony Thwaite and Philip Larkin*. Despite this title, only one brief chapter of Osterwalder's study really dealt with Larkin, and that chapter mainly repeated arguments made by earlier critics that Larkin's style was more Romantic, and more Symbolist, than Larkin himself had suggested.[15] This view, by the early 1990s, had become increasingly common. A 1991 article by G. J. Finch, for instance, argued that Larkin's verse often showed a strong (but not simplistic) semi-Romantic attachment to nature and rural life – an attachment always qualified (but never entirely negated) by the poet's irony. Such ambivalences (Finch contended) were central to the poet's creativity as well as to his popular appeal: nature, for Larkin and his readers, could seem as mysterious as human life itself.[16] Also concerned with Larkin's irony was a 1991 article by Peter MacDonald Smith. He argued that Larkin often presented his spokesmen (his alter egos) ironically, regularly undercutting them and their views.[17] Meanwhile, another helpful 1991 essay – by James Booth – explored Larkin's use of rooms as settings and images. Booth noted that rooms, in Larkin's early verse, tended to be associated either with social responsibilities or with personal freedom, and he also discussed the impact on Larkin's writings of various rooms the poet had actually lived in. Sometimes these featured symbolic windows, but as Larkin grew older and less psychologically secure, he began to associate rooms with confinement, so that they sometimes functioned as (and foreshadowed) symbolic coffins.[18]

Most of the commentary from 1991 discussed so far was generally respectful and even laudatory. Commentators usually took Larkin's importance for granted. Although this assumption would come under increasing assault with the publication of Larkin's *Selected Letters* in 1992, there was already, in 1991, a first glimpse of later controversies. In an article ominously titled 'Larkin's Conceit', Peter Snowdon criticised the poet's implication that his own dark view of life was one his readers should share. Snowdon claimed that Larkin rejected connections with life and other people, offering instead a barren alienation rooted in personal resentments. He found Larkin's texts emotionally reductive, small in topical range, and simultaneously egocentric and self-denigrating. Larkin (Snowdon argued) could neither feel happiness himself nor concede others' joy: he assumed his own gloominess was typical rather than abnormal and peculiarly personal. Refusing joy or transcendence, Larkin assumed that joy and transcendence were impossible.[19] In Snowdon's words:

> ■ All Larkin's poetry revolves around this generalisation of a quite specific emotional response hinging on an arbitrary and irrationally masochistic rejection of experience. To present Larkin as a poet who remains true to poetry as the rendering of experience is simply absurd. Larkin posits experience as a beyond into which he has no desire to enter. ... By assuming the knowledge before experience, that others who think they are better off than him are only more deceived, and thus modelling all their lives on his own failures, the poet sentences himself to imprisonment in a world in which there is nothing which might help him to escape from his own limitations.[20] □

Not since the 1950s and early 1960s, perhaps, had Larkin been so forcefully attacked (with the possible exception of Janice Rossen's book from 1989, with its misgivings about his views of women). Snowdon's comments, however, would seem mild by the mid-1990s.

As 1992 opened, two important books on Larkin appeared. Neither, significantly, referred to the as-yet unpublished *Selected Letters*, and so both treated Larkin with real regard. This was especially true of James Booth's *Philip Larkin: Writer*, a brief overview of the poet's whole career.[21] Already, though, Booth found himself defending Larkin against Janice Rossen's charges of misogyny and against overly political interpretations of Larkin's verse. For Booth, the poems seemed frequently both true and beautiful and should be appreciated for both qualities. Discussing Larkin's style, he noted its debts to imagism and symbolism, its apparent simplicity but actual complexity, and its rejection of didacticism and easy political propagandising. He reviewed Larkin's life; commented on the early poetic influences of Auden, Yeats, and even Dylan Thomas; noted Larkin's increasing self-assurance as he matured; and discussed the ways the poet's relations with various women affected what and how he wrote. Booth then discussed Larkin's novels, summarising their plots, comparing and contrasting Larkin's fiction with that of his friend Kingsley Amis, and indicating, interestingly, that parts of two other novels were available in manuscript.

Commenting on Larkin's verse, Booth thought it reflected the continuing influence of both Yeats *and* Hardy, and he downplayed similarities between Larkin and Betjeman, finding Larkin less simply 'English' than the older, more conventionally patriotic poet. Booth noted Larkin's concern for animals, the growth in his range of tones, and the complexity of tones within single works (such as 'Ambulances'). He noted the poet's stylistic preference for abstract nouns, the resemblances between him and most of his first-person speakers, and his tendency to use poems not to satirise others but to argue with himself. Thematically, Booth noted the poet's unusual frankness in alluding to masturbation and sexual frustration, his emphasis on the gap between sexual ideals and sexual realities, and his stress on tensions between the sexes, especially men's annoyance with women. Booth defended Larkin against simplifying readings, especially of 'Sunny Prestatyn', a poem sometimes interpreted as misogynistic. All in all, Booth found Larkin's attitudes towards women less hostile than was sometimes assumed. He ended by discussing Larkin's dealings with such themes as death, age, and absence, suggesting that, as Larkin aged, his treatment of these issues darkened. Booth's close attention to individual poems meant that he made few large-scale generalisations. His method, though, reflected his basic assumption that what mattered most about Larkin were the successes of particular works rather than broad, abstract issues.

Significantly different was another important book from 1992 – Stephen Regan's *Philip Larkin: An Introduction to the Variety of Criticism*.[22] Regan offered a comprehensive overview of commentary from the 1950s to the 1990s, but he also advanced arguments of his own.

Reflecting the renewed interest in history common among critics in the 1990s, he recommended reading Larkin's works as both reflections of and responses to their specific historical contexts. Challenging the idea (implied by Booth) that truth and beauty could ever be absolute, Regan often attacked allegedly naïve interpretations.

Regan opened by situating Larkin and the other so-called 'Movement' poets within their historical contexts. He saw their writing less as a reaction against the Romanticism of such writers of the 1940s as Dylan Thomas as a pulling back from the politically engaged poetry (such as Auden's) of the 1930s. Regan suggested numerous reasons for this growing rejection of politics – an effort he thought could never succeed because even apolitical stances had political implications. He saw the writing of Larkin and his colleagues as rooted in a kind of middle-class liberalism that emphasised caution, scepticism, individualism, and a disguised self-interest that was also the interest of a middling social class (neither proletarian nor aristocratic). Larkin and other 'Movement' poets were (Regan thought) mostly passive conformists with little interest in really challenging the social, political, or economic status quo. They were literary rebels in only a very modest sense, and their attempts to appear neutral ended, eventually, in a growing willingness to adopt and display conservative convictions.[23]

Regan conceded that Larkin did indeed return repeatedly to such themes as time, chance, choice, change, and death, but he contended that none of these issues was timeless: responses to them were inevitably affected by historical trends and events. To assume otherwise would be to take Larkin's verse at face value rather than examining it historically. Regan maintained that formalist criticism, by emphasising literary skill, poetic beauty, and enduring ideas and ideals, reduced Larkin's thoughts to clichés and bromides. He repeatedly faulted previous critics for failing to examine Larkin's works in context. Linguistic and structuralist approaches also often struck Regan as similarly limited. Critics who overlooked the historical dimensions of literature (Regan thought) ignored whatever real meanings and effects literature could have.[24]

He supported this argument by showing how interpretations of Larkin's verse had evolved: a poem that might have been seen one way in 1955 might seem something significantly different in 1985. Regan particularly noted that by the early 1980s critics had begun arguing that Larkin was a more Modernist, more Symbolist poet than he himself had claimed, partly because many poems in *High Windows* had seemed so allusive and obscure. Discussing such commentators as Seamus Heaney, Barbara Everett, and Andrew Motion, Regan argued that they tended to simplify poets' writings, making Yeats and Hardy (for instance) seem less complex than they really were by setting them against each other as opposite and competing influences on Larkin. Once again, Regan saw a need to historicise – to read *all* writers and works within their specific cultural contexts and not make sweeping generalisations about their styles and meanings. For Regan, Yeats did not simply contrast with Hardy, and the impact of both poets on Larkin was far from simple.

Regan then developed his own 'historicist' approach more fully and independently, concerning himself less with other critics and more with specific poems and Larkin's overall development. He thought Larkin's poetry was much concerned with the perceived loss of post-war English power, that it extended the range of language used in English verse, and that poets of the 1930s (such as Auden and MacNeice) had had a far greater impact on Larkin's early poems than was usually realised. The war, however, helped turn Larkin towards Yeats, so that the poems published in *The North Ship* were less overtly sociological and political than others left unpublished. The early poems (Regan argued) were agnostic about both religion and love – a cautiousness partly caused by the war:

> ■ It is clear now that Larkin's response to the work of Auden and his contemporaries was not one of rejection but one of careful modification within the context of war, and the persistence of this influence can be detected in poems as late as those of *High Windows* (1974). The insecurities of wartime Britain helped to shape poetry of restricted choices, quietistic moods and disappointed ideals, but in a more positive way produced a poetry of tenacious survival and vigilant awareness.[25] □

Regan saw Larkin's post-war poetry as typifying middle-class political attitudes of the time: cautious, restrained, concerned with preserving individual freedom, less interested in the good of the community than in the good of oneself, sceptical about large ideals, uninterested in actual socio-economic complexities, fearful of commitment. The politics the poem implied (Regan maintained) focused on individual desires, satisfactions, and disappointments rather than on any broader ideals. The yearning for liberty in *The Less Deceived* never became broadly or overtly political. Larkin's speakers were concerned with their own problems, not with the problems of society at large.

The poems in *The Whitsun Weddings* (Regan contended) reflected England's growing post-war affluence, especially in the late 1950s and early 1960s – an affluence Larkin sometimes satirised, especially when it promoted shallow consumerism. But Larkin never imagined a real, viable alternative to the kind of materialistic society his poems often disdained. Instead, his glimpses of England as a genuine community seemed fleeting, nostalgic, and somewhat impotent. By the 1970s, when real political tensions were beginning to appear in Britain, Larkin's poetry (especially in *High Windows*) reflected the growing breakdown of the post-war political consensus. His poems now became increasingly and openly political (often in ways Regan clearly regretted as too conservative or reactionary). The poet longed for a greater sense of community, but he did so in ways still rooted in middle-class individualism and desires for personal liberty. Ultimately this was (according to Regan) an empty vision:

> ■ As the fragile post-war consensus begins to break down, Larkin's poetry is increasingly caught between a liberal perception of oppressed humanity and an agnostic apprehension of infinite nothingness. ... *High Windows* is a work of political liberalism, not Marxism, and yet its mood of dissent is so powerful and sustained that it cannot help but reveal the essential contradiction in a society that asserts the need for human community at one level and stresses the need for competition at another.[26] □

One real value of Regan's book was its strongly historical and political approach – an approach few previous critics had pursued.

Other examples of academic commentary on Larkin in 1992 were more conventional. Barbara Richardson, for instance, discussing Larkin's 'Early Influences', especially emphasised his youthful enthusiasm for D. H. Lawrence, suggesting that Lawrence was appealing partly as a literary outlaw, partly for writing so openly about sex, partly because he satirised industrialisation and social snobbery, and partly because his idiom was so conversational. Eventually (Richardson showed) Larkin abandoned Lawrence, finding him insufficiently ironic and too prone to illusions.[27] Larkin's own rejection of illusions and of comforting thoughts was the focus of a 1992 article by Rowland Molony, who thought Larkin was always willing to escape from confinements, even consoling ones, in order to face vast unknowns and the limits of human knowledge.

Larkin in Decline 1992–94

Molony obviously admired Larkin, but in that respect his essay would soon seem old-fashioned. The appearance of the poet's *Selected Letters* in 1992 revealed aspects of his personality that disappointed many readers. The Larkin of the letters could seem selfish, sexist, racist, and reactionary – a chauvinist in practically every sense. Already statements criticising his politics had appeared in Stephen Regan's 1992 volume, but such statements pervaded a 1992 article by Tim Trengove-Jones, who mentioned the letters in his notes. Trengove-Jones saw Larkin as an English nationalist at a time when Europe was seeking greater integration. He associated Larkin's Englishness with racism and xenophobia, but he contended that the more Larkin tried to distance himself from other languages and traditions, the more they paradoxically influenced his writing: by defining himself *against* others and otherness, Larkin implicitly acknowledged their inescapability. For Trengove-Jones, Larkin ultimately symbolised the kind of parochialism that threatened greater European unity.[28]

If this had been all Larkin now symbolised, his reputation would not have suffered much. But by the end of 1992, as more people read and responded to the *Selected Letters*, his reputation could seem irreparably damaged. Jonathan Raban, expressing more sorrow than anger, found himself 'embarrassed for Larkin', especially concerning the letters' 'inexhaustible flow of self-concern'. Raban said that on 'politics, as on sex, Larkin sounds like a man out of control. There's the same shrilling note'. He could 'think of no other writer whose life had been so exposed' by his correspondence, calling himself 'shocked, depressed, ... and angry at his publishers for having turned Larkin out into the street in such a defenseless condition'.[29] Other commentators, however, were less concerned about damage to Larkin than about the damaging racism which (they felt) Larkin had embraced and helped authorise. Tom Paulin, for instance, accused him of 'race hatred', suggesting that omissions from the letters had probably minimised his actual prejudice, and later he spoke of 'Larkin's racism, misogyny, and quasi-fascist views' – 'monstrous views' that revealed 'the sewer under the national monument Larkin became'.[30]

Commentary published in 1993 was often just as negative. In fact, the 1993 appearance of Andrew Motion's major biography of Larkin often did further damage in many people's eyes.[31] Motion's lengthy, fact-filled volume presented a Larkin whom many readers found personally, ethically, and politically unappealing, but Motion also often commented insightfully about particular poems and about larger artistic issues. Discussing *The Whitsun Weddings*, for instance, he suggested that despite its wide range of topics, it reflected a coherent way of looking at things.

■ Compared to The Less Deceived, in which traces of Larkin's Yeatsian and Symbolist inheritance rub against a simpler manner, The Whitsun Weddings is a more uniform book. Its gaze is steadier, and it more precisely illustrates the qualities associated with The Movement, even though it appeared nearly a decade after The Movement had been identified. It tackles the big, central issues of ordinary life in the language of ordinary speech, and makes them numinous. Its details (posters, pet-shops, parents) are the details of the everyday; the truths it wrings from them are abiding. Intensely lyrical, it is nevertheless often discursive, speculative and argumentative.[32] □

In contrast, Motion found *High Windows* far angrier than its predecessors, and he also considered it more Yeatsian or Symbolist than the collections for which Larkin had become best known. Yet he also thought *High Windows* reassuringly accessible, not only in its style but also in the topics it treated, including nature, ageing, and approaching death.[33]

Motion's biography, however, pulled no punches in dealing with unattractive aspects of Larkin's life and character, including remarks that certainly sounded racist, classist, and xenophobic. Peter Ackroyd, reviewing the book, alleged that Larkin had 'descended into a maelstrom of bigotry', indulging in a 'rancid and insidious philistinism' and producing little more than a 'drab monologue of misery and self-pity' in both his letters and his poems. Ackroyd thought Larkin had made 'a small talent go a very long way', dismissing him as 'a minor poet' who had become 'a foul-mouthed bigot'.[34] In a long, often funny piece titled 'Alas! Deceived', the playwright Alan Bennett – once a genuine advocate for Larkin – now expressed profound disappointment. Suggesting that the poet himself had once respected Hitler, Bennett mocked his enthusiasm for Margaret Thatcher, lamented his incorrigible sadness and gloom, condemned his racial and other prejudices, and lampooned his interest in prizes and awards. At times Bennet's tone seemed as crude as anything Larkin had written, but he concluded by indicating that, despite being disappointed in Larkin's life, he felt he had lost a friend and suggested that the poems, though hard to reread without thinking about the biography, were still very much *worth* rereading.[35]

Christopher Carduff blamed part of the negative impact of Motion's biography on Motion himself, accusing him of condescending to Larkin so that by the book's final pages Motion was 'wholly out-of-sympathy, unable or unwilling to imagine Larkin from the inside out'.[36] Dana Gioia, who considered Larkin one of the four best British poets of the twentieth century (along with Hardy, Yeats, and Auden), continued to praise his verse but regretted that the letters 'bristle with racist remarks, misogynistic sneers, crude sexuality, and personal invective'. Gioia, though, still admired the art and artistry even if he had lost some respect for the artist.[37]

Ian Hamilton, in a long, serious review, thought the *Selected Letters* had shown 'Larkin to be a fairly unpleasant piece of work, mean-spirited and – yes – foul-mouthed', but he thought the resulting 'widespread outrage seemed excessive'. He compared some of Larkin's personal flaws to Hardy's, but in general he, like Gioia, continued to admire the verse if not always the poet.[38] Penelope Fitzgerald, reviewing the *Selected Letters*, conceded that Larkin had attacked many contemporary writers but noted that he had also attacked many great authors of the past: he habitually (at least in the letters) condemned numerous persons, beliefs, and institutions. Even the generally forgiving Fitzgerald, however, provided further evidence for the prosecution, reporting that when she

> ■ was working in an unimportant capacity for the British Arts Council Literary Panel, Larkin was asked for advice on the funding of ethnic arts centers. He replied that anyone lucky enough to be allowed to settle here had a duty to forget their own culture and try to understand ours.[39] □

Far less tolerant of Larkin's flaws than Hamilton, Gioia, and Fitzgerald was Edward Hirsch. While commenting helpfully on Larkin's poetry (including ways it reflected and articulated post-war English decline), Hirsch condemned Larkin the man for his general misanthropy and especially his racism, and he also suggested that Larkin's diaries – which the poet had requested be destroyed – were even worse than the letters. Hirsch argued that Larkin personified the worst traits of both of his parents (his mother's worries and his father's despotic impulses), and although Hirsch showed some continuing respect for the art he had little patience for the person who had produced it.[40] Clive James, always a great admirer of Larkin, issued one of the strongest defences of the poet. He thought the letters showed 'how thoroughly Larkin could indulge in racism, sexism, and all the other isms when he was trying to shock his unshockable friends', but he argued 'that if Larkin made racist remarks in order to be outrageous, then he was no racist. A racist makes racist remarks because he thinks they are true'. James continued to consider Larkin 'fundamentally a decent man' who remained a great poet, and he offered evidence that Larkin was not nearly as prejudiced as the letters sometimes made him seem. He condemned many of Larkin's critics as 'mediocrities' who sought to improve their own stature by lowering the poet's, 'matching his feet of clay with their ears of cloth'.[41] His defence of Larkin was unusually vigorous, but Jonathan Raban, another admirer of the poet, was less forgiving. Raban suggested that in interviews Larkin had tried to blend the sarcasm of W. C. Fields with the self-deprecation of Eeyore the donkey. But he thought the letters 'an ugly hemorrhage [sic]', sometimes 'snappishly funny' but 'also petulant, smutty, and inexhaustibly self-concerned', often childish in their offensive racist phrasing and immature in other ways as well. Raban respected Larkin less after reading the letters than he had before.[42] This seemed far less true of Stuart Wright, who found the letters darkly humorous – designed more to seem outrageously over-the-top than to unleash deep-seated hatreds. Wright noted that the letters contemptuously mocked practically everyone and everything (including the English), and he also noted that the many women who had interacted with Larkin praised him as a perfect gentleman. Larkin was less antagonistic towards women (Wright suggested) than towards marriage, and his joking contempt for children was a running gag (much as it had been for W. C. Fields), not any evidence of fundamental misanthropy.[43]

As even this random sampling of opinion from 1993 will suggest, both the *Selected Letters* and the Motion biography damaged Larkin's standing in the eyes of many readers, even some who continued to love his poetry. Clive James and Stuart Wright were Larkin's rare enthusiastic defenders; most commentators either condemned both the writer and his writings or carefully distinguished between the two. Not all 1993 Larkin commentary concerned the letters and/or biography (although much of it did). Some critics (who perhaps had written their essays before the correspondence and biography were published) carried on as usual, discussing the poetry rather than the man. Neil Covey, for instance, explicitly noted that he had written his article before reading the letters and the life, but he felt that both sources only confirmed conclusions he had already reached. Discussing Larkin's ambivalent attitudes towards modern readers, Covey found the tone of his poetry anti-heroic, his view of his audience somewhat distanced (and even superior and occasionally condescending), and even his treatment of people in his poems (such as 'The Whitsun Weddings') frequently patronising.[44]

T. J. Ross, who apparently wrote before the *Selected Letters* or biography appeared in 1993, assessed mainly Larkin the poet, not Larkin the person. He noted Larkin's basically apolitical interest in everyday experience (unlike the often politically motivated interest in unusual topics favoured by such Modernists as Yeats and Pound). He also variously (1) noted the influence on Larkin's early verse of the kind of 'end of the century' art-for-art's-sake views of Oscar Wilde; (2) praised the value of Larkin's own literary criticism; and (3) suggested that Larkin's concern with everyday life in England, far from being merely parochial, was relevant to the everyday lives of readers anywhere.[45] Meanwhile, in another article from 1993, Paul Volsik helpfully considered the kind of audience the poetry implied and also discussed how variously Larkin's verse might be considered postmodernist in emphasising various kinds of ambivalence:

> ■ There is the use of personae who are in some sense – but only at certain moments – groping and uncertain, who verge on the parodic but who are presented against the ground of an astonishingly flawless form; there is the structuring of poems around debates between two voices neither of whom is reliable; there is the constant playing with a possible identification (or lack of identification) between the persona and the author; there is the ambivalence about Larkin's position on any of the major thematic spaces he deals with ...; there is ... the cunning working from an 'I' to a 'we' which integrates the reader into a universe where s(he) is rarely at ease or which

is anyway self-imploding; there is the yoking of opposites in paradoxes of an oxymoronic type ...; there is the contiguity in the published collections of radically different poems ...; there is the use of notoriously ambivalent and unsettling aesthetic devices like the 'politically' problematic black comedy (?) of 'Sunny Prestatyn'; there is the magnificent use of all the possibilities of linguistic modality from negation, through conditionals, to questions (real questions) and modalising interpretations of the 'perhaps', 'well', 'I don't know' sort; there are the wonderful 'visionary' conclusions which counterpoint the often squalid and realistic narratives of the poems; there is the antiphony generated ... by the playing off of the violently demotic and the intensely lyrical ...; there is the use of the possibilities of rhyme and line – ambivalences that only poetry can produce.[46] ☐

It would be hard to imagine a more comprehensive single-sentence listing of Larkin's traits than this. The fact that Volsik kept his attention so squarely on the poetry despite having read the letters was a sign that Larkin criticism might be returning to a focus on the literature rather than becoming obsessed with the man.

Commentary on the *Selected Letters* and on Motion's biography continued to appear in 1994, but it came mainly from the United States, where the books had been published later than in Britain. An essay by Joseph Epstein, for instance, began by highly praising Larkin's poetry in all the by-now standard ways. Epstein shared the common opinion that the letters revealed an unpleasant man, but he argued that the kindest letters were those to women, including women from whom Larkin had nothing to gain. He also suggested that Larkin's politics were not so much reactionary as anti-Left, and ultimately he found Larkin a generally decent person with a good sense of humour that he often used to make fun of himself.[47] Less sympathetic than Epstein, but more sympathetic than some others, was John McCormick, who stressed Larkin's racist views but suggested that the poet often, in commenting harshly on most things in the letters, was trying to be funny. McCormick ultimately judged Larkin a talented poet but a complex, sad human being.[48] Finally, Gary Kissick, in an essay titled 'They Turn on Larkin', offered a helpfully balanced review of the commentary evoked by the letters and the biography, citing many assessments, both negative and positive.[49]

In a 1994 article on Larkin's 'obscenity', Joseph Bristow helpfully listed many of the responses (including two television programs) prompted by the *Selected Letters* and biography. He thought both publications had damaged Larkin's stature but also argued that the new understanding of Larkin the man helped explain some broader flaws in recent English culture and politics. Larkin's obscenity, which had once made him seem honest and plainspoken, now became (for Bristow) another indication of his reactionary politics. Bristow warned that some of Larkin's critics risked being as intolerant as the man whose intolerance they attacked, but he also maintained that the turn against Larkin signalled larger changes in what it meant to be a British academic. He suggested that Larkin's expressed contempt for women and workers meant (paradoxically) that both groups impacted the kind of poetry he wrote.[50] Bristow considered Larkin a more Modernist writer than he had wanted to be – an increasingly common argument developed even more fully in 1994 by Nigel Alderman. Alderman saw evidence for this claim in Larkin's love of jazz, in the breadth of his reading, in some of his critical vocabulary, and in his yearning for (but final refusal of) the kinds of epiphanies celebrated by Modernists. The ideals Larkin pursued (Alderman suggested) were ones he could never quite achieve, whether they involved a satisfying sense of nationhood or a secure sense of self.[51]

Another 1994 essay, by Steve Clark, explored Larkin's attitudes towards (and treatment of) sex, finding it odd that England's most prominent post-war poet had had such misgivings about sexual relationships and marriage. Larkin's poems (Clark suggested) often described women in distanced ways (in advertisements and photographs) and frequently shifted from focusing on women to examining other topics as the poems developed. Clark compared and contrasted the ways Larkin and Yeats dealt with sex, exploring individual works in some detail but ending by suggesting that Larkin, by refusing merely to accept or endorse common views of gendered relationships, sometimes transcended (as in 'An Arundel Tomb') common ideas about the domination of one gender over the other. Yet even if Larkin struck some readers as occasionally misogynistic (Clark noted), such readers would have to admit that misogyny has had a long tradition in English literature.[52]

Larkin in Recovery: 1995–99

Oddly, few essays on Larkin appeared in 1995 (perhaps academics had been spooked by the controversies following the letters and biography), but a new book *was* published that year: Andrew Swarbrick's *Out of Reach: The Poetry of Philip Larkin*.[53] Swarbrick immediately announced his belief in Larkin's importance, his intention to depict him as less parochial than was often assumed, and his rejection of recent charges of political incorrectness. Larkin, Swarbrick asserted, was interesting far more for his poems than for his life. Central to many poems (Swarbrick argued) was a preoccupation (involving both fear and desire) with death and nothingness, making the verse more challenging and modern than some critics believed. Swarbrick suggested that no easy equations could be made between the poet's life and works, although he did examine the life in some detail while also commenting on many individual texts and on each major collection. He also cited numerous particular remarks by many different critics, providing a good compendium of much previous commentary.[54]

Swarbrick suggested that the early poems had already indicated the oscillation between aspiration and irony that would mark so much of Larkin's later work. The poet, he argued, was influenced in his youth by Auden, Thomas, and Lawrence, with each leaving a particular trace on his writing. From Auden he took an interest in contemporary life and language; from Thomas he borrowed some of his music; and from Lawrence he derived his sense of his literary goals and social attitudes. Swarbrick especially stressed (as did Larkin) the early impact of Yeats – an impact he never completely escaped. Swarbrick also discussed Larkin's early aspirations and achievements as a novelist and the ways his prose writing affected his verse. In fact, it was partly Larkin's failure to produce a satisfactory third novel that led him (Swarbrick thought) both to the mood and to the motives that produced *The Less Deceived*. The poetry he now began to write showed not only the new influence of Hardy but also the lingering influence of Yeats. The newer poems reflected the loss of British power on the world stage even as they also implied Larkin's sense of his own loss of power as a novelist.[55]

Interestingly, despite claiming to be interested less in Larkin's life than in his writings, Swarbrick often situated his numerous discussions of particular poems in clear biographical contexts. He tended to discuss specific poems one-by-one, making relatively few generalisations, although he did suggest how the self-mocking poems of *The Less Deceived* represented an advance over the Yeatsian Romanticism of *The North Ship* and how the emotions expressed so openly in Larkin's first book were expressed more subtly later. Swarbrick discussed ambivalences in the mature work, especially regarding sex and death (particularly in *The Less Deceived*) but also involving Larkin's attitudes towards 'the Movement'. But Swarbrick saw underlying continuities in Larkin's concern with questions of identity and in his distrust of academic theorising. Like other critics, he commented on the variety and interactions of different tones in Larkin's poems, particularly interactions of irony and compassion in *The Whitsun Weddings*. Larkin sometimes wrote monologues, but his works (according to Swarbrick) were in fact rarely monological. Instead, they often involved real dialogue within their speakers' minds and voices, dialogue that often displayed oscillating disdain and sympathy for the persons the poems depicted but that also often implied the poet's self-criticism.[56]

Swarbrick's praise for *The Whitsun Weddings* helped emphasise his misgivings about Larkin's next book, *High Windows*. The later volume, he argued, showed a breakdown in the kind of balance displayed earlier and a rise in anger, bitterness, and dogmatism. Larkin was now more critical, less lyrical, and more philistine than previously, although he was also closer in some poems to the kind of imaginative writing done by the Symbolists. Intriguingly, Swarbrick considered 'The Old Fools' merely sarcastic rather than at all compassionate, and he also found 'High Windows' itself essentially full of anger and jealousy. Like other critics, he disliked Larkin's overtly political texts, finding them too simplistic and merely prejudiced. But Swarbrick also found much to admire, especially in the more lyrical, affirmative works (particularly 'The Explosion'). Finally, Swarbrick discussed the performative, dialogical aspects of Larkin's writings while also tracing, through numerous quotations, the development of critical responses to the poet's work.[57]

By the second half of the 1990s, the controversy was beginning to die down. Increasing numbers of writers now once again began to take Larkin's stature for granted, feeling less need either to attack or defend him. In 1996, an article by Terry Whalen argued that Ireland and Irish writers (besides Yeats) had significantly and positively influenced Larkin's own work. Whalen mentioned Oscar Wilde's wit, George Moore's realism, and Flann O'Brien's humour as such influences and noted that his years in Ireland (1950-55) were among his most productive. Larkin's positive responses to Ireland and its culture showed (Whalen argued) that he was less insular than he often claimed.[58] Also in 1996, Salem K. Hassan traced Larkin's poetic references to women, linking them to his quest for (and development of) a mature style.[59] All three essays took Larkin's importance for granted and said almost nothing about the recent biographical controversies.

Perhaps the clearest indication of Larkin's surprisingly quick recovery from earlier attacks was the publication, in 1997, of no fewer than five books dealing with his work. Two, admittedly, were brief guides for students and general readers, but that fact alone is telling: publishers thought they could profit from broadly introducing Larkin, thereby suggesting that he was still being widely read and widely taught. Warren Hope, for instance, made a strong case for Larkin's literary importance, whatever his personality and politics. Hope discussed style, themes, forms (especially stanza forms), personae, sense of humour, anti- or un-heroic attitudes, and biographical and stylistic development. Especially interesting were his comments on the politics of Larkin's father. He argued that the older man was less politically predictable than had often been claimed (with, for instance, a strong interest in socialism) and that his politics were not unusual in pre-war England. Hope speculated that domestic problems had led to Larkin's childhood stammer, that he was fixated on his mother, and that this alleged fixation affected his views of his sister and other women. Hope considered 'An April Sunday brings the snow' Larkin's first mature poem and emphasised the ways he ordered his poems in collections. Like other critics, he was less impressed with *High Windows* than with *The Whitsun Weddings*, and he ended by intriguingly suggesting that if Larkin's mature verse began with a poem about the death of his father, it eventually petered out after his mother died.[60]

Laurence Lerner's 1997 booklet dealt with Larkin's life, novels, three major poetry collections, persona, and critical attitudes. He saw the early poems as more influenced by Yeats's *sounds* than by his views, and he interestingly suggested that many readers still considered *The Less Deceived* Larkin's best book. Escaping deception was (Lerner argued) one of Larkin's central motives and themes, as 'Church Going' demonstrated. In *The Whitsun Weddings*, Lerner especially admired 'Mr. Bleaney', a poem he thought established Larkin as his era's spokesman. Lerner defended the poetry from Larkin's off-hand political remarks, although he indicated that troubling political poems still remained unpublished in 1997. Surprisingly, Lerner found a non-political poem, 'The Old Fools', deeply offensive. Particularly interesting was Lerner's suggestion of similarities between Larkin and Eliot.[61]

Unlike the brief introductions by Hope and Lerner was a substantial volume by A. T. Tolley titled *Larkin at Work*. Intended mainly for dedicated scholars, this book discussed and reproduced many notebook drafts of individual poems. Tolley discussed in detail Larkin's methods of composition and revision, but his concluding chapter offered various valuable generalisations:

> ■ When he had got his first line, Larkin did not have great difficulty in drafting his first stanza, which would frequently consist of physical details of the circumstance of the poem. Finding a way forward might present some difficulty; but, once this had been done, narrative details would often come very easily. It was at the point at which Larkin had to discover the way that the poem was to end – the point at which he had to make his poem move in that direction – that created the greatest difficulty and saw the most drafting, often with no immediately clear sense of direction. This might be described as the *peripeteia* of the poem – the turning point at which it revealed itself to both author and reader.[62] □

Tolley also commented valuably on the general stylistic traits of Larkin's verse, but his book was designed more for specialists than for readers at large.

Probably the widest-ranging book from 1997 was Stephen Regan's edited collection.[63] Regan reprinted previously published essays by Barbara Everett (1980), Andrew Motion (1982), Stan Smith (1982), Seamus Heaney (1988), Graham Holderness (1989), David Lodge (1989), Janice Rossen (1989), Tom Paulin (1990), Alan Bennett (1993), Steve

Clark (1994), and Andrew Swarbrick (1995), as well as a new essay by James Booth – an essay also published in a 1997 collection edited by Michael Baron and titled *Larkin with Poetry*.[64] Booth's essay explored Larkin's interests in such topics as Englishness, nationalism, and masturbation, finding him less political than had often been claimed and championing his work's artistry over its supposed ideological dimensions. Larkin (Booth contended) dealt with large human themes from an English perspective, and he even suggested that if Alice Walker (the black American writer) could celebrate masturbation without being accused of sexism, perhaps Larkin deserved the same courtesy. Both writers (Booth thought) presented masturbation as one method of escaping social expectations and pressures concerning sex, and Booth generally defended Larkin against charges of misogyny. He even likened Larkin to Salman Rushdie (whom Larkin once mocked) since both writers were willing to challenge authority and insist on their own individual visions. Booth, in short, was fighting a rear-guard action in defence of Larkin, although by 1997 the tide seemed to be turning in Larkin's favour.[65]

Marion Lomax's 1997 essay wittily discussed 'Larkin with Women', noting his admiration for Christina Rossetti, Barbara Pym, Stevie Smith, Emily Dickinson, and Sylvia Plath, the last of whom was, like Larkin, a confessional poet. Lomax discussed his rejection (at least in his verse) of many traditionally male attitudes towards women; his use of female speakers; and the kind of vulnerability he shared with many women of his time.[66] She defended Larkin from charges of simple sexism with considerable aplomb. Stephen Regan's essay reviewed Larkin's reputation, especially in the years since his death. It pulled no punches when condemning the poet's racism and sexism, but Regan also reviewed discussions of such matters as Larkin's symbolist dimensions, his Englishness and its relations to postcolonialism, formalist challenges (mainly from James Booth) to the postcolonial critique of Larkin, and Regan's own reasons for preferring historical, ideological interpretations – interpretations that emphasised the post-war sense of England's decline.[67] Finally, Andrew Swarbrick briefly discussed the challenges and pleasures of teaching Larkin to older adolescents.[68]

Articles on Larkin from 1997 included another essay by James Booth, who distinguished between aesthetic and political responses to the poet, citing the appreciation of Larkin's poetry by Derek Walcott (an important poet and a person of colour) and contrasting that reaction to the political indictments recently issued by such commentators as Tom Paulin, Nigel Alderman (who, Booth thought, simply misread many poems), Joseph Bristow, and even Seamus Heaney. All these commentators, Booth contended, wanted Larkin to use his poetry to teach lessons when Larkin in fact had no lessons to teach, only poetry to offer.[69]

More complicated than Booth's piece was a dense 1997 essay by Gary Day, who argued that Larkin's own comments about poetry and readers were defensive, conservative, naïve, confused, and ahistorical. Larkin (Day asserted) tried to control readers' interpretations in ways he simply could not. He projected ideal readers who were versions of himself and tried to ensure closed readings that were impossible to dictate. Day speculated about the psychological grounds of Larkin's writing (including a possible death wish) and suggested that wherever Larkin sought firm control and identity he found that neither was possible.[70] Finally, another essay from 1997 – by David Ward – suggested that however unappealing Larkin may have been as a person, he kept his obscenity out of his poems, focusing instead on loneliness, even if this sometimes meant an interest in voyeurism and masturbation, the latter of which meant freedom from human entanglements.[71]

1998 saw the appearance of various articles, including an extended discussion of 'Aubade' by William Kerrigan,[72] and a piece by Janice Rossen arguing that Larkin had had a major hand in revising *Lucky Jim*, the widely successful first novel by his friend Kingsley Amis.[73] An intriguing essay by Antony Rowland depicted Larkin as a representative post-war humanist who accepted the idea of individualism even as he attempted to embrace the notion of a classless community despite (or perhaps because of) his condescension towards the working class. Rowland ended by proposing that a class-based approach to Larkin's poetry might be more fruitful than still more aesthetic analyses.[74] A 1998 essay by Dale Salwak suggested that Americans had been more forgiving of Larkin's transgressions than some of their British counterparts. Salwak surveyed American commentary and then wrote movingly of his own relationship with Larkin.[75] Finally, a 1998 essay by Martin Scofield mocked some of Larkin's more extreme critics; conceded that some of his political satires were shallow; and praised him for dealing with class in ways that suggested a deeper, more common humanity. Scofield defended Larkin against charges of misogyny and ended with stirring praise of his artistry. By 1998, it would seem, much of the firestorm ignited by the letters and by Motion's biography had died down. More and more, Larkin was being treated primarily as a poet again.[76]

One indication of this change in emphasis was the publication, in 1999, B. J. Leggett's *Larkin's Blues: Jazz, Popular Music, and Poetry*. Leggett quickly reviewed the biographical controversies, noted Larkin's tendencies to adopt different (often playful) roles, and then emphasised Larkin's life-long love of jazz, especially the older, more traditional, pre-war forms to which he had become addicted in his youth. Leggett argued that Larkin's obsession with jazz had been under-explored, and he particularly contended that the moody, melancholy jazz known as 'the blues' had had a major impact on the phrasing, tone, and atmosphere of Larkin's verse. Jazz influenced his poetry (Leggett maintained) partly because it seemed authentic, accessible, realistic, and anti-elitist (although, in Britain, it was popular among a relatively small, self-selected group of self-styled individualists – another attraction). Leggett questioned Larkin's own account of his dislike of Modernist, post-war jazz and suggested that his tastes were broader and more inclusive than he sometimes proclaimed.[77]

The blues, Leggett argued, tended to combine sadness with a sense of stoic resignation *and* a frustrated desire to escape – all traits also found in Larkin's mature verse as well as in much of his early poetry and prose. Leggett discussed in great detail not only the several poems that obviously deal with jazz but also the many others that seem to reflect the influence of such music in their plots, phrasing, and attitudes. Larkin's poetry (Leggett maintained) was richly intertextual, although the poet's allusions to other texts (especially jazz texts) were not always obvious to readers less familiar with jazz than he was. Leggett thought that Larkin drew on jazz forms and structures as well as phrasing and moods. He even argued (for example) that 'Aubade' owes more to jazz than to previous English literature, and he emphasised the ways that poem refuses, in unprecedented ways, all the standard ways people comfort themselves when faced with thoughts of death. Leggett also discussed the ways Larkin, like composers of popular songs (such as Cole Porter), used common clichés to give their writing vernacular authenticity. They wrote in the ways regular people actually spoke, and although Larkin said and implied ambivalent things about his imagined audiences, his creative use of clichés (on which he drew both for phrasing and for structures) was in Leggett's opinion unprecedented in the work of a major English poet.[78]

Leggett's book, with its closely argued attention to particular texts and its emphasis on Larkin's subtle artistry, seemed to symbolise a shift away from the political and personal controversies that had dominated Larkin criticism in the middle years of the 1990s. Instead, as a new century began, Larkin was increasingly being treated as a writer again – and less as a writer of offensive letters than as a writer of permanently valuable poems. The next chapter will trace his critical reputation in the first decade of the twenty-first century.

CHAPTER FIVE

Larkin Triumphant Once More: The 2000s

By the opening of the new century, Larkin's critical fortunes were rebounding. The damage done to his reputation in the early 1990s by the publication of the *Selected Letters* and Andrew Motion's biography had begun to recede. The Philip Larkin Society had been formed in 1995 and was growing each year, and more and more 'new' texts by Larkin – that is, texts that had long existed but had not been previously published or collected into books – began to be studied and printed. These included many of his writings on jazz (2001), much of his unpublished prose fiction (2002), and a collection of the early poems and juvenilia (2005). Larkin continued to be widely read, widely studied, and widely valued by an audience that included not only academics and students but also thousands of 'regular' readers as well.

Larkin in the Early 2000s

One especially clear indication of the continuing and indeed growing interest in Larkin was the publication, in 2000, of an essay collection titled *New Larkins for Old*. The collection opened with an essay by Barbara Everett titled 'Larkin's Money', which began by examining a poem titled 'Money' and then moved to broader issues. Everett (1) suggested how Larkin's colloquial style contributed to the compression and intensity of his poems; (2) clarified the meaning of this particular text (which, she argued, alluded to a quarterly savings statement, not – as some had assumed – to a monthly pay cheque); (3) explored the symbolic role of money and commodification in general in Larkin's work; and (4) emphasised the importance of role-playing in his writings, including the letters. Everett challenged some of Andrew Motion's interpretations of Larkin's life, discussed the development of the poet's style, and preferred (unusually) *High Windows* to *The Whitsun Weddings*, particularly praising the beauty of 'The Explosion'.[1]

Edna Longley, in 'Larkin, Decadence and the Lyric Poem', discussed the ways Larkin's poetry now seemed increasingly to reflect an earlier culture, noted the influence on his work of the 'decadents' of the 1890s, emphasised the influence of Cyril Connolly's book *The Condemned Playground; Essays 1927-1944* (1946), and explored Larkin's early 'aestheticism', with its strong commitment to lofty ideals of art. Considering Larkin's attitudes towards women, Longley suggested that his personality was quite literally borderline narcissistic, even comparing him to Woody Allen in many of his attitudes and dealings with others, including women. She explored different sorts of sentimentality in Larkin's work, stressed his self-pity, and commented on the intense emphasis on intensity in many of his poems.[2]

Another essay from 2000 – John Carey's 'The Two Philip Larkins' – began by finding fault with Larkin's most famous poem ('This Be the Verse'), using that work to call attention to the existence of many Larkin texts containing two voices – one aggressively masculine and the other more sensitively thoughtful and feminine. Carey heard these voices (sometimes alternating, but often present in the very same texts) in numerous works, including letters, fiction, and poetry, beginning with Larkin's college days if not before. Like other contributors to Booth's collection, Carey explored Larkin's 'feminine' aspects, particularly as reflected in his youthful novels featuring lesbian characters, plots, and themes. He singled out 'The Explosion' for special praise, although he argued that it represents mainly the 'female' voice in Larkin's work, unlike, say, 'An Arundel Tomb', where he thought both voices are heard in the final stanza – a stanza that struck him as simultaneously affirmative and sceptical.[3] Carey concluded that:

■ Taking 'This Be The Verse' as my starting point was in a way misleading, because it seems to equate the male voice with coarseness and obscenity. Those are potentials of the male voice, but it is capable of much else – of wit, humor, skepticism, self-mockery, realism, intelligence, acuity. Despite its versatility it is – or so my argument claims – persistently and creatively distinguishable from another voice, its complement and opposite, which I have called the female. This voice feels where the first thinks, it transcends the reality that the first voice analyses, it inclines more to religion and the supernatural, and it overrides the prejudices which, however jocularly assumed, are still the prejudices of the male voice. From the two there emerges what Larkin is – or is for me.[4] □

George H. Gilpin's essay – 'Patricia Avis and Philip Larkin' – recounted Larkin's affair in the early 1950s with a married woman. Avis actually became pregnant by Larkin but soon miscarried. Their relationship, intense at first, eventually wound down, but Gilpin's article offered interesting insights into Larkin's capacity for love.[5] M. W. Rowe's essay, dealing with the early lesbian novels (written under the pseudonym Brunette Coleman), suggested that writing these works helped Larkin overcome an early case of writers' block. Rowe argued that Larkin, while at Oxford, had had strong homosexual attractions, that these partly repelled him, and that by writing about lesbians he could express certain elements of his personality without feeling self-disgust. Like many other scholars, Rowe maintained that the best elements of Larkin's personality displayed themselves when he was writing letters to women rather than to male friends, and Rowe also argued that Larkin's feminine aspects produced his best creative work.[6]

Liz Hedgecock's essay focused on 'Mythology and Exile' in Larkin's work, especially his novels. She noted similarities between Larkin himself and his main character (John Kemp) in the novel titled *Jill*, and she also explored the author's creation of female characters in all his early major works of fiction.[7] Meanwhile, Terry Whalen argued that Larkin, especially as a young man but also later, was strongly influenced by the personal example, social attitudes, and literary works of D. H. Lawrence, especially *Lady Chatterley's Lover*. According to Whalen, Larkin shared Lawrence's dark, depressed view of modern English society, his profound scepticism about industrialisation and his perception of spiritual decay, and his deep dislike of the values and identities of many modern, middle-class males. Whalen believed that Lawrence and Larkin both challenged their society's standard assumptions about gender, especially about male heroism but also about the restrictions imposed on women.[8]

In another essay, Stephen Regan discussed Larkin's little-known 1947 collection of poems titled *In the Grip of Light* – a collection submitted to six different publishers in 1948 and rejected by all. Regan explored this collection's use of nature imagery; the ways it anticipated such later characteristic themes as agnosticism and scepticism; the continuing influence of Yeats and Edward Thomas on the style of these poems; the absence of any obvious influence from Hardy; and the place of the collection in Larkin's development as a thinker and writer.[9] Raphaël Ingelbien's essay dealt with the uses of symbolism by Larkin and T. S. Eliot. Ingelbien suggested that Larkin admired Eliot more than was commonly realised and had more in common with him, both stylistically and thematically, than was often acknowledged. Both poets, Ingelbien argued, were in some respects 'symbolist' writers, although Larkin's scepticism meant that he could not share Eliot's belief in the ideal of a Christianity community or indeed in any kind of permanent transcendence.[10]

John Osborne's essay suggested that Larkin was in some ways a forerunner of British postmodernism, especially in his emphasis on fundamental uncertainties. According to Osborne, Larkin underestimated the degree to which jazz (which he loved) had always been a modernist art form, and he found Larkin's own writings far more influenced by Modernist poets such as T. S. Eliot than Larkin himself ever admitted. In fact, Larkin's verse (Osborne maintained) was open to many more non-English influences than he let on, and his scepticism about consumerism anticipated the similar scepticism of later 'postmodernists'. It was, however, Larkin's repeated stress on contradictions and irresolvable conundrums, as well as his emphasis on questioning, fractured selves, undecidability, and doubts about the authentic self that made him a proto-postmodernist in thought if not in form and style (since in both ways he was invested in English phrasing and structures).[11] Steve Clark, writing on Larkin and empire, noted many allusions in his works to Britain's status in the world, even in apparently non-political poems, and suggested that ultimately Larkin was less a British imperialist than a critic of American cultural and geopolitical domination.[12]

Ian Almond discussed the way Larkin saw mystical elements in mundane experience but did not embrace a transcendent sense of mystery.[13] James Booth, contributing his own essay to the book he edited, compared and contrasted Larkin's sense of place with that of the poet Seamus Heaney, his great Irish contemporary. Booth suggested that Heaney's works were far more attached to specific geographical places (especially Irish locations) than Larkin's were, with the partial effect that Larkin's verse seemed much less overtly political than the work of Heaney and other recent writers. Booth argued, in fact, that political approaches to Larkin were sometimes inaccurate and usually irrelevant to the greatness of the poetry *as* poetry.[14] Meanwhile, V. Penelope Pelizzon, taking a dialogical approach, compared and contrasted his poems with traditional English 'Punch and Judy' puppet shows, both because of their carnivalesque elements and because of their rollicking humour and masculine aggressiveness. She saw the puppet shows and Larkin's verse as both unruly and conservative, making them 'dialogical' in that sense as well as many others.[15] Finally, in a last essay for the 2000 Booth volume, István D. Rácz discussed Larkin from an East European perspective, focusing on his distinctive Englishness and zeroing in particularly on 'Mr. Bleaney' as an exemplary Larkin poem.[16]

The 16 essays collected by Booth and published at the beginning of the new century admirably fulfilled the volume's titular promise to offer *New Larkins for Old*. Contributors stressed the importance of recently available early texts, the value of non-traditional approaches and kinds of analysis, and the ways Larkin continued to seem relevant as a new millennium began. Contributors also responded, either explicitly or implicitly, to many negative charges levelled against Larkin in the early to mid-1990s. Thus the Booth volume was one of the clearest indications that the poet had weathered the storm touched off by the *Selected Letters* and the Motion biography and had regained much of his earlier social and literary status. The rest of the 2000s would see the publication of many more books and essays not only discussing Larkin but also, in some cases, forthrightly championing him.

Critics, in other words, had now increasingly returned to actual literary criticism and had begun to turn away from assessments of Larkin's personality. This literary emphasis could be seen, for instance, in Alex R. Falzon's book from 2000 titled *Negative Indicative: Philip Larkin in the Forties: A Study in Transformation*. Falzon studied the under-examined poems Larkin produced before he achieved his distinctive Larkinesque style in the 1950s. He argued that although Larkin during the 1940s was more open to Symbolist, Modernist, and even late Romantic literary techniques than he later seemed, it was the early Yeats (with his seductive music) who had most greatly influenced his writing during that period. This influence led Larkin (Falzon suggested) to produce poetry that seemed more abstract, artificial, obscure, and distant from the poet's own experiences than his later work, and the break with this Yeatsian influence was, he argued, far less sudden than Larkin himself had suggested and than various critics had assumed. Falzon noted many flaws in the early poems (partly to emphasise the kinds of changes that later produced Larkin's mature style), but he also saw continuities between the early and later works, as in their use of traditional formal structures – structures Larkin tended to transform rather than merely imitate.[17] Falzon argued that the first real hint of Larkin's mature style initially appeared in 'The Dancer', but he also discussed various other works from the 1940s that foreshadowed later developments, especially 'Going' but also 'Modesties' – a poem that unfortunately remained unpublished for many years. However, Falzon agreed with other scholars that it was in the poem 'An April Sunday brings the snow' – written in response to the death of Larkin's father – that his mature style first fully appeared. Falzon's emphasis was almost entirely stylistic rather than sociological.[18]

Another indication that critics were now more and more interested in Larkin's writings than in his personality or political opinions appears in a 2000 article by Stan Smith. Smith discussed the stylistic differences between Larkin's early verse and his later writings, but his essay was especially valuable for heavily emphasising statistics, particularly when discussing the number, nature, and frequency of various particular words Larkin had employed throughout his career. He stressed the sheer variety of words Larkin used (more than the number employed by T. S. Eliot, and nearly as many as W. B. Yeats, who wrote many more lines than Larkin did). According to Smith, Larkin used 7038 distinct words throughout his poetic canon, with 4648 of those coming in the later, more mature phase of his career. Interestingly, Larkin used the word 'I' 418 times, making it the seventh most commonly used term in his oeuvre and indicating the heavy emphasis his verse places on the personal experiences of individual speakers.[19] Even more technically detailed than Smith's essay was a 2001 article by Peter Groves dealing with the scansion, or metrical analysis, of Larkin's lines, showing that to an unusual degree they begin with accented syllables, thus disrupting the typical rhythms commonly found in much other English poetry and thereby bringing his verse closer to the sounds of actual colloquial speech.[20]

Interesting in its own ways was an intriguing 2002 essay by Roger Craik, which called attention to Larkin's strong interest in reading and writing poems about animals. Craik argued that Larkin had an extraordinary ability both to sympathise and especially empathise with animals, without ever imposing his own thoughts upon them. Craik criticised approaches to Larkin that allegorised such poems, as if they really dealt merely with human issues, not animals themselves. According to Craik, one reason for the poems' appeal was that Larkin treated animals with the dignity they deserved – but so rarely received – in literature, and he noted that Larkin's will left a large portion of his fortune to the RSPCA.[21]

More political was a 2002 chapter in a book by Raphaël Ingelbien, who challenged various ideological, nationalistic interpretations of Larkin, including ones that appropriated his verse either for the left or the right. Leftist interpretations of Larkin's references to England tended (Ingelbien claimed) to see his nationalism as 'postcolonial' – that is, as emphasising England's status as a small, relatively powerless nation in the post-war period. Opposite interpretations tended to see Larkin as harkening back, if only nostalgically, to Britain's imperial past; these interpretations either praised or criticised that sort of sentimentality. Ingelbien, focusing especially on such poems as 'Here', argued that neither kind of approach stressing Larkin's supposed nationalism did full justice to the broader, darker, more humanistic dimensions of his writing, which had implications for people everywhere rather than simply for one part of the British Isles.[22] Also stressing Larkin's interest in larger human questions was a 2002 essay by Andrew McKeown. It argued that Larkin's attitudes towards religion were neither entirely affirmative nor entirely sceptical but sometimes one or the other and sometimes somewhere in between. McKeown suggested that Larkin was far more interested in religion that either he or his critics sometimes let on and that he found religion intriguing if not always appealing.[23]

In 2003, Raphaël Ingelbien published another fine essay on Larkin, this time arguing that in writing about ageing, the poet was influenced first by a somewhat Romantic Yeats, then by a more fatalistic Hardy, and then finally (as Larkin himself became older) by Yeats again. Ageing (Ingelbien) showed, had always been a strong interest of Larkin's: sometimes he wrote empathetically about the old, but as he grew older himself he became more bitter about age, following, in that respect, Yeats's lead – not Yeats the Romantic, the symbolist, or the modernist but Yeats the old man angry about *getting* old.[24] In another essay from 2003, however, Victoria Longino traced a different development in Larkin's verse, this one involving his ideas about gender.[25] Longino pointed to what she considered to be 'a significant achievement':

> ■ [Larkin's] empathic attention to gender ... took root in his early poetry, continued into the novels, and expanded in the three books of poetry that followed. This poetic expansion is evident in Larkin's focus on the uniqueness of the female experience in *The Less Deceived*, his vision of women and men as distinct yet joined in life's journey in *The Whitsun Weddings*, and his perception in *High Windows* of women and men as more similar than different as they go about the daily business of living. In his poetry and novels, Larkin reveals a maturing and deepening vision of woman and man as he portrays aspects of gender, of being female and male apart and together in the world.[26] □

The Larkin who, in the mid-1990s, was often depicted as simply sexist emerges in readings such as Longino's as something more subtle and complicated. Critics were now increasingly willing to challenge perceived simplifications about Larkin, whether those came from Larkin's critics or even from Larkin himself. John Osborne, for instance, in a 2003 article, was one of a growing number of writers who took issue with Larkin's controversial claims about jazz. Larkin had famously asserted that he disliked post-war trends because they had made jazz modernistic. Osborne asserted, in contrast, that jazz had always been a modernistic art form, and that Larkin's real objection to post-war jazz was that it was increasingly inaccessible and less appealing to popular tastes. Larkin, who loved pre-war jazz but who detested artistic Modernism, could not bring himself (Osborne maintained) to admit that jazz had always been the pre-eminent modern art form.[27]

2004 saw the publication of Stephen Cooper's *Philip Larkin: Subversive Writer*. Cooper devoted much of his book to discussing Larkin's early novels, including the lesbian-inflected 'Coleman novellas' (featuring female students) as well as various unfinished fiction. These previously unpublished texts had only recently become widely available in a 2002 collection edited by James Booth, and one of the main features of Larkin scholarship in the 2000s was a growing interest in these and other previously unpublished writings. As Cooper's title suggested, he saw Larkin as a writer willing to challenge conventional thinking and behaviour, especially regarding imperialism, class, gender, and sexual relations. The 'new' texts, along with as-yet unpublished letters, thus undercut or at least complicated the view of Larkin as a reactionary – a view apparently supported by the *Selected Letters* and by Motion's biography. Even the reactionary attitudes found in those sources (Cooper suggested) were often parodied there, and a whole range of other writings in the Larkin archives helped challenge (in Cooper's opinion) the now-common view of Larkin as a hidebound traditionalist. Larkin (he argued) had been more open to a wide range of ideas and influences (including James Joyce and Virginia Woolf) than was often assumed.[28]

Discussing *Jill* and the 'Coleman novellas', Cooper argued that Larkin showed himself far more sympathetic to women – and far more critical of traditional masculine values – than some of his later comments (in the *Selected Letters* as well as the poems) might lead one to believe. The same was true of Cooper's commentary on *A Girl in Winter* and the unfinished novels, which he read as variously critical of establishment ideas and ideals, including nationalism and male privilege. Thus it did not surprise Cooper that Larkin's early poetry – including *The North Ship* – was more subversive than many critics assumed, partly because this work so strongly reflected the impact of W. H. Auden and Louis MacNeice, perhaps the foremost leftist poets of Larkin's youth. Cooper saw *Letters from Iceland* (co-authored by Auden and MacNeice) as a particularly important influence on Larkin's early poetry, not only on its attitudes but also on its style. Similarly, he also stressed the liberating impact of Larkin's deep friendship during the 1940s with James Sutton, who had encouraged Larkin's own tendency to think unconventionally about politics, war, economics, and sexuality. Here again, Cooper drew on unpublished materials (especially letters to and from Sutton) to support his claims.[29]

Cooper spent his last chapter arguing for stylistic and thematic continuities between Larkin's early works and the later, major poems. He argued, for example, that the later poetry reflects Larkin's early experiences as a realistic novelist interested in distinct characters, voices, and plots. Even the ways Larkin composed poems resembled (Cooper maintained) the ways he composed novels, with a strong emphasis on narrative and drama, whether literal or figurative. Cooper particularly stressed Larkin's unconventional thinking about gender in the later poems, but he also explored the poet's scepticism about jingoism and all sorts of social regimentation.[30] Cooper conceded that the *Selected Letters* were often troubling, but he argued that Larkin was ultimately more complicated than the letters alone suggested:

> ■ There are, it seems, two Larkins: one is the idealistic rebel deconstructing the dogmas of the other entrenched conformist persona, unwriting or parodying the vindictive tirades expressed in the letters. Such aspects of Larkin cannot be ignored. But these 'limitations' are mapped onto the geography of the poems, where they are ridiculed, taunted and rejected so that – aesthetically transformed – they become enlisted in Larkin's career-long campaign against clichéd narratives.[31] ☐

Larkin the man, in other words, revealed flaws that are mocked and subverted by Larkin the writer.

Larkin in the Mid-2000s

Cooper's 2004 monograph was soon followed in 2005 by yet another book by James Booth, who was now establishing himself not only as the dean of Larkin scholars but as one of the poet's most impassioned defenders. In *Philip Larkin: The Poet's Plight*, as in previous writings, Booth strongly argued for viewing Larkin first and foremost from an artistic perspective rather than emphasising historical, political, or social contexts and judgments. Yet Booth's own approach, at least in this book, was often biographical. He set many poems in specific personal contexts, especially when discussing poems about women and love. As so often before, Booth focused on offering detailed close readings of particular texts, so that it was often hard to summarise larger claims. This was less true, however, of his study's opening chapters, where he did offer intriguing generalisations about the poet's style.[32]

Booth began by stressing the sheer popularity of Larkin's poems – the ways he had used words skilfully and made his phrasing memorable, often by using a distinctive vocabulary or 'idiolect'. He noted, for instance, Larkin's frequent use of words ending in 'ing', which Booth interpreted as evidence of Larkin's emphasis on movement rather than stasis. Larkin also (according to Booth) often used words with negative connotations, such as 'not' or words beginning with 'un-', which enhanced his works' sense of scepticism and darkness. And, although Larkin famously used common words, he also (Booth showed) often employed many unusual terms, frequently using hyphenated compounds to create distinctive words of his own. Larkin was so good at coining memorable phrases that some of them (Booth demonstrated) had worked their ways into common speech, so that regular people often found themselves alluding to Larkin without conscious intent, as in references to 'mum and dad' and the idea that 'work has to be done'. In this especially fine opening chapter, Booth also discussed Larkin's varied use of rhymes, his skill in distinct genres, and the subtle, deliberate arrangement of poems in particular volumes.[33]

Booth's focus now became increasingly biographical. He discussed Larkin's eventually frequent hostility towards Auden, their different views of a poet's roles, Larkin's commitment to his job as a librarian, his attitudes towards money, and his relations with various women and the different impact each of them had had on the kinds of poems he wrote. These women included (1) his mother; (2) a girl named Ruth Bowman, who inspired many poems and to whom he was briefly engaged; (3) a friend named Winifred Arnott, who eventually married someone else; (4) Patsy Strang, a married woman with whom he had a sexual fling; (5) Monica Jones, a free-spirited academic who was the closest Larkin came to having a wife; (6) Maeve Brennan, a devout Catholic who found herself in a lengthy competition with Jones for Larkin's attention; and (7) Betty Mackareth, his long-time secretary.[34] Booth showed the impact each relationship had had on specific poems, concluding that

> ■ Larkin's love-life appears at first sight a miscellaneous *bricolage*: a traumatic broken engagement, routine life-long monogamy, a prolonged mutual narcissism, two brief affairs twenty years apart. His 'nothing if not personal' work presents perhaps the widest spectrum of different intimacies in twentieth-century poetry. Each of the seven women who appear in his work focuses a distinct personal relationship with a 'real girl'. There is a mutuality in Larkin's work rare in conventional love poetry. He submits with humility to the different women in his life. ... In this openness and vulnerability to others Larkin approaches the sacramental submission to Life of his idol D. H. Lawrence.[35] □

Booth next explored Larkin's relationships with history in general. Critiquing various historical approaches to the poet's work, he noted that Larkin used the word 'history' only once in his verse. Booth's own comments on this topic were rooted in detailed discussions of specific poems, but his comments on Larkin's politics were more general. He suggested that Larkin had mixed feelings about his father's right-wing views, that Larkin himself often played games when writing his letters, and that much evidence suggested that Larkin was more tolerant in person than when joking with certain correspondents. Few of Larkin's poems (Booth contended) express political opinions, and although he was sometimes associated with a strident English nationalism, the growing popularity of his poetry throughout the world suggested that his appeal was not merely or even mainly jingoistic.[36]

The closing chapters of Booth's book accomplished various objectives. They explored Larkin's use of room imagery; argued that his poetry was more metaphorical than was often admitted; maintained that even the plots and structures of some poems were rooted in metaphors; and noted the ways his depictions of rooms changed over the course of Larkin's career. Booth concluded by stressing the elegiac nature and forms of much of Larkin's verse, especially in his use of 'self-elegy', or poetry mourning the impact of approaching death on the speaker himself. In an appendix, Booth printed texts of two more previously unpublished poems, demonstrating once again how much of Larkin's work still remained to be issued.[37] Clearly Booth's monograph was the major contribution to Larkin criticism during 2005, although an article published that year by Dan Jacobson was also worth consulting, especially for its emphasis on Larkin's complexities, self-contradictions, self-divisions, debts to Modernism, unusually vivid emphasis on English summers, and exceptional use of run-on stanzas – stanzas that flow, without punctuation, from one into another.[38]

Also valuable was Richard Bradford's 2005 book *First Boredom, then Fear: The Life of Philip Larkin*.[39] This volume, the second major biography of the poet, often dealt as much with Larkin the writer as with Larkin the man and commented often on such matters as his transition from aspiring novelist to successful poet, on the circumstances that helped produce specific poems, and on the general reception of his successive volumes of poetry. Bradford suggested, for instance, that in his mature verse Larkin often wrote poems tightly tied to his own life; that most writers initially associated with the so-called 'Movement' began to distance themselves from it almost immediately; that 'Mr. Bleaney' was Larkin's 'first full excursion into mordantly dark comedy'; and that 'An Arundel Tomb' is far less affirmative than is sometimes imagined.[40] Bradford also commented on such issues as the sense of separateness that underlay many Larkin poems from 1956-60; on the frequency with which people of the lower classes appear in *The Whitsun Weddings*; on Larkin's relative disinterest in politics in the early 1960s (despite a temperamentally conservative orientation); and on the unusual personal vulnerability he displayed in a poem titled 'The Dance'.[41] Additionally, Bradford variously argued that public debates about 'The Movement' helped to renew public interest in poetry in general and to ignite interest in Larkin's work in particular; that a 1964 television broadcast about Larkin helped to confirm his status as his own man and to refute attacks made by his enemies; and that Larkin felt freer and freer, in the 1960s, to use his poems to deal with his own complicated attitudes towards romance, sex, and marriage.[42] As Larkin aged, however, his poetry more and more reflected his sense of isolation:

■ From 1970 onwards virtually all of Larkin's poems involve what can only be described as a reluctant presence. Read as a sequence they are informed by a mood which has no exact precedent. Literature is replete with figures beset by various conditions – mental, emotional, and physical – from which they seek release, but none comes close to the effect created by Larkin in these pieces where a condition of claustrophobic unease seems to surround each word or phrase, irrespective of its meaning.[43] □

Ultimately (Bradford argued), Larkin withdrew increasingly from poetry until he finally fell almost completely silent.

Yet however silent Larkin himself may have become, by the mid-2000s scholars and critics of Larkin were more and more active. 2006 saw the publication of *Philip Larkin and the Poetics of Resistance*, edited by Andrew McKeon and Charles Holdefer.[44] It included contributions both from various well-known Larkin scholars and from 'new' voices as well. Thus Raphaël Ingelbien discussed how to interpret Larkin's well-known (and perhaps ambiguous) rejection of so-called 'foreign poetry'. He suggested that Larkin was less genuinely hostile to such verse than his off-hand comments sometimes suggested; his real problem, Ingelbien maintained, was with the over-emphasis on foreign models promulgated by Ezra Pound and other American writers – an over-emphasis that Larkin feared would distort the nature of English poetry.[45] Interestingly enough, Ingelbien's piece was followed by comments from Larkin's French translator, Jacques Nassif, discussing both the challenges and rewards of trying to render Larkin's famously 'English' style of poetry into a different language.[46]

Jean-Charles Perquin then emphasised the beauty of Larkin's verse, its rejection of sentimentality, its subversion of moments of potential transcendence, and its desire to say things difficult to articulate. Perquin highlighted the various tensions in Larkin's poetry, its emphasis on conflicting ideas and attitudes, and the ways even the structures, shapes, and stanzas of the poems resist rigid confines.[47] Charles Holdefer, meanwhile, examined Larkin's 'camp' sensibility as a way of exploring his contradictions, his desire for truth but his scepticism about attaining it, his appreciation of surface beauty, and his melancholy persona.[48] István Rácz emphasised Larkin's recurring concern with time both as continuous and as divisible (as well as Larkin's efforts to resist time),[49] and Martine Semblatt intriguingly explored Larkin's 'Classical Prosody' – that is, his use of traditional metres, rhythms, and rhyme schemes. Semblatt noted the diminishing number of different stanza forms Larkin used as his career progressed, his keen interest in different kinds of rhymes, his prosodic skill, and the ways his understated but clever use of rhyme reinforces the modest impressions conveyed by his personae. Semblatt commented that even the poems apparently written in free verse are relatively consistent in beats per line, and she explored the ways Larkin managed to make his verse look and sound simultaneously traditional and innovative, especially in the ways rhyme schemes sometimes subverted stanzaic structures. But she also noted how Larkin's poems often returned to regularity in their final lines. Larkin frequently (according to Semblatt) stressed predictable rhymes and rhythms, both to reinforce humour as well as to lighten moods. He also (she showed) used different rhythms for different speakers within single poems, and in general Semblatt produced one of the clearest, most persuasive discussions of Larkin's sound effects anyone could want.[50]

Another essay – this one by Helen Goethals – argued that Larkin's early verse should be read as war poetry, not because it mentioned war very explicitly but because it was written in wartime and was thus conditioned by wartime moods and experiences. Wartime in England had been darker and less heroic than it often seemed in official propaganda and standard historical accounts, and Larkin's neo-Romantic wartime poetry frequently reflected (Goethals claimed) this gloominess and sense of the absurd, often in comic ways.[51] A 2006 article by Stephen Cooper repeated many arguments already made in his book from 2004,[52] while a 2006 piece by David Ten Eyck began by noting Larkin's resistance to Modernism as well as his rejection of standard notions of political progress. Ten Eyck mainly focused, however, on various kinds of stylistic and thematic resistances or conflicts *within* the poems, particularly ones about love and desire.[53] Meanwhile, an essay by Adrian Grafe interestingly catalogued many varied ways in which Larkin was concerned with transience:

> ■ [Larkin] is the poet of trains, train journeys and changing stations; ... of rented rooms; of hotels and old peoples' homes, of not feeling at home at 'Home' and of the sheer non-existence of home ...; of ambulances, hospitals, and hospital wards. ... He is the poet not only of places of passage but of rites of passage – witness 'Born Yesterday', or 'Annus Mirabilis', or 'Church Going', or the wedding poems, amongst others; of arriving and of leave-taking: *The Less Deceived* alone includes poems entitled 'Coming', 'Going', 'Poetry of Departures', 'Absences', and 'Arrivals, Departures'.[54] □

Grafe also emphasised Larkin's interest in death, memory, methods of memorisation, and preservation, but he additionally stressed Larkin's ambivalence about language – an ambivalence that could variously result in silence, frankness, obscenity, and stalemated endings of which the poet eventually grew weary so that he ultimately stopped writing.[55] Finally, James Booth made a strong case for the many biographical and poetic similarities between Larkin and T. S. Eliot, especially in their use of self-mockery, their longing for annihilation of self, and their light-filled epiphanies. Booth conceded, to be sure, important differences: he saw Eliot as more authoritarian, less worldly, more elitist, and more experimental than Larkin. But he noted many intriguing resemblances, including domineering fathers, close relationships with mothers, a fondness for private obscenity, and, most interestingly, a tendency to work out their personal problems in their poems despite a proclaimed preference for privacy.

The year 2006 also saw the publication of Tijana Stojković's book *'Unnoticed in the Casual Light of Day': Philip Larkin and the Plain Style*, which sought to explain Larkin's famously clear phrasing, showing why and how he wrote as he did and why his style was actually more complex than was often assumed.[56] Stojković surveyed much previous writing on Larkin's 'plain' phrasing, setting his methods within the historical contexts of the plain style tradition (especially during the Renaissance and the eighteenth century) and discussing the political and social implications of a style that sought to make poetry accessible to a wider than usual modern audience by emphasising the possibility and desirability of communication. Stojković noted the emphasis on 'ordinary language' among philosophers at Oxford when Larkin studied there, suggesting that this emphasis, along with various other mid-century influences, helped move Larkin towards the plainness for which he later became famous.[57]

Stojković often engaged in detailed analyses of particular poems before offering larger generalisations about Larkin's methods. She contrasted, for instance, his notably successful poem 'Church Going' with an earlier, less successful (because less clear) poem on a similar subject titled 'A Stone Church Damaged by a Bomb', and she used similar discussions of particular rhetorical strategies in specific poems to explain how Larkin's plain style reflected an empiricist philosophy that featured particularity, storytelling, anti-pedantic diction, visualisation, and numerous references to looking and seeing. This philosophy also stressed concrete imagery, use of parables, parenthetical asides, epigrammatic and proverbial expressions, familiar logic, traditional ideas (often subjected to investigation), and an almost cinematic presentation of particular scenes and events. Stojković suggested that some of Larkin's poems were inductive (moving from the particular to the general) while other poems that were deductive or discursive reversed that process:

■ Although they don't exhibit the same inductive movement as the earlier-mentioned poems, the poems belonging to this discursive type are similar in that they attempt to develop and convey an idea through what looks like a common thought-process. The speaker's mind moves in an orderly and 'logical' fashion, each thought deriving from the previous one, and often capturing a recognisable 'pattern' on a certain subject. 'Aubade' is probably the best example of such an analytical style. ... From beginning to end, the speaker's mind is revealed in an elaborate contemplation of one subject – death.[57] □

Stojković noted, in fact, that Larkin's poetry often explored rhetorical 'commonplaces' – that is, standard ideas or topics that had often, throughout history, been common subjects of speeches, essays, and poems. This tendency was one of many that helped make his verse seem relevant and accessible to a broad audience, and the same effect resulted from his use of speakers to whom many readers could relate. Stojković also examined Larkin's use of various typographical tactics, such as the use of italics and question marks to set off distinct voices within poems, thereby complicating by multiplying the different tones of voice specific works could convey. She likewise explored Larkin's use (and interrogation) of various common themes, such as his questioning of standard gender roles, his investigations of human relations in a materialistic culture, his attraction towards ideal communities and traditions, his celebrations of nature, and his tendency to extol the beautiful and the mystical. All in all, Stojković explored and extolled Larkin's plain style while showing that it was capable of complexities and complications that made it anything but simplistic.[58]

Another important book on Larkin, this one by Sisir Kumar Chatterjee, also appeared in 2006. Titled *Philip Larkin: Poetry that Builds Bridges*, it was one of several works produced in the first decade of the twenty-first century by scholars from India. This fact itself is significant, given Larkin's supposed prejudice against non-English persons, particularly persons of colour. Chatterjee obviously loved Larkin's poetry and produced an exceptionally thorough and lengthy study with an especially intriguing overall argument. He contended that Larkin had very definitely 'developed' over the course of his career, both thematically and stylistically, even though Larkin himself had often mocked the idea of poetic development. Chatterjee provided close, insightful readings of practically every poem in the main Larkin corpus and also showed detailed familiarity with previous scholarship, offering an excellent survey of that commentary in his opening chapter.[59] He was not afraid to take issue with previous interpreters but always showed a thorough understanding of any claims he disputed (or endorsed).

Chatterjee moved patiently through Larkin's whole career, carefully examining one poem after another, wasting no words but producing thoughtful analyses all along the way. His larger argument was perhaps best summarised in the following passage:

■ In *The North Ship* the poet was obsessed with himself and wrote in a vein of self-pity and sentimentality. The poems in this volume are steeped in a feeling of sweet pain and languishing melancholy. Here Larkin's attitude to life is irredeemably gloomy. In *The Less Deceived*, however, the poet turns his attention to other people's lives, and even while speaking about himself shows a desire to stand face to face with truth, naked, and shorn of all illusions. Here his attitude both to himself and to other people who seek to make life bearable by deceiving themselves with various illusions is ironic and satirical. Quite differently, in *The Whitsun Weddings* Larkin not only becomes less self-obsessed and more outward looking, but even his treatment of other people, the victims of life, is largely compassionate. His perspective on life here takes on a definitely affirmative turn, though the expression of this affirmation is at times ambiguous. Lastly, in *High Windows* there is hardly any poem in which the poet speaks about himself, and there is very little negative in his general outlook on life. Here he shows more occasions to appreciate the beauty of small things even in the rituals of ordinary, day-to-day life. The last collection presents a panoramic, almost epical, canvas of life, embodies a sunnier vision and celebrates the invincible dignity of human life, despite all its inherent limitations.[60] ☐

Chatterjee's assessment of *High Windows* ran against the grain of some previous Larkin scholarship, which had tended to see the poet growing gloomier in his final book. But Chatterjee carefully supported his claim and paid much attention both to stylistic and thematic developments. The fact that such a strong book emerged from India said much about Larkin's international appeal – an appeal also evident in a helpful, very clearly organised 2006 study guide produced by the Indian scholar B. G. Tandon and also published in the subcontinent. Tandon, unfortunately, died before the book could be completed, preventing discussions of some important poems by Larkin from being included. But the book's structure made it an unusually lucid overview of Larkin's writings in general and of many specific poems in particular.[61]

Also helpfully designed and very beneficial to students and 'regular readers' was Nicholas Marsh's 2007 book *Philip Larkin: The Poems*. It was intended to guide readers not only through Larkin's verse but through increasingly advanced ways of interpreting literature in general. Each chapter built on the one before it, making this book a fine, methodical introduction to basic approaches to interpretation. Marsh built his book inductively around readings of individual poems – readings from which he then drew broader conclusions about Larkin's verse in general. He emphasised the dramatic nature of many poems, their use of speakers, the ways dilemmas in the poems reflected dilemmas inherent in the speakers' characters, and the use of multiple, often conflicting tones within individual works. He stressed Larkin's effective use of silence, his recurring theme of death, and the ways he drew on other writers. Marsh explored Larkin's mastery of such technical devices as metre, rhythm, rhyme, alliteration, onomatopoeia (in which words sound like the things they describe), stanza form, repetition, sentence structure, imagery, and various other methods for which there are no simple names. In short, Marsh provided readers with a solid grounding not only in the meanings of Larkin's works but also in how those meanings were technically accomplished and conveyed.[62] Subsequent chapters became increasingly complex, but each chapter ended by helpfully reviewing that chapter's basic points. Marsh especially explored such typical Larkin themes as deception, self-deception, dilemmas leading to inaction, and the force of external pressures on individual lives. Also discussed were Larkin's varied uses of satire, his emphasis on lonely males, his concern with personal and spiritual emptiness, and the ways money and consumerism were now used to fill gaps left by the retreat of traditional ways of giving meaning to life. Particularly interesting were Marsh's comments on the ways Larkin presents women. The poems (Marsh contended) treat women as objects because the personae who speak the poems are often neurotic men whose views Larkin depicts without necessarily endorsing them himself.[63] Later Marsh's book emphasised Larkin's atheism, his attraction to social rituals as substitutes for religion, his relative lack of interest in politics, and his deterministic view of life. Marsh also explored the poet's interest in journeys (both literal and metaphorical), his use of framing devices (such as windows) when offering descriptions, and his tendency to associate views of the sky with recognitions of humanity's absurdly small place in an indifferent universe.[64] All in all, Marsh produced a lucidly organised study helpful not only for its specific and general comments on Larkin but also for its usefulness as a basic guide to critical interpretation.

Larkin in the Later 2000s

Essays on Larkin published in 2007 covered varied topics. Terry Castle, for instance, emphasised his interest in lesbianism, lesbian pornography, and lesbian fiction (which he both read and wrote). She praised *Jill* for its self-critical depiction of men, suggested a lesbian subtext to the book, and discussed the ways Larkin used his own 'schoolgirl' fiction to explore his personal sense of loneliness.[65] Stephen Regan offered the increasingly common opinion that Larkin had been less anti-Modernist than he often appeared, especially in his modern questioning of complacent assumptions about the possibilities of discovering and knowing truth.[66] Finally, Robert Lance Snyder argued that Larkin's poems rarely alluded to specific English locations or place names, partly because he was less interested in space than in time and partly because he stressed dispossession, rootlessness, and alienation. Snyder thought that Larkin often tried to bridge the divide between the profane and the secular but could rarely succeed in doing so, and he also stressed the poet's disappointed attempts at final closure, his tendency to undercut symbols of transcendence, the integrity with which his speakers confronted nothingness, and his postmodern preference for irony and evasiveness despite a continuing yearning for human connectedness.[67] Meanwhile, in 2008, A. Banerjee offered an essay that emphasised Larkin's preoccupation with death, noted his avoidance of issues of large historical horrors (such as genocide), and compared and contrasted him with such other gloomy twentieth-century writers as Kafka, Camus, and Beckett:

> ■ Whereas Beckett leaves one paralyzed with the understanding that 'nothing can be done' in the face of hopelessness, the English poet unobtrusively emphasises the virtue of enduring. In fact, Larkin's writing is curiously uplifting because of the way he shapes the sadness of life into poetry. Like Hardy before him he believed that the poet's sensitivity to human sadness can be spiritually nourishing. ... One of the devices that Larkin deploys for suggesting life's possibilities is the uplifting note at the end of many of his poems. He recognises that despite man's sadness and suffering he retains a hunger for transcendence that neither can be appeased nor ignored.[68] □

It was also in 2008 that John Osborne produced an especially lively, thought-provoking volume: *Larkin, Ideology and Critical Violence: A Case of Wrongful Conviction*. Osborne vigorously defended Larkin against all the various fault-finders who had attacked the man and the poet since the early 1990s.[69] He argued that the poetry should be judged first and foremost as poetry, not as private expressions of Larkin the individual, and he maintained that critics often had to import biographical details into poems that Larkin himself had created to be deliberately general and non-specific. Even Larkin's admirers (Osborne claimed) read the poems biographically although the poems often offered no biographical details. Both opponents and defenders of Larkin, then, were guilty of a 'biographical fallacy' that reduced the range of the poems' possible meanings, turning their speakers into carbon copies of the poet and interpreting the poet himself as far more limited in his thinking than he actually was. Like increasing numbers of previous critics, Osborne argued that Larkin resembled twentieth-century Modernists far more than he liked to admit, but some of Osborne's other claims were significantly more original. He contended, for instance, that the poet was at heart a radical sceptic who questioned practically everything, thus undermining many certitudes and faiths that other people took for granted, whether those certitudes involved politics, gender, nationalism, personal identity, or the nature of life in general:

> ■ Larkin's focus upon doubt, alterity, and undecidability is so drastic in its implications as to anticipate Deconstructionism. [Using a variety of techniques, Larkin] instantiated unfixity in the very fabric of his verse. These techniques (ellipses, split similes, double negatives, oxymora, paronomasia, asymmetrical stanza length and rhyme schemes, etc.) are the implements of Larkin's home-grown Deconstructionism. ... this deconstructive approach was applied by Larkin to the subjects of nationality, gender, politics and identitarianism. The effect in every case is such as to de-naturalize, de-essentialize and de-stabilize the discourses of power – sometimes with gratifyingly unexpected results. Hence, Larkin's political detractors see him as reprehensibly Tory; but the only poem he wrote on commission for the Conservative Party was so little to their liking that they brutally censored it before publication. Similarly, the miserable racism of Larkin's private correspondence has lured certain biographical critics into smearing his poetry .... Yet as even the titles of his poems attest ('Going', 'Strangers', 'Arrivals, Departures', 'Home is so Sad', 'The Importance of Elsewhere'), Larkin's sense of deracination, exile, and incomplete belonging is ... akin to that of ethnic minorities and immigrants ....[70] □

Sometimes, as in the last quoted sentence, Osborne's arguments risked sounding strained, but no brief quotation or summary can do justice to the actual subtlety and thoroughness of his claims, especially the assertions rooted in historical facts. Osborne made Larkin sound like a postmodernist before postmodernism had even been philosophically formulated. His basic contention was that Larkin rarely embraced either/or thinking, so that the poet's verse could be reliably recruited to serve no large, simple, simplistic 'truths'. Osborne's feisty, colloquial style (not really well represented in the passage quoted above) made his book stimulating to read, especially since he did not hesitate to step – and sometimes stomp – on the toes not only of Larkin's detractors but even, sometimes, of Larkin's admirers. The Larkin who emerged from Osborne's book seemed highly unconventional – different and better as a poet than he sometimes was as a correspondent.

Another 2008 volume – Richard Palmer's *Such Deliberate Disguises: The Art of Philip Larkin* – was helpful in its own ways. Like various other recent critics, Palmer was especially interested in Larkin's attitudes towards jazz. He found the poet more open-minded in his actual reviews of jazz recordings than some of his most famous comments about that art-form might have suggested. Larkin, in other words, seemed to Palmer actually more tolerant of avant-garde jazz than he might have presented himself as being, and this tolerance suggested a corresponding openness to Modernism in literature as well. Palmer also discussed such matters as Larkin's similarities to the poet R. S. Thomas, his abiding interest in spiritual matters, his strengths as a chronicler of social changes, and his interest in myth despite his claims to the contrary.[71]

Palmer's main interest, however, concerned Larkin's attitudes towards jazz. He considered these attitudes important because they showed (he thought) that Larkin was not only more tolerant of Modernism but also far less actually racist than his letters might have suggested. Although Larkin wrote only five poems explicitly dealing with jazz, his love of such music (Palmer claimed) was central to his personality. Palmer stressed the importance of some of Larkin's lesser-known writings about jazz – writings that revealed his attitudes to be far more open-minded than was usually supposed, not only in his views of music but also in his appreciation of black people and the beautiful music they produced.[72] Later chapters in Palmer's book suggested that Larkin's early prose fiction – including the lesbian writings and the novel *Jill* – were generally weak, although Palmer did think *A Girl in Winter* had some strengths. He thought Larkin's fiction showed little real interest in the psychology of its characters and that Larkin was not especially adept at writing works of great length. He questioned Larkin's supposed debts to Hardy, suggested that in general Larkin's own pronouncements about his work should be scrutinised rather than simply accepted, and argued that Larkin was interested in spirituality even if he rejected religion. To Palmer, Larkin seemed less pervasively gloomy and negative (even in the famously dark poem titled 'Aubade') than had often been claimed, and he also suggested that Larkin feared death less than insanity.

Far more deliberately wide-ranging was a two-volume study of Larkin by Sunil Kumar Sarker published in 2009. Amounting in total length to over six hundred pages, Sarker's *A Companion to Philip Larkin* provided further evidence of the continuing interest in this poet (especially in the 2000s) by scholars from India. Volume I of the Sarker set examined Larkin's life and psychology, surveyed his various works, discussed his novels, and then offered detailed readings of representative poems from *The Less Deceived* and *The Whitsun Weddings*. Volume II offered similar readings of poems from *High Windows* and then moved on to broader issues. Sarker discussed, for instance, why Larkin both could and could not be classified as a 'modern' poet, offering solid reasons for both claims but slightly favouring the latter. Sarker agreed with Larkin himself in disputing his alleged affiliation with 'The Movement', and then he surveyed distinctive features of Larkin's own poetic theory. These included his emphasis on poetic pleasure, his interest in appealing to many readers, his lack of interest in odd formal experimentation, his agreement with Wordsworth that poems were born spontaneously and should focus on common life, his concern for emotion in poetry, and his distrust of lofty notions of poetic inspiration.[73]

Commenting on Larkin's style, Sarker discussed his characteristic uses of such techniques as imagery (especially similes and metaphor), dramatic monologues, irony and satire, variations in tone and diction, traditional methods of syntax and prosody (metre), preference for normal rather than poetic language, conversational colloquialism, indirection, and occasional (and purposeful) indulgence in clichés and vulgarity. Sarker agreed with previous critics who argued that Larkin's phrasing tended to be more realistic and less metaphorical than the phrasing of various other poets, and he also concurred with analysts who had emphasised Larkin's keen interest in stanza forms. He additionally noted the typical structures of Larkin's poems (involving a movement from an opening situation to an emotional response to a final reflection and often a sudden final twist). When Sarker turned to discussing Larkin's characteristic themes, he drew on previous critics who had emphasised such topics as death, time, innocence, sadness, dark humour, memory, modern England, personal relationships, the individual and society, and appearance vs. reality. Sarker then discussed the appearance of some of these themes in various poems, concluding that Larkin's crucial concerns were with time and death, with the former leading to the latter. Although Sarker conceded that Larkin was often glum and pessimistic, he saw Larkin as hardly unique in this way and even suggested that his tone was occasionally (but only occasionally) flecked with brightness.[74]

Later sections of Sarker's book discussed Larkin's talent as a mimic of varied voices – a skill perhaps explainable as a reaction against his early stammer, and a talent useful in promoting his poetry's lyricism, enhancing its parodic nature, and giving his verse a strong dialogical dimension. Sarker reviewed the critical controversy over whether Larkin had or had not 'developed', ultimately siding with those who claimed that he had not by arguing that Larkin's relative lack of development by no means made him an inferior poet. Sarker contended that Larkin's use of bawdy language (a use resembling Shakespeare's) disqualified him from being labelled genteel, but he did think Larkin could be classified as a typical Englishman nostalgic for, and admiring of, English imperialism. He cautioned against the tendency to over-emphasise the autobiographical dimensions of Larkin's verse, suggested that most of the symbols Larkin used occurred in his early verse, and concluded that although Larkin was basically a realistic writer his poetry was sometimes tinged with Romanticism. He agreed with Roger Day that Larkin's verse could basically be classified as either personal or public and that the public poems could be further classified into four smaller groupings: poems involving observation, satirical poems, poems about death, and poems of celebration. One virtue among many of Sarker's two-volume set was its clear design: issues were openly stated (for instance, whether Larkin was a love poet) and just as clearly answered. Sarker demonstrated extensive familiarity with the whole Larkin canon and with much previous criticism.[75]

The appearance of Sarker's two hefty volumes at the very end of the first decade of the twenty-first century indicated, in several ways and for various reasons, just how strongly Larkin's critical fortunes had rebounded. Sarker gave Larkin's poems (and indeed practically every aspect of his poetic career) both thorough and thoughtful attention. The fact that he was Indian, and that his scholarly study was published in India, suggested that Larkin's appeal was not only worldwide but was strong even among people who, arguably, had good reasons to ignore or even disdain his work. If Larkin had been (as some insisted) a racist, xenophobic imperialist, those charges did not seem to matter much to Sarker or the other Indian scholars who, during these years, wrote so admiringly about his talent. For them, as for increasing numbers of other readers, it was the work that mattered far more than the man. The next and final chapter explores the newer approaches to that work which emerged in the second decade of the present century.

CHAPTER SIX

Newer Approaches to Larkin: The 2010s

As the second decade of the twenty-first century began, Larkin studies were stronger than ever. The controversies of the mid-1990s had largely receded, and in 2012 Larkin's *Complete Poems*, presented by Archie Burnett in the first true scholarly edition, provided interested readers with thorough, reliable, and fully annotated texts. Larkin's poems continued to attract critical attention, some of it deliberately at odds with earlier interpretive views. Many previous approaches to Larkin persisted, especially the ever-growing tendency to find him more Modernist, more Symbolist, even more Surrealist than he himself claimed. Critics also continued to study his connections with various earlier writers, especially those from the 1920s and 1930s. History in general was important to critics of the early 2010s, but their interest in historical detail was often combined with close (sometimes *very* close) attention to precise textual details. Other topics discussed during this period concerned Larkin's relationships with his audiences, the connections between his early poems and his later works, and the political and psychological dimensions of his writing.

Larkin in the Early 2010s

During the first half of the new decade, a new monograph on Larkin appeared practically every year, beginning in 2010 with Gillian Steinberg's *Philip Larkin and His Audiences*.[1] As its title suggested, Steinberg's book was especially concerned with the roles of audiences both inside and outside the poems. She particularly noted Larkin's 'stated interest in recreating his own emotions in readers', but she also explored various other matters, including the following:

■ ... the creation of spaces in the poems into which readers can insert themselves; the regular use of first-person plural pronouns that include the reader even when he wishes not to be included; the positioning of the poems' speakers as audience members themselves to create an alignment with the poems' readers; the explicit calling into question of the observer's role in any scene; and the use of media outside the poems to play games with audience expectations.² □

Steinberg, like many critics of the early 2000s, saw Larkin as far more complex than he often seemed and even *wanted* to seem. Also like other recent critics, she questioned the reliability of his own pronouncements about his art. She contended, for instance, that he had been more influenced by Modernism than he liked to admit and that in general his poetry was more complicated than he sometimes liked to pretend. She stressed his allusiveness, his emphasis on readers inside his poems, the ways his speakers' self-presentations appeal to a broad readership, and the ways his positioning of readers differs from the methods used by many earlier poets, such as the Romantics. Larkin's poems (Steinberg argued) implicate readers in ways that more obviously autobiographical and personal lyrics do not. His works make readers share the speaker's emotions, particularly fears (especially fear of death), in ways less true of more obviously lyrical poets, who tend to stress the poetic 'I' rather than the poetic 'we'. In fact (Steinberg contended), by implying his speakers' shared connections with his readers, Larkin found some sense of comfort and community as he faced the terrors that haunted him, especially the terror of death. Offering detailed readings of particular poems, Steinberg consistently argued that Larkin gently, subtly, even kindly implicated his readers in his speakers' thoughts and emotions.³

However, just as Steinberg maintained that the positions of Larkin's audience were often more complex than was usually assumed, so she made the same argument about his speakers: the tones, attitudes, and roles of his personae often changed within poems, and the attitudes the poems seemed to express were often far more complicated than a quick final summary might suggest. Equating the speakers of the poems with Larkin himself only simplified the real richness of many texts, making Larkin seem a less inventive, sophisticated poet than he actually was. Larkin's poems could be and often had been interpreted in contradictory ways – belying (in Steinberg's view) the idea that they were predictably clear or simple. His speakers' thoughts and feelings often altered over the course of poems, prompting readers' reactions to evolve as well, and encouraging readers to continually rethink their own responses. Like various other recent critics (especially John Osborne), Steinberg urged readers to trust the poems themselves rather than turn to Larkin's biography or rely on his own pronouncements about his writings. She pointed to 'The Whitsun Weddings', in particular, as an example of a poem far more complicated in positioning both speaker and audiences (both within and outside the work) than was often assumed, and she found the poem far from easy to interpret. Neither Larkin's essays, nor his interviews, nor his letters could be as easily construed as they had been by various readers, Steinberg suggested; views that he might seem to endorse were views that he often questioned or contradicted.[4]

Steinberg next discussed Larkin's dislike of change and his fear of death, as well as the general consistency of his tastes in literature, music, and other arts. But she also challenged the idea that his poetry was intended merely to preserve the past – an ideal the poems showed to be impossible to achieve and not especially desirable. In Larkin's treatment of time as in his treatments of other subjects, Steinberg found him complex, neither merely endorsing nostalgia nor merely distrusting innovation. She associated him with less strident, more subtle Modernist writers such as Wallace Stevens and William Carlos Williams (rather than Pound and Eliot), and she argued that he was less opposed to artistic innovation than he sometimes made himself out to be. He wanted, according to Steinberg, to appeal broadly – a goal that did not exclude sophisticated readers but one that rejected focusing on them exclusively. In treating memory and change, as in dealing with so much else (including his views of jazz), the poems seemed to Steinberg far richer than standard critical assumptions or even Larkin's own pronouncements suggested.[5]

The same was true in Steinberg's chapter on 'Religion and Empathy', where she argued that Larkin was far kinder and more compassionate in the poems, especially in treating various characters, than the letters might lead readers to suspect. The poems revealed far more open-minded, tolerant, and empathetic speakers than Larkin the man may himself have been, but even Larkin the man (Steinberg suggested) was more complicated than his private writings sometimes implied. His poems, for instance, seemed to Steinberg significantly more tolerant of religion than Larkin claimed he was as a person: religious settings, events, and topics appear frequently in the poems, and Larkin's speakers often show themselves capable of understanding, if not always accepting, the psychological impulses that lead people to religious belief. In this way as in so many others, he made his art appeal to readers whose opinions he may not have shared but whose thoughts and feelings he could seem to understand. He was capable of comprehending why people were religious even if he could not be religious himself. Even a poem such as 'Faith Healing' is, according to Steinberg, more empathetic than it initially appears.[6] In an especially fine and efficient summary of her overall argument, she asserted (concerning the poems about religion) that the

■ empathy these poems present, not only for their created characters but also for their implied readers, demonstrates one of the most profound ways that Larkin reaches out to his audience. And so, in addition to speaking explicitly about and to his readers; using multiple voices to create dialogue as well as confound reader expectations; writing candidly about the interactions between individuals and memory; and presenting himself and his speakers as members of a viewing, listening audience, Larkin also chooses a topic [religion] about which his own skeptical views are widely known and offers nuanced connections to people whose views are utterly different from his own. The presumed incomprehensibility of others' minds is made comprehensible in these religiously-themed poems, wherein a poet so often accused of insularity, provinciality, narrow-mindedness and self-absorption creates characters who reach outside themselves, look elsewhere for answers, expand their perspectives, and embrace the needs of others.[7] □

Steinberg's book was one of an increasing number of studies in the 2010s that took for granted that Larkin's poetry was richer, more diverse, less predictable than even Larkin himself had often claimed.

Another such argument was made, for instance, in a 2010 article by Sam Perry, who saw in Larkin's verse unexpected affinities with twentieth-century surrealist writers. Agreeing with earlier critics (such as Barbara Everett) who had already made a case for Symbolist influences on Larkin, Perry called attention to new evidence (especially from the poet's library) suggesting that he was, in general, more attuned to French literature than had often been supposed. During his college years (Perry maintained), Larkin had been more open to Symbolism, Modernism, psychoanalysis, and even surrealism than had often been realised. He was intrigued by the idea of unconscious psychological forces that affected thought and emotion – an interest that led him, for a time during his college years, to study Jungian psychology and keep detailed records of his dreams. Perry argued that Larkin's early interest in psychoanalysis encouraged in him, as in the surrealists, an opposition to capitalist notions of reality, and Perry also linked Larkin's interest in the unconscious to his interest in jazz and other kinds of unpremeditated art, including surrealism. His early writing was (Perry contends) more experimental and unconventional than was often grasped, and even in Larkin's later work Perry found evidence of subversions of common sense and standard logic. He challenged traditional gender roles, linked artistic innovation with political radicalism, and probed beneath the surface of the apparently ordinary and mundane in ways that (according to Perry) linked him with the surrealists and with other members of the twentieth-century avant-garde.[8]

Another article from 2010 – this one by Daniel Weston – also emphasised the importance of symbolism in Larkin's poetry, although Weston's definition of 'symbolism' was broader than that of some other critics. He argued that major Larkin poems often began with mundane empirical details and then moved towards the broader, deeper implications of the situations they described. He found this pattern evident, for instance, in such major works as 'Church Going', 'The Whitsun Weddings', and 'An Arundel Tomb'. Weston, like various earlier critics, suggested that Larkin's poetry frequently involved a complex dialogue between different kinds of voices, tones, and registers, often working towards an ultimate balance rooted in and promoting a consensus view of reality that rejected opposed extremes.[9]

M. W. Rowe's book on Larkin from 2011 also stressed the poetry's Symbolist dimensions (with a capital 'S'). Rowe began by explicitly acknowledging the impact of Barbara Everett's influential article on Larkin and French Symbolism, using it as a jumping-off point for his own discussion of Larkin and aestheticism – that is, an 'art for art's sake' view that puts art at the very centre of life. Rowe argued that Larkin constantly tested his high artistic ideals against the realities of everyday existence, so that nothing phony, pretentious, or derivative would survive in his final work. According to Rowe, Larkin often based later poems on ones he had written earlier, so that his mature work was often in a dialogue with previous efforts: later poems often revisited topics, themes, and even specific works from the poet's youth. Throughout his career (Rowe maintained), Larkin was deeply interested in connections between the self and art in a way that made him variously comparable to the French writer Gustave Flaubert. By examining a number of Larkin's most representative works in rich detail, Rowe (himself a philosopher) sought to show not only how Larkin was motivated by aesthetic ideals but also how his poetry often explored significant philosophical issues.[10]

Rowe's book was structured around exceptionally detailed close examinations of five different, representative poems. He started with a lyric titled 'Here', setting it in various stylistic, biographical, and philosophical contexts and arguing that the text is less about an actual journey than an imaginative one. According to Rowe, the poem is less realistic and less straightforward in its meanings than it might at first appear, so that as soon as readers discard naïve assumptions about its style and meanings the more compelling it appears. Rowe compared and contrasted 'Here' with other poems about journeys included in *The Whitsun Weddings* (a collection he regarded as the least obviously Symbolist of Larkin's books) and examined the poem's metrics, its stanza-by-stanza development, its grammar, the length of its sentences, its use of alliteration and assonance, various moments of obscure phrasing, and many other matters. Rarely before had single poems by Larkin been treated so minutely, so that Rowe's book was exemplary in the sheer depth of its close readings. Ultimately Rowe pulled back from 'Here' and offered wider-ranging thoughts on the importance of close reading itself, especially the value of artistic pleasure and aesthetic attention. His ideas could be seen as part of a larger return to critical formalism that was beginning to take place at the start of the second decade of the twenty-first century.[11]

In a chapter on Larkin and Flaubert, Rowe compared and contrasted the two authors' lives, psychologies, and modes of writing, suggesting Larkin's real interest in his French counterpart and the basic attitudes they shared towards art and the artist's place in society. Rowe thought Larkin, like Flaubert, was interested in aesthetics first and foremost and argued that in both cases this attitude led to an increasingly dark attitude and social withdrawal. Both men, Rowe contended, became political conservatives, drifted towards misanthropy, and rejected social or personal obligations that interfered with their devotion to their art. These obligations even involved such potential distractions as women and marriage, so that both writers' closest relationships were with males who shared their artistic visions, although each man also developed and acknowledged a strongly feminine side.[12]

Rowe's third chapter returned to close readings of actual texts, in this case the three sections of a poetic sequence titled 'Livings'. Rowe noted that many readers had found these poems puzzling, partly *because* they seemed less straightforwardly realistic than much of Larkin's other work. Once again, Rowe employed various methods of close analysis to examine and explain the poems, paying particular attention to such matters as stanza form, imagery, music, apostrophising, geographical and temporal settings, the relations between the work's distinct parts, and the relevance of biographical evidence. Ultimately he concluded that although 'Livings' remained mysterious, it did convey meaning, achieve unity, and reflect important aspects of Larkin's own life, including his relations with places in general and homes in particular.[13]

Rowe next dealt with the poet's attitudes towards the supernatural and the likely influence on his writing of various ghost stories by M. R. James. Here again Rowe tied his discussions of the work to the life, partly explaining interest Larkin's in the supernatural by noting his characteristic obsession with death. As when discussing Flaubert, Rowe here drew parallels between Larkin's life and the life of James, suggesting how variously James and his writings may have influenced 'Church Going' in particular. Ultimately he argued for parallels between feelings of eeriness and creepiness and the feelings that, in Larkin's case, inspired poetry: in both cases (Rowe noted) the person feeling either creepy or poetically inspired is alone, lonely, hyper-sensitive, and thinking and feeling in primitive ways. In Larkin's case, these moods often arose when he was staying in strange places, when he was thinking about absent women, and when he felt almost that he was being visited by a kind of muse beyond his personal control.[14]

Perhaps Rowe's best chapter dealt with one of Larkin's most intriguing poems – 'Aubade', one of his last works and often considered one of his very finest. Rowe discussed such matters as the significance of the poem's title, Larkin's understandings of the word 'aubade', the ways that word has been interpreted by others, Larkin's familiarity with previous poems in the 'alba' or 'aubade' genre, and the ironies of thinking of the poem in relation to traditional morning songs. Rowe also discussed the work's relative de-emphasis on sensory imagery, how the poem's development can be traced over the course of Larkin's notebooks, how Larkin modified the text's diction and tone as he worked on each version, and how the poem's language and structure differ from those of works in *High Windows*, the book that immediately preceded the publication of 'Aubade'. Rowe noted differences between 'Aubade' and other long poems by Larkin, both in metre and in subject matter, and he also discussed the poem's bearing on traditional Christian ideas about life and a possible afterlife. As in previous chapters, Rowe here suggested various specific influences on the poem, such as the writings of Cardinal Newman's *The Dream of Gerontius* and the musical setting of that text by Edward Elgar. Yet Rowe also paid very close attention to the poem's sheer artistry, discussing the implications of specific works and even sounds while also setting it within a clear biographical context.[15] Indeed, Rowe even speculated about why 'Aubade' *was* Larkin's last major poem:

> ■ 'Aubade' is the poem where death is clearly and unequivocally confronted for the first time: death is not screened by the process of dying, or merely glanced at, or called by soft names. But why should this affect his creativity? It could be that the significance of this topic, and the conclusiveness of the poem, dwarfed all other subject-matters, making them seem trivial and peripheral. It could be that a repressed horror of death coloured and animated his poetry, in a way that the same horror confronted, dissected and analysed could not.[16] □

In other words, Larkin – having finally and at length stared death squarely in the face, and having shown why he thought there were no alternatives or consolations – could no longer summon the muse that had inspired him earlier. Admittedly this argument is speculative, but the real strength of Rowe's book lay in his meticulously detailed attention to the actual phrasing of specific poems.

No major book of literary criticism about Larkin appeared in 2011, but of the critical articles published that year, one of the best was Peter Holbrook's essay on Larkin and Shakespeare. Holbrook noted Larkin's high opinion of the Bard, and, although he could cite only three specific allusions by Larkin to Shakespeare, he argued more broadly that the two poets were part of an important 'empiricist' tradition in English verse. This tradition emphasised the importance of everyday life, of a sane, level-headed approach to existence, and of a basically irreligious, non-dogmatic approach to human experience. Both writers (according to Holbrook) avoided prejudging life according to any pre-formulated, traditional doctrines, especially any transcendental or religious dogmas. Both took life as they found it, and part of what they both found included such facts as constant, fundamental change, the transience of beauty, and the inevitability of death. Holbrook pointed particularly to similarities between Larkin's poems and Shakespeare's sonnets, especially in their shared focus on mutability, on life pervaded by death, and on the idea that nothing, finally, undergirded the values humans value most. Both Larkin and Shakespeare, Holbrook claimed, emphasised a somewhat selfish view of the demands love placed on people, and both valued solitude and self-assertion rather than complete surrender to others, even or perhaps especially loved ones.[17] Summarising his argument, Holbrook concluded as follows:

> ■ Like Larkin's poems, ... the *Sonnets* are among the bleakest documents in our language. But there is another side to them that makes them exhilarating, notwithstanding their melancholy grasp of life as inevitable failure. I mean their defiant self-assertion, the way in which they insist upon the speaker's identity as, if not exemplary, as least his own. The speaker is in the end simply and sincerely himself: he can be no other.[18] □

And of course this view of Shakespeare applied, in Holbrook's view, equally to Larkin: both the later poet and his famous forbear wrote in ways that were utterly believable, and both created speakers who were convincing first and foremost as credible, complex human beings.

Also interesting among the articles published in 2011 was an essay by S. J. Perry arguing that Larkin's writing often makes it difficult to distinguish appearances and reality. Drawing on Freud's idea of the 'uncanny', with its emphasis on the ways the familiar and unfamiliar could be hard to separate, Perry suggested that Larkin was frequently concerned with the issue of whether things were really as they seemed. He compared Larkin's verse in this respect to T. S. Eliot's *The Waste Land*, particularly in their shared emphasis on speakers feeling rootless and dislocated. Perry commented on the ways Larkin's five-year residence in Ireland allowed him to see England as a lost home – a perception that changed when he actually returned to his native country and felt, in a sense, even more homeless than before. Larkin (Perry maintained) felt rootless in various ways throughout his life, from his childhood forward, a fact that made the ideal of a stable place attractive to him but always beyond his grasp.[19]

One last essay from 2011 seems worth mentioning: Carol Atherton's article on her experience teaching Larkin to students in their late adolescence. She suggested that Larkin particularly appealed to readers at that stage of life, commenting that his works had often been used in England as texts for comprehensive exams, sometimes as the unanimous choice of teachers devising the examinations (although sometimes, too, with some grumbling or resistance). Attempting to explain why Larkin's works often seemed so appealing both to teachers and students, Atherton discussed several possibilities:

> ■ Part of it, I'm sure, is because of the accessibility of his poetry: part of it is undoubtedly due to his confiding, colloquial narrative voice. But there's something else about his verse that's important; something that seems particularly attuned to the moods of late adolescence. Perhaps it's the persistent sense of ambivalence: the push and pull of divergent attitudes, captured by Andrew Motion in a list of opposites that I remember discussing in an A-level essay: 'sociability and singleness, work and idleness, resolution and despair'. Perhaps it's the trying-on of different identities, a way of keeping the self at a defensive arm's length. Swarbrick has written of the self-protective irony that distinguishes much of Larkin's work, commenting that this is an attitude that students 'almost instinctively know about ... as a mode of discourse and, in their case, almost as a way of life'. Perhaps it's the fact that its narrative voice is prepared to confront its own shortcomings, owning up to the sense of ridiculousness that we all feel but flinch away from looking at directly. But also, crucially, there's the sense of a search for an ungraspable ideal, summed up by Larkin himself in an interview with John Haffenden as a 'long[ing] for infinity and absence, the beauty of somewhere you're not'. □

Little wonder, then, in Atherton's view, that Larkin attracted the real, interested attention of both students and their instructors.[20]

Relatively little work was published on Larkin in 2012, but an essay by Francis O'Gorman did discuss the relative absence of sound as a topic in his poems (including a surprising lack of attention to jazz), as opposed to his much greater use of visual imagery. Indeed, O'Gorman argued that silence itself was often a topic of Larkin's works and that even an emphasis on mysteriously unheard sounds began to appear in some of his later poems.[21] But O'Gorman's emphasis on imagery and phrasing in their own rights differed from the historical and political emphases found, for instance, in an article by Graham MacPhee published in 2013, which examined Larkin's treatment of Englishness, his attitudes towards nationality in general, and his thinking about the decline of the British empire. Challenging John Osborne's claims that Larkin was thoroughly deconstructive, MacPhee argued instead that Larkin's treatment of nationality was less clearly subversive than Osborne thought, so that Larkin emerged as a more conservative, nostalgic writer than Osborne had suggested.[22] Meanwhile, another article from 2013, by Adam Piette, was even more explicitly biographical. Piette contended that the wartime bombing of Coventry, Larkin's boyhood hometown, gave Larkin a chance to erase much of his childhood from his mind and ritually bury the impact of his father, who had been a fascist before the war.[23]

Larkin According to Osborne

Unlike the preceding two years, 2014 was an important year for Larkin studies because of the appearance of a second book by John Osborne, a feisty, innovative scholar who in 2007, as we saw in the previous chapter of this Guide, had already produced one of the most stimulating studies (and defences) of Larkin ever written. In his new book, *Radical Larkin: Seven Types of Technical Mastery*, Osborne continued to argue that Larkin's texts were far more complex than other critics often assumed. In particular, Osborne asserted that many previous studies of the poems had been handicapped by attempts to link the works to details of the poet's life. Biographical interpretations, Osborne maintained, were inevitably limiting: they tied the works too tightly to the specific facts of Larkin's own existence, and even the validity of those presumed 'facts' were often doubtful. Moreover, Larkin criticism in general had often made assumptions about the poems that were not warranted by the actual texts themselves. Interpreters often assumed, for instance, that the poems' speakers were white, male, English, middle-class, heterosexual, and so on, when the actual phrasing of the poems often provided no such details. The effect of Osborne's book was to destabilise or deconstruct many standard assumptions about Larkin and his works. Osborne returned readers again and again to the words on the page, suggesting that the texts were far more open to a variety of possible interpretations than critics and regular readers tended to think.

In introducing his book, Osborne noted all the various, conflicting interpretations that had been offered of Larkin's life, many of the contradictory claims that had been made about the biographical circumstances of particular poems, and the tendency of critics to rely on Larkin's personal claims about his works when offering their own interpretations – claims that were themselves often contradictory or otherwise unpersuasive. Osborne, in short, often used biographical evidence to argue *against* biographical interpretations. He often showed how a fuller understanding of the biographical details of Larkin's career *undermined* confidence in biographical readings of the poetry. The more readers knew about Larkin's life (Osborne suggested), the less certain they were likely to feel about any simple, unequivocal readings of the poems. Rather than ignoring historical or biographical evidence, Osborne used the sheer complexity of such information to undercut allegedly simplistic interpretations of Larkin's life *and* works. Osborne contended that Larkin scholars had sometimes been simply and demonstrably *wrong* in making various assertions about the texts, including even assertions about their phrasing, punctuation, dating, and so on. He also challenged many common assumptions made not only by defenders of Larkin but especially by his fiercest critics, such as Tom Paulin, who came in for much sceptical inquiry in the pages of Osborne's book. As he ended his introduction, Osborne offered a tour-de-force sentence (too long to quote here) in which he laid out his book's numerous objectives. These included an intent to examine major representative poems quite closely from across Larkin's career; an intent to relate Larkin's rich, complex artistry to the kinds of techniques used by modern and postmodern authors; and an intent to show how the poems deconstruct not only standard assumptions about Larkin's life and views but also standard views about life in general. Osborne saw Larkin as a deconstructor and postmodernist before those terms had even been invented, especially in his sceptical questioning of all kinds of commonplace certitudes.[24]

Osborne's first main chapter dealt not with poems by Larkin but rather with his early novel *A Girl in Winter*, which Osborne considered one of Larkin's most interesting but least appreciated works. He linked the novel to various 'Modernist' tendencies in novel writing as well as to many specific Modernist novels. But he also showed how these tendencies can also be found in Larkin's poetry, arguing that Larkin was far more indebted to the works of T. S. Eliot (especially 'The Love Song of J. Alfred Prufrock') than he often let on. Additionally, Osborne maintained that many of the same critical tendencies that limited interpretations of Larkin's poems also narrowed interpretations of this novel. For instance, he showed that various critics had come to varied, contradictory views of the main character's nationality when the novel itself was anything but clear about this contested issue. According to Osborne, critics of the novel, as well as of the poems, often filled in blanks that had been left *deliberately* blank by Larkin. They made assumptions that the texts themselves often did not warrant. The novel (Osborne claimed) was often ambiguous despite critical efforts to erase its ambiguities, and its ambiguities resulted not from Larkin's incompetence but from his habitual tendency to undermine easy assumptions about such matters as nationality, gender, politics, and other tendencies to see things in terms of unchanging essentials when such essentials did not (for Larkin at least) exist.[25]

Osborne's second chapter focused on three poems in particular – 'An Arundel Tomb', 'The Card-Players', and 'Lines on a Young Lady's Photograph Album' – to make an argument crucial to his larger project. He contended that Larkin often composed his works with other works of art very much in mind, whether those other works were poems, novels, paintings, pieces of music, and so on. Larkin, who often presented himself (and was interpreted by others) as a simple realist was, in Osborne's view, in fact an author familiar with a wide range of previous works of art. His tendency to present himself as a somewhat unlearned philistine was, according to Osborne, merely a joking pose – a role he sometimes adopted because he disdained pretension, but a role that never really affected his writing. According to Osborne, Larkin's texts not only often alluded to previous works of art but also often took works of art as their subjects, including by focusing on sculpture, painting, and photography (respectively) in the poems already mentioned. In these works, Larkin often implicitly explored philosophical issues, such as the relative stability of visual (or physical) and verbal works of art as well as the human capacity to know, with any certainty, both the past and the present. Here, as in his other chapters, Osborne sought not only to deconstruct alleged critical certainties but also to show how Larkin's works themselves deconstructed supposed certainties in numerous different ways. Throughout his book, Osborne did not merely rely on 'the text itself' to make his claims. Rather, he explored much historical and biographical evidence to show how difficult it could be to interpret Larkin's works in simple or simplistic ways. By offering painstaking, detailed readings of individual words and phrases, as well as by setting the poems in complex contexts, Osborne showed how difficult interpretation could be and how Larkin's texts subverted standard methods of interpreting almost anything.[26]

Osborne offered similar arguments in his third chapter, which focused especially on 'At Grass', 'March Past', and 'Church Going'. In discussing these works, he challenged common tendencies to specify the locations the poems supposedly implied. He responded especially to interpretations of Larkin's work by Irish critics (such as Tom Paulin and Seamus Heaney) who sought to define Larkin as narrowly 'English', either to condemn him (as Paulin did) or to celebrate him (as did Heaney). Once more Osborne demonstrated deep familiarity with numerous historical, textual, and biographical data and used such data to challenge conclusions he considered too easy and simple, particularly in their political or ideological implications. Osborne repeatedly argued that Larkin's poems are rarely as specific in their settings or other details as critics have often assumed, and he sought to show how texts external to the poems themselves – such as television documentaries about Larkin, photographs of him, and even personal interviews – had been used, illegitimately, to authorise interpretations of the poems not supported by the poems themselves.[27] In a typical passage, Osborne showed how difficult it can be to determine any precise meaning for even a single small detail of any poem, including (for instance) the speaker's reference (in 'Church Going') to donating 'an Irish sixpence' when he visits a church:

> ■ If the poem is set in England and the church is Protestant, the donating of an Irish sixpence may be a gesture of contempt, indifference or flippancy from a narrator who is clearly not religious. However, if that same narrator carries Irish coinage because he is from the Republic or of Irish ancestry that same gesture combines religious unbelief with a hint of political disaffiliation from the UK. If that Irish narrator was brought up a Catholic, though now an unbeliever, the donation may register a degree of denominational as well as political dissidence. These same possibilities are much exacerbated if we follow Larkin's claim that the church [that Larkin wrote about] was in Northern Ireland. Although Irish coinage was legal tender in Ulster, so that the donation is not financially invalid, the gesture carries strongly republican implications, the more so if the church is Protestant. If the church is Catholic … such a choice of coin might still suggest an identification with the persecuted minority despite the narrator's personal loss of faith.[28] □

Osborne's point was not to try to establish any single one of these possible interpretations but rather to show how difficult it would be to settle a matter – nationality – not especially important to the poem in any case. It was critics, Osborne argued, who had interjected nationality into the poem in ways that the poem itself largely ignored. Once again, then, Osborne urged readers to trust the evidence provided by the poem itself, not to import extraneous information and perspectives.

Similar arguments appeared in Osborne's chapter on 'The Whitsun Weddings', where he again drew on a multitude of conflicting biographical data to undercut simple biographical readings.[29] By showing how variously the work had been biographically situated, Osborne cast doubt on tendencies to read it as rooted either in some simple prior experience or merely in Larkin's life at all. Using charts (here and elsewhere) to great explanatory advantage, Osborne contended that the poem closely reflected aspects of the plot of Larkin's novels *A Girl in Winter* and *Jill*, so that the poem seemed grounded as much in art as in some particular biographical incident. Osborne then suggested that the poem alluded to many other texts besides ones written by Larkin himself, especially writings by T. S. Eliot, D. H. Lawrence, and various others, so that the poem was full of echoes:

> ■ We have already said enough to demonstrate that far from being generically pure, the text of 'The Whitsun Weddings' is a hybrid which freely appropriates constituent granules from plays, films, novels, ballads, schoolroom classics, canonical masterpieces, music-hall songs and hardcore modernist epics. Far from being insistently 'English', the narrative voice is a transatlantic medley encompassing contributions from Brits (Blake), Americans (Longfellow), Americans who became naturalized British citizens (Eliot) and Englishmen who became naturalized Americans (Auden). Far from being repressively masculinist, the narrative welcomes on an equal basis intertexts from gay men (Auden), bisexual women (Woolf), the sexually tepid (Eliot, Hardy), and the sexually feverish (Lawrence).[30]

Thus Osborne once again found multiplicity where others allegedly found singleness or simplicity. His tendency, as always, was to relate Larkin's texts to numerous *other* texts, so that neither the speakers nor the meanings of the poems could be easily pinned down or seen as one-dimensional.

Osborne argued, in his next chapter, that Larkin admired the Modernist writers more than he usually said; that even the work of his poetic hero, Thomas Hardy, was more complicated (especially in its sexual overtones) than was often realised; and that both Larkin *and* Hardy were far more allusive writers than they are usually credited with being, with Larkin himself alluding to Hardy in unexpected ways. Discussing Larkin's sense of humour, Osborne suggested not only how pervasive and various it was but also the numerous ways in which it was both funny and served serious purposes. In a typically detailed discussion of 'This Be The Verse' (with its infamous opening line, 'They fuck you up, your mum and dad'), Osborne explored the poem's allusiveness and also suggested how this and similarly humorous poems by Larkin worked to subvert humourless assumptions about various important topics, such as family, parents, children, life after death, and so on. Osborne also noted how the relaxation of legal censorship of obscenity in Britain in late 1960 coincided with a far more common use of such language in Larkin's poetry after that date than before.[31]

Osborne next argued that the endings of Larkin's poems, far from providing firm, strong resolutions, often did just the opposite: they often subverted such resolutions, frequently ending a poem with deflation, anti-climax, and fragmentation. The poems often concluded with reversals rather than with firm completions because Larkin's typical instinct was to see life in terms of opposites, contradictions, and irresolution rather than in terms of simple harmonies. Even a listing of the titles of many of his poems suggested, to Osborne, Larkin's tendency towards a kind of poetic double vision or an emphasis on ambivalence and ambiguity, as in such poems as 'Coming' and 'Going' or 'Arrival' and 'Poetry of Departures', among many others. He examined, for instance, the various instabilities in the poem 'Verse de Société', including the ways in which the very title toyed with Larkin's reputation as a xenophobe; the ways the poem involved a kind of complicated dialogue with a poem titled 'Reasons for Attendance'; and especially the ways the ending of 'Vers de Société' can be read as significantly ambiguous. Larkin, Osborne argued, had a postmodern interest in false endings. Whereas other critics saw clear meanings and firm resolutions in many of Larkin's poems, Osborne saw just the opposite – not because Larkin lacked the skill to produce closure but because he lacked the interest.[32]

Closing his own book with a discussion of Larkin's last great poem ('Aubade'), Osborne characteristically challenged simple definitions of lyric poetry, emphasised the ways such definitions have changed over time, and then situated Larkin's poem in the long and varied tradition of morning poems, showing how Larkin's text deliberately undermined earlier conventions. He contended, for instance, that Larkin's poem undercut even the most basic aspects of the aubade genre:

> ■ every one of the five characteristics enumerated above as the means by which we recognize a poem as an *aubade* is systematically eviscerated [in Larkin's text]. Hence, (i) the sex of the narrator is not disclosed, the poem (like so many of Larkin's) being resolutely non-gender-specific; (ii) there is no declaration of love, whether proffered below the beloved's window or from within a shared bed; (iii) indeed, there is no beloved, whether of the opposite or the same sex, no addressee implied or directly summoned into a dialogue; (iv) it is not even morning – 'Waking at four to *soundless dark* (my emphases) – the poem being set towards the end of the night rather than the start of the day; (v) this redefining of the *aubade* as less a dawn song than an hour-before-dawn song setting the stage for the poem's dark theme, the dispelling of the erotic by a terminal morbidity. Unresting sex has been nullified by 'Unresting death'.[33] □

According to Osborne, Larkin undercut the aubade genre as relentlessly as he used this poem to undercut conventionally consoling views of death, and once again Osborne heard in the poem many allusions to previous works – allusions that worked to make the text seem even less simple and straightforward than it might appear. Earlier authors or traditions echoed in the poem included (according to Osborne) Orwell, the blues, Edward Thomas, Siegfried Sassoon, Kingsley Amis, *Hamlet*, Robert Frost, C. Day Lewis, Randall Jarrell, Dylan Thomas, T. S. Eliot, Oscar Wilde, the Bible, Lucretius, Arthur Hugh Clough, *King Lear*, *As You Like It*, Cardinal Newman, Virginia Woolf, and many, many others, including Larkin himself.[34] Finally, Osborne argued that Larkin's 'Aubade' challenged earlier ways of dealing with death (of trying to make sense of it), including Epicureanism, Stoicism, and existentialism. In this poem (Osborne suggested), Larkin confronted death with an unflinching honesty made possible both by his historical circumstances and by his own predilections.[35] As in his earlier book on Larkin, Osborne provided arguments that were both dense with detail but also utterly clear.

Larkin in the Mid-2010s: Booth's Biography and New Critical Studies

Much the same might be said of another book published in 2014 – James Booth's lengthy biographical study titled *Philip Larkin: Life, Art, and Love*.[36] Greeted by many reviewers as the best overview of Larkin's life so far issued, Booth's study not only traced the development of the author's career but also offered many passing comments about particular poems and poetic tendencies as well as other matters relevant to Larkin's writing. Booth suggested, for instance, that in the 1950s Larkin leaned more to the left than to the right politically; that by 1964 he had begun to revisit some of the symbolist aspects of his earlier style; that during the same year he abandoned the theme of marriage, which had been so prominent in his previous poems; that from this point forward he now began to focus on the topics of growing old and dying; and that his style at this point began to become increasingly ironic, self-mocking, allusive, and even (occasionally) hard to follow.[37] By 1968 (Booth contended), Larkin had begun to write 'a widely spaced series of ever more subtly successful poems about failure' while continuing to write in ways that showed the artistic impact of jazz forms on his verse compositions.[38] Booth challenged ideas that Larkin was genuinely racist; disputed Larkin's own alleged anti-Modernism; noted the poet's growing political and social conservatism in the period from 1964-70; and suggested that Larkin's poetry was becoming increasingly private in tone and orientation.[39] Booth argued that such later poems as 'The Building', 'The Old Fools', 'Show Saturday', and 'Aubade' were the latest in a series of 'long Keatsian odes or reflective elegies' that also included such earlier works as 'At Grass', 'Church Going', 'An Arundel Tomb', 'The

Whitsun Weddings', 'Here', and 'Dockery and Son', but he also perceived a change in Larkin's style in the period from 1972–74:

> ■ Since his forty-fifth birthday poem, 'Sympathy in White Major', Larkin's poems had been distilled intertextually from earlier literature or art, or had evoked a reified historical past or an exotic location. Now he returned to the contemporary social scene of his middle-period work. But the modulations were more abrupt and the tone harder.[40] □

As Booth traced the changes in Larkin's poetic career of the 1970s, he inevitably traced a gradual diminishment in the number of poems produced and a gradual darkening of their mood, until eventually Larkin had written himself into a kind of silence that lasted until his death in 1985. Rather than publish bad poems in his final decade, Larkin chose to write almost none at all.

Other publications from 2014 varied in their claims and critical orientations. Peter Krahé, for instance, discussed issues of solitude and isolation in relation to a number of specific poems,[41] while Piers Pennington commented on the poet's tendency to use images of straight lines in his works, particularly railway lines.[42] Perhaps the most interesting essay, however, was Ryan Hibbett's article on the poet's use of obscene language. Hibbett suggested that Larkin often used such words when writing letters to certain friends (such as Kingsley Amis) and also when dealing with conflicts between generations. Yet Hibbett also related Larkin's obscenity to issues of class, maintaining that he deliberately appropriated terms typically used, in his day, by people of lower socio-economic status, thus giving his verse a broader appeal by making it sound more realistic and more convincingly English. Attempting to explain the acceptance and indeed popularity of Larkin's obscenity, Hibbett suggested several possibilities.

> ■ One answer has to do with his selectivity in swearing, and its connection to the persona he fashioned; when the blatant obscenities of *High Windows* finally appeared, they had the effect of something long stifled, though hinted at, being released – a sense of the guarded, private self finally venting to the public. This effect was probably intensified by the historical moment, when the politer 'f-word' expression, along with similar euphemisms, was being used more frequently. The evolution of Larkin's expletives can be traced from an old-school 'damn' in *The North Ship* ('XX'); to a figurehead's 'golden tits' ('Next, Please') and 'take that you bastard' ('Poetry of Departures') in *The Less Deceived*; to *The Whitsun Weddings*' 'cock and balls' ('Sunny Prestatyn') and declaration of books as 'crap' ('A Study of Reading Habits'); to, finally, the blatant 'fucks' of *High Windows*. The sudden baring of what had previously festered below the surface

invited approval; as Alan Bennett puts it, Larkin's 'ordinary voice' made him 'someone to like, to take to...whose voice echoed one's inner thoughts...a shared secret'.⁴³ □

Hibbett maintained that Larkin, by using blatant obscenity as his career drew to a close, both resembled and differed from the kind of 'punks' who became increasingly common in British culture of the 1970s. Larkin assimilated obscenity in ways that made it acceptable to other people of his class and educational background, even as he also used it to express antagonism towards various kinds of youth whom he disdained.⁴⁴

Relatively little on Larkin appeared in 2015, but as the new century's second decade crossed over into its second half, interest in Larkin seemed as strong as ever. 2016, for instance, saw the publication of a book by István Rácz titled *Philip Larkin's Poetics: Theory and Practice of an English Post-war Poet*. The fact that Rácz was Hungarian indicated that Larkin's work could appeal beyond the British Isles and even the English-speaking world, just as it also indicated that Larkin was now recognised even by non-Britons as one of Britain's leading recent poets. Rácz stressed, among other matters, Larkin's genuine interest in using his poems to preserve experience, his diminishing use of dialogue in his poems as his mature career developed, and his double-sided attraction to both Yeats and Hardy, the first associated with aspirations towards transcendence and the latter associated with a more earth-bound, realistic approach to life and writing.⁴⁵

In subsequent chapters, Rácz explored such issues as the importance of the word 'almost' as a key term in Larkin's phrasing, his attraction to nothingness as a poetic theme, his tendency to think of time in distinct units, the way this tendency almost transforms time into space, and the ways both of these traits help explain his interest in photography, with its emphasis on discrete moments frozen forever. For Larkin (according to Rácz), the goal of privacy almost inevitably proves elusive or illusory; beauty is associated with community; and truth is associated with isolation. Rácz argued that Larkin often implied a distinction between the speaker of a poem and the larger meaning of a work, as in both 'Church Going' and 'High Windows', where the speaker initially seems shallow but the final message of the poem seems far more profound. Similarly, Rácz contended that Larkin's poems often involved shifts of language from phrasing rooted in sensation to phrasing involving contemplation.⁴⁶

In a later chapter, Rácz compared and contrasted Larkin and Auden, suggesting that while the former saw poetry as a way of transferring thoughts and feelings to the reader, the latter saw poems as methods of transforming experience. Yet Larkin was, according to Rácz less anti-intellectual than he pretended to be, so that his poems are actually more indebted to previous literature than he suggested. Both Larkin and Auden were (Rácz claimed) less political in their poems than in their lives, and he thought that the aspect of Auden's work that Larkin admired most was its anti-Modernism, especially in Auden's first three books. While Auden later found some solace in Christianity, Rácz noted that Larkin never achieved such consolation.[47] His thought remained restless, and the same was true of his self-presentation. Throughout his book, Rácz was interested in Larkin's various masks or personae, even suggesting at one point that as a young man the poet wanted to be female but noting that his more common persona, in his mature poems, was a person who very much resembled himself without necessarily being identical to himself.[48]

Rácz later argued that pain not only helped motivate Larkin to write poetry but was one of his key themes. 'Pain and joy', Rácz suggested, 'are contrasted in Larkin as knowledge and ignorance' – an 'antagonism ... which is never resolved in his texts'. This antagonism had various consequences for Larkin's writing:

■ 1. The paradox of gaining insight through pain is that it also prevents the subject from being initiated into adult society. 2. The consciousness of death, which is the ultimate result of pain, sets the limits to the knowledge gained through suffering: death is both an ontological and epistemological end. 3. Identifying suffering as the only road leading to knowledge is a traditionally religious approach to the problem of human understanding, but Larkin's agnosticism (which he shared with Hardy) prevented him from finding consolation in it. These three consequences of pain as 'a positive quality' are richly problematized in his fiction and poetry.[49] □

By usually analysing particular poems rather than offering many larger generalisations, Rácz sought to show how the arguments just cited affected the phrasing of specific works. In particular, he argued for the impact of agnosticism and materialism on Larkin's diction, including his frequent use of images of nothingness and his recurring emphasis on matters of time.[50] According to Rácz, Larkin saw time as continuous but divisible and thus tended to focus not only on particular moments as the temporal settings of his poems but also on ageing and mutability as major themes. When Larkin dealt with time as an experience of individuals (Rácz argued), he thought of it as leading inevitably towards death. When he thought of it as something shared and experienced by communities, he emphasised the ideal of continuity, although even such shared continuities could be threatened.[51]

Rácz's book seems an appropriate one with which to conclude this survey, not only because by the mid-2010s it was the most recent monograph on Larkin but also because it epitomised so many main trends of previous Larkin criticism. Its emphases on time, ageing, and death would, by themselves, have made it a typical work of Larkin scholarship, but the same was also true of its interest in Larkin's relations with previous writers (especially Yeats and Hardy), its concern with the typical structures of his major poems, and its comments on his philosophical attitudes, such as his materialism and agnosticism. If Rácz's book said little that was radically new, that was part of its value: it summed up many areas of critical consensus. It simultaneously drew on, was strengthened by, and in some ways extended a critical heritage that was now at least six decades old – a heritage from which future readers of Larkin could profit and on which future students of Larkin could build.

CONCLUSION

In the years since Philip Larkin's death in 1985, his stature as one of England's greatest twentieth-century poets has only grown. Admittedly, his reputation was badly damaged by the appearance of his *Selected Letters* in 1992 and the publication of Andrew Motion's biography in 1993. In the immediate aftermath of those events, Larkin was often intensely condemned for his alleged racism, misogyny, and general political incorrectness. But even at that time he had his defenders. They argued that the charges were overblown and that whatever Larkin's faults may have been as a human being, his poetry remained, and would always remain, superb. In the two decades since then, this attitude has increasingly prevailed. The two newest major biographies are more sympathetic than Motion's was, and Larkin remains widely read, widely taught, and widely admired. In 2015 he was even the subject of yet another nationally broadcast television documentary (*Return to Larkinland*; one of at least three since 1964).[1] And, in late 2016, he is scheduled to be memorialised in Poets' Corner at Westminster Abbey. Whatever damage was done to his stature by the events of the early 1990s seems to have diminished. There may have been far better human beings living between 1922 and 1985, but there were few better poets.

Larkin Up Till Now

This text has offered the first thorough overview of critical commentary about Larkin covering the entire range of his reception, from the mid-1950s down to the present day. It has surveyed the consistencies of opinion as well as the critical controversies that have arisen as serious students of Larkin have discussed and debated his work. Most critics have agreed that Larkin's voice was distinctive in the poetry of his time, not only because of his typical style but especially because of his typical subject matters. Most commentators have concurred that Larkin wrote in a way that seemed plainer, clearer, more colloquial, and more accessible than the style often associated with High Modernism – the style, say, of some of Ezra Pound's later *Cantos* or the poetry of David Jones, Gertrude Stein, and various other members of the avant-garde. Few readers have trouble understanding most of Larkin's best and most famous poems; to say this, however, is not to imply that the poems are in any sense simple. Instead, they reveal genuine depths of meaning and technical accomplishment as soon as they are examined closely, and most critics agree – and have almost always agreed – that Larkin is anything but an unsophisticated writer.

Yet almost as appealing as Larkin's style (if not even *more* appealing to some readers) have been the topics he wrote about. His frequent interest in such topics as nature, animals, community, traditions, work, everyday life, everyday relationships, love, longing, disappointment, mutability, and many others made him a poet who seemed to 'speak' to the genuine experiences and concerns of numerous readers. Even his near-obsession with ageing, sickness, and death made him seem a strikingly and unforgettably *honest* poet – one who did not look the other way when faced with human limitations but who instead confronted them directly. Larkin has always been the kind of poet who appeals to readers who are (to paraphrase Larkin's own lines from 'Church Going') 'forever surprising a hunger in themselves to be more serious'. But he has often, too, been a poet of great humour – able to be both laugh-out-loud funny and deadly grim (sometimes even in the same poem).

Critical discussion about Larkin has long reflected interest in a number of key issues. These have included the relative influence on his verse of Yeats and Hardy (and others, but especially those two); his involvement with the so-called 'Movement' writers of the 1950s; the question of whether or in what ways he 'developed' as a poet; and the issue of whether he is too parochial, too English, and too much a poet of his own place and time to appeal to non-English readers or even to English readers of different eras, classes, or backgrounds. (His popularity beyond England would seem to suggest otherwise.) Some critics have faulted Larkin for a narrowness of range, tone, and subject matter; in contrast, others have replied that he repeatedly deals with some of the most important issues, events, and concerns any human being can face. Some commentators have seen an almost complete identification between Larkin himself and his speakers; others have argued for significant distances between the two; some have even suggested that there is no necessary connection whatsoever. These latter critics have argued, instead, that Larkin's poems rarely say anything about his speakers' race, class, sexual orientations, or even gender. The relative importance of biographical evidence in interpreting the poems has also been much discussed, and even scholars who agree that such evidence is important have often come to strikingly different conclusions about what to make of it in particular cases.

In the period since the 1970s, and especially in the 1980s and beyond, critics have increasingly questioned Larkin's presentation of himself as anti-Modernist. If anything, the impact of various Modernist writers and aesthetic tendencies on his writing has been stressed so heavily in recent decades that one sometimes wonders what Larkin himself would have made of this critical trend. It now seems undeniable that he was *less* anti-Modernist (and more influenced by Symbolism with a capital S) than he sometimes claimed, but perhaps the argument is in danger of being pushed too far. In any case, the precise nature of Larkin's aesthetic assumptions and accomplishments has been much discussed and is worth even more discussion. Comparisons and contrasts between Larkin's early works and his later writings have long been made, and increasingly his poetry is compared and contrasted with his early prose fiction – not only the two major early novels but even the playful works set in girls' schools that he composed in the 1940s. Likewise, the relevance of his interest in (and many writings about) jazz has also received increasing attention. And, as more biographical evidence becomes available about Larkin in ensuing decades, especially in the form of letters to and testimony from more people who knew him, the more important biographical insights and criticism are likely to prove.

Larkin in the Future: New Resources?

Where are Larkin studies likely to go in the future? Where *should* they go? The possible answers to these questions are numerous. One hopes, for instance, that it will not be too long before a complete and fully annotated scholarly edition of all Larkin's works (both in poetry and in prose) will be undertaken. Archie Burnett's splendid 2013 edition of *The Complete Poems* is a model of its kind,[2] but one could easily imagine (and greatly desire) an edition with even fuller annotations and commentary. This sort of 'Larkin *Variorum*' edition – like the ones that already exist for John Donne and other important poets – would provide interested readers (especially non-English audiences and readers who were not Larkin's contemporaries) with fuller explanations of some of his diction, allusions, and likely meanings. An ideal edition of *The Works of Philip Larkin* would include everything he wrote in verse and prose and would be annotated in great detail, and a companion set would include as many of the letters as could reasonably be expected to be published. Of course, the existence of the Internet now means that an edition of the letters need not be confined to print; it could also be put online, and the same would ideally be true of other Larkiniana, especially facsimiles of the complete notebooks. The advantages of putting as many as possible of all Larkin documents online are obvious: they would be fully and easily searchable, and (if facsimiles of everything accompanied the edited texts) they would be illuminating in all sorts of ways. An excellent model of such work would be the recent *Cambridge Edition of the Works of Ben Jonson*, which exists both in print and in a constantly updated electronic version.[3]

In addition to making Larkin's texts available in full scholarly editions, it would also be helpful to have a Larkin encyclopaedia – that is, a handy one-volume reference (of the sort produced for many other authors, including some far less significant than Larkin). This kind of book would put at readers' fingertips a comprehensive overview of numerous data, including a detailed chronology of Larkin's life and times; brief biographies of important friends and associates; summaries of Larkin's literary and critical texts (and summaries of critical responses to those texts); summaries of important letters; and extensive bibliographies. A Larkin encyclopaedia would be immensely valuable to students and teachers and would make available, in compact form, a wealth of information to readers who might never consult a full scholarly edition. Equally valuable would be a detailed annotated bibliography of critical studies – a bibliography of the sort that R. Neil Scott has prepared for Flannery O'Connor and that John R. Roberts has prepared for various writers of the seventeenth century.[4] Additionally, a collection of newspaper and magazine reviews, similar to the one that Scott prepared for readers of O'Connor, would be a very worthwhile contribution to Larkin studies.[5]

More valuable to scholars, perhaps, than to 'regular readers' would be a full, annotated catalogue of surviving books from Larkin's library. Scholars would thus be able to see what Larkin read and could try to determine how his reading may have influenced his thinking and writing. Especially valuable would be a catalogue of any annotations Larkin made in his books; readers would then have yet another source of information about the ways his mind worked and about how his own writings were shaped in and through dialogue with writings by others. Ideally this resource, like all the others so far mentioned, would eventually be made available online in a continuously updated form so that new information could be added as it became available.

Larkin in the Future: Possible Topics and Approaches

Even without the existence of the potential new resources just mentioned, the possibilities of rich new work in Larkin studies abound. It would be helpful, for instance, to have fuller discussions of Larkin's aesthetic assumptions, especially any changes or developments in those assumptions as his career evolved. How consistent were his ideas about art from, say, the 1950s to the 1970s? What evidence can the nonfiction prose (including the letters but also the essays) offer about the ways he thought about art over the years and about why he thought as he did? What can his comments about other poets (not only Hardy and Yeats and Pound but many others) tell us about his own priorities and ideals? How did he respond to poets of the recent and distant past, and how did he also respond to the writings of his contemporaries – and why? Obviously some work along these lines has already been done, but much more remains worth doing. How did his contemporaries interact, poetically, with *Larkin*? The present book surveys the reactions of scholars and critics to Larkin's works, but what can the responses of other poets (such as Seamus Heaney or Ted Hughes or Derek Walcott) tell us about Larkin's own art as well as theirs? And how did Larkin influence the work of other writers of his own day and in the years since? John Osborne has dealt to some degree with the latter question (making a case that Larkin has had an important impact on various 'postmodern' writers), but much more work remains to be done. What influence has Larkin had in countries beyond England, and how and to what degree was Larkin influenced by writers from other lands? Increasingly, the impact of French writers on his texts has been discussed, but one suspects that there is more work to be done on his similarities to and differences from such American poets as Robert Frost, Emily Dickinson, and others.

The poems that Larkin himself did not publish in collections during his lifetime often deserve much more attention than they have yet received. But also meriting further work is the question of Larkin's published collections *as* collections – as groups of poems artfully and intelligently arranged by the poet himself with a sure eye to the poems' interactions and dialogical resonances within the covers of single books. Part of the aesthetic impact of Larkin's collections derives from the ways those collections are organised, and the whole question of whether and how Larkin wanted the books to be read *as books* is worth discussing in greater detail.

By this point in the history of Larkin criticism, defences of Larkin from various attacks (personal, political, or aesthetic) have seemed less and less necessary. Readers who are likely to reject his writings because they dislike his personality and/or politics will probably not easily change their minds. Many are unlikely to be swayed to set aside their evaluations of him as a person and respond simply to his art. Perhaps such disentanglement of art from life is not really possible or even desirable. As Britain becomes an increasingly multicultural nation (or collection of distinct nations) than it already is, one wonders how Larkin's writings will fare. Will he (despite John Osborne's best efforts) come to be seen as simply a spokesmen for white, privileged, middle-class *English* males with sometimes unsavoury views of various minority groups?

Or will he manage to appeal to readers of various colours, ethnicities, sexes, genders, and social status? Readers, scholars, and critics who love Larkin may find themselves needing to defend his work all over again, either by trying to explain it as a product of its times or by trying to argue for its universal relevance and appeal.

In the end, it will always be (to most people) Larkin's poems that matter most of all. Most persons who become interested in Larkin are drawn to him first and foremost as a poet, and it is the poems that will always merit ever closer attention. By now, some of them have received exceedingly close attention indeed, and it would be helpful to have a very fully annotated edition of 'Larkin's greatest hits' – an edition that would present his best poems alongside very full analyses of them, especially analyses from diverse and even competing perspectives. This kind of 'pluralistic' approach to Larkin (one that looked, for instance, at 'Church Going' or 'The Whitsun Weddings' from perhaps 20 different theoretical and critical perspectives) might help readers appreciate just how richly and variously even the best-known of Larkin's poems can be interpreted. By examining the poems from multiple perspectives arranged side by side (or one after another), we would not only appreciate Larkin's poetry in new ways but would also better perceive just how thought-provoking critical interaction and dialogue can be. It is this sort of dialogue the present book has been designed to explore, as well as to promote.

Notes

INTRODUCTION

1. On Larkin's life, see especially Andrew Motion, *Philip Larkin: A Writer's Life* (London: Faber & Faber, 1993), Richard Bradford, *First Boredom, Then Fear: The Life of Philip Larkin* (London: Peter Owen, 2005), and James Booth, *Philip Larkin: Life, Art and Love* (London: Faber & Faber, 2014).
2. Philip Larkin, *The North Ship* (London: Fortune, 1945).
3. Philip Larkin, *Jill* (London: Fortune, 1946) and *A Girl in Winter* (London: Faber and Faber, 1947).
4. Philip Larkin, *XX Poems* (Belfast: privately printed, 1951).
5. Philip Larkin, *The Less Deceived* (Hull: Marvell Press, 1955).
6. Philip Larkin, *The Whitsun Wedding* (London: Faber and Faber, 1964).
7. Philip Larkin, *The North Ship* (London: Faber and Faber, 1966).
8. Philip Larkin, *All What Jazz: A Record Diary* (London: Faber & Faber, 1970).
9. Philip Larkin, ed., *The Oxford Book of Twentieth-Century English Verse* (Oxford: Clarendon, 1973).
10. Philip Larkin, *High Windows* (London: Faber and Faber, 1974).
11. Philip Larkin, *Collected Poems*, ed. Anthony Thwaite. 1988. (Rev. ed. London: Faber and Faber, 1990.)

1 LARKIN ARRIVES: THE 1950s AND 1960s

1. Anthony Hartley, 'Poets of the Fifties', *The Spectator* (27 August 1954), pp. 260–1. [261]
2. Donald Davie, 'In the Movement', *The Spectator* (1 October 1954), pp. 399–400. [400]
3. Richard Murphy, 'Three Modern Poets', *The Listener* (8 September 1955), pp. 373–5. [373]
4. Anonymous, 'Poetic Moods', *The Times Literary Supplement* (16 December 1955), p. 762.
5. Anonymous, 'Philip Larkin', *The Times Educational Supplement* (13 July 1956), p. 933.
6. Samuel French Morse, 'Five Young English Poets', *Poetry* 89 (December 1956), pp. 193–200. [196]
7. John Holloway, 'New Lines in English Poetry', *The Hudson Review* 9 (Winter 1957), pp. 592–7. [594]
8. John Wain, 'The Immediate Situation', *The Sewanee Review* 65 (July–September 1957), pp. 353–74. [362]
9. Wain, 'The Immediate Situation', p. 366.
10. Wain, 'The Immediate Situation', p. 369.
11. Charles Tomlinson, 'The Middlebrow Muse', *Essays in Criticism* 7 (April 1957), pp. 208–17.
12. *Mavericks: An Anthology*, ed. Howard Sergeant and Dannie Abse (London: Editions Poetry and Poverty, 1957), p. 13.
13. Derek Brewer, 'The Modern English Literary Temper and the Crisis of Expansion', *Proteus: Studies in English Literature* (1958), pp. 233–61. [253–9]
14. William Van O'Connor, 'Philip Larkin: The Quiet Poem', in *The New University Wits and the End of Modernism* (Carbondale: Southern Illinois University Press, 1963), pp. 16–29.
15. Geoffrey Moore, *Poetry To-day* (London: British Council, 1958), pp. 45–9.

16. A. Alvarez, 'Poetry of the 'Fifties in England', *International Literary Annual* 1 (1958), pp. 97–107.
17. G. S. Fraser, 'An Imaginary Parallel', *London Magazine* 6.11 (1959), pp. 11–14. [13–14]
18. M. L. Rosenthal, 'Tuning in on Albion', *The Nation* (16 May 1959), pp. 457–9. Rosenthal's indictment of Larkin was repeated nearly verbatim in his book *The Modern Poets: A Critical Introduction* (New York: Oxford University Press, 1960), pp. 222–4. Alun R. Jones's refutation of Rosenthal, which is quite detailed, champions Larkin for many of the same reasons others did in the late 1950s and early 60s; see his article 'The Poetry of Philip Larkin: A Note on Transatlantic Culture', *Western Humanities Review* (Spring 1962), pp. 143–52.
19. C. B. Cox, 'Philip Larkin', *The Critical Quarterly* 1 (Spring 1959), pp. 14–17.
20. G. S. Fraser, *Vision and Rhetoric: Studies in Modern Poetry* (London: Faber and Faber, 1959), pp. 242–8.
21. Fraser, *Vision and Rhetoric*, pp. 261–3.
22. Derek Roper, 'Tradition and Innovation in the Occidental Lyric of the Last Decade, I: English Poetry and the Tradition, 1950–1960', *Books Abroad* 34.4 (Autumn 1960), pp. 344–8.
23. G. S. Fraser, 'English Poetry in the 1950s', *Audience* 8.2 (Spring 1961), pp. 42–57.
24. Boris Ford, ed., *The Pelican Guide to English Literature*, vol. 7: *The Modern Age* (Baltimore: Penguin, 1961), pp. 471–2.
25. Charles Tomlinson, 'Poets and Mushrooms: A Retrospect of British Poetry in 1961', *Poetry* 100.2 (May 1962), pp. 104–21. [117]
26. Donald Davie, 'England as Poetic Subject', *Poetry* 100.2 (May 1962), pp. 121–3.
27. Patricia Ball, 'The Photographic Art', *A Review of English Literature* 3 (1962), pp. 50–8.
28. John Press, 'English Verse Since 1945', *Essays by Divers Hands* 31 (1962), pp. 146–84.
29. Anthony Thwaite and Jon Silkin, 'No Politics, No Poetry?', *Stand* 6 (1963), pp. 7–23. [11–12]
30. Anonymous, 'Undeceived Poet', *The Times Literary Supplement* (12 March 1964), p. 216.
31. Philip Hobsbaum, 'Where are the War Poets?', *Outposts* 61 (Summer 1964), pp. 21–3.
32. Ian Hamilton, 'Poetry', *London Magazine*, 4 (1964), pp. 70–4.
33. Colin Falck, 'Essential Beauty', *The Review*, 14 (December 1964), pp. 3–11; rpt. in *The Modern Poet*, ed. Ian Hamilton (New York: Horizon Press, 1969), pp. 101–10.
34. Francis Hope, 'Philip Larkin', *Encounter* (22 May 1964), pp. 72–4.
35. Anthony Thwaite, *Contemporary English Poetry: An Introduction*, 3rd edn. (London: Heinemann, 1964), pp. 146–9.
36. John Wain, 'Engagement or Withdrawal? Some Notes on the Work of Philip Larkin.' *Critical Quarterly* 6.2 (1964), pp. 167–78.
37. Martin Dodsworth, 'The Climate of Pain in Recent Poetry', *London Magazine* 4.8 (November 1964), pp. 86–95.
38. William Dickey, 'Poetic Language', *The Hudson Review* 17.4 (Winter 1964–65), pp. 587–96.
39. Norman Holmes Pearson, Untitled review of *The Whitsun Weddings*, *The Kenyon Review*, 27.2 (Spring 1965), p. 384.
40. Louise Bogan, 'Books: Verse', *The New Yorker* (10 April 1965), pp. 193–6.
41. William Stafford, 'Losses, Engagements, and Privacies', *Poetry*, 106.4 (July, 1965), pp. 294–5.
42. Louis Martz, 'Recent Poetry: The Substance of Change', *Yale Review* 54.4 (1965), pp. 605–20.
43. Anonymous, 'A Solitary Sensibility', *Time* (19 February 1965), pp. 101–2.
44. Christopher Ricks, 'A True Poet', *The New York Review of Books* (14 January 1965), pp. 10–11.
45. Joseph L. Featherstone, 'A Poetry of Commonplaces', *The New Republic* (6 March 1965), pp. 27–9.
46. Harriet Zinnes, Untitled review, *Books Abroad* 39.4 (Autumn 1965), p. 462.

47. J. M. Newton, '... And a More Comprehensive Soul', *The Cambridge Quarterly* 1 (1965), pp. 96–101.
48. Frederick Grubb, *A Vision of Reality* (London: Chatto and Windus, 1965), pp. 226–35.
49. Richard Kell, 'Poetry Selection, 1964', *Critical Survey* 2.2 (Summer 1965), pp. 109–12.
50. Norman Page, 'Philip Larkin's "Myxomatosis": A Critical Appreciation', *Critical Survey* 2.3 (Winter 1965), pp. 169–70. For an entirely different kind of close reading, see J. McH. Sinclair, 'Taking a Poem to Pieces', in R. Fowler (ed.), *Essays on Style and Language: Linguistic and Critical Approaches to Literary Style* (London: Routledge and Kegan Paul, 1966), pp. 68–81, a highly technical discussion of the grammar and syntax of Larkin's poem 'First Sight'.
51. Anonymous, 'The More Deceived', *Times Literary Supplement* (6 October 1966), p. 916.
52. John Carey, 'Early Larkin', *New Statesman* 82 (September 1966), pp. 482–3.
53. Elizabeth Jennings, 'The Larkin Tone', *Spectator* (23 September 1966), pp. 385–6.
54. J. M. Cohen, *Poetry of This Age: 1908–1965* (London: Hutchinson, 1966), pp. 244–5.
55. D. J. Enright, *Conspirators and Poets* (London: Chatto and Windus, 1966), pp. 141–6.
56. J. D. Hainworth, 'A Poet of Our Time', *Hibbert Journal* 54 (1966), pp. 153–5.
57. Peter Davison, 'The Gilt Edge of Reputation: Twelve Months of New Poetry', *The Atlantic* (Jan. 1966), pp. 82–5.
58. Alun R. Jones, 'The Poetry of Philip Larkin: A Note on Transatlantic Culture', *Western Humanities Review* (Spring 1962), pp. 143–52.
59. M. L. Rosenthal, *The New Poets: American and British Poetry since World War II* (New York: Oxford University Press, 1967), pp. 233–44.
60. Patrick Swinden, 'Old Lines, New Lines: The Movement Ten Years After', *Critical Quarterly* 9.4 (Winter 1967), pp. 347–59.
61. Philip Gardner, 'The Wintry Drum: The Poetry of Philip Larkin', *Dalhousie Review* 48 (1968), pp. 88–99.
62. Gardner, 'The Wintry Drum: The Poetry of Philip Larkin', pp. 90–1.
63. Peter Faulkner, 'Philip Larkin: A Poet of Our World', *The Humanist*, 84 (May 1969), pp. 145–7.
64. Keith Sagar, 'Philip Larkin: "Church Going" and "Wedding Wind": Commentary', in Maurice Hussey (ed.), *Criticism in Action: A Critical Symposium on Modern Poems* (London: Longmans, 1969), pp. 117–26.
65. Sagar, 'Philip Larkin: "Church Going" and "Wedding Wind": Commentary', p. 126.

2 LARKIN RISES: THE 1970s

1. Anthony Thwaite, 'The Poetry of Philip Larkin', *The Survival of Poetry: A Contemporary Survey* (London: Faber, 1970), pp. 37–55.
2. A. Kingsley Weatherhead, 'Philip Larkin of England', *ELH* 38.4 (Dec. 1971), pp. 616–30.
3. Donald Davie, 'Landscapes of Larkin', in *Thomas Hardy and British Poetry* (London: Routledge & Kegan Paul, 1972), pp. 63–82.
4. Dieter Welz, '"A Winter Landscape in Neutral Colours": Some Notes on Philip Larkin's Vision of Reality', *Theoria* 39 (1972), pp. 61–73.
5. David Timms, *Philip Larkin* (Edinburgh: Oliver & Boyd, 1973), pp. 4–21.
6. Timms, *Philip Larkin*, pp. 22–35.
7. Timms, *Philip Larkin*, pp. 54–91.
8. Timms, *Philip Larkin*, pp. 92–120.
9. Timms, *Philip Larkin*, pp. 121–31.
10. Anthony Thwaite, 'Larkin's Recent Uncollected Poems', *Phoenix* 11/12 (1973/74), pp. 59–61.
11. Edna Longley, 'Larkin, Edward Thomas and the Tradition', *Phoenix* 11/12 (1973/74), pp. 63–89.

12. George Hartley, 'No Right of Entry', *Phoenix* 11/12 (1973/74), pp. 105–9.
13. Harry Chambers, 'Some Light Views of a Serious Poem: a footnote to the misreading of Philip Larkin's "Naturally the Foundation Will Bear Your Expenses"', *Phoenix* 11/12 (1973/74), pp. 110–14.
14. Frederick Grubb, 'Dragons', *Phoenix* 11/12 (1973/74), pp. 119–36.
15. John Bayley, 'Too Good for this World', *TLS: The Times Literary Supplement* (21 June 1974), pp. 653–4.
16. Dan Jacobson, 'Profile 3: Philip Larkin', *New Review* 1 (June 1974), pp. 25–9.
17. Clive James, 'The New Larkin: Wolves of Memory', *Encounter* 42 (June 1974), pp. 65–71.
18. Alan Brownjohn, 'The Deep Blue Air', *New Statesman*, (14 June 1974), pp. 854–5.
19. William Bedford, review of *High Windows*, *Agenda* 12.3 (1974), pp. 18–26.
20. Humphrey Clucas, review of *High Windows*, *Agenda* 12.3 (1974), pp. 13–17.
21. James Naremore, 'Philip Larkin's "Lost World"', *Contemporary Literature* 15.3 (Summer 1974), pp. 331–44.
22. Lolette Kuby, *An Uncommon Poet for the Common Man: A Study of Philip Larkin's Poetry* (The Hague: Mouton, 1974).
23. Kuby, *An Uncommon Poet for the Common Man*, pp. 9–27.
24. Kuby, *An Uncommon Poet for the Common Man*, p. 28.
25. Kuby, *An Uncommon Poet for the Common Man*, pp. 28–42.
26. Kuby, *An Uncommon Poet for the Common Man*, pp. 43–57.
27. Kuby, *An Uncommon Poet for the Common Man*, pp. 58–69.
28. Kuby, *An Uncommon Poet for the Common Man*, pp. 70–140.
29. Kuby, *An Uncommon Poet for the Common Man*, pp. 141–80.
30. Calvin Bedient, 'Philip Larkin', *Eight Contemporary Poets* (London: Oxford University Press, 1974), pp. 69–94.
31. Richard Murphy, 'The Art of Debunkery', *The New York Review of Books* (15 May 1975), pp. 30–2.
32. George Hartley, 'The Lost Displays', *Phoenix* 13 (1975), pp. 87–92.
33. David C. Nimmo, review of *High Windows*, *Dalhousie Review*, 55 (1975), pp. 383–5.
34. Kerry McSweeney, 'That It Can't Come Again', *Queen's Quarterly*, 82 (1975), pp. 317–20.
35. William H. Pritchard, 'Larkin Lives', *The Hudson Review*, 28.2 (Summer 1975), pp. 302–8.
36. J. R. Watson, 'The Other Larkin', *Critical Quarterly*, 17 (1975), pp. 347–61.
37. Stephen S. Hilliard, 'Wit and Beauty', *Prairie Schooner*, 49.3 (Fall 1975), pp. 270–1.
38. Walford Davies, 'An Ordinary Sorrow of Man's Life', *The Sewanee Review* 84.3 (Summer 1976), pp. 523–7.
39. Edward Lucie-Smith, 'Between Suicide and Revolution: The Poet as Role-Player', *Saturday Review* (19 April 1975), pp. 14–18.
40. Hermann Peschmann, 'Philip Larkin: Laureate of the Common Man', *English* 24 (1975), pp. 49–59.
41. Peschmann, 'Philip Larkin: Laureate of the Common Man', p. 55.
42. Steven David Lavine, 'Larkin's Supreme Versions', *Michigan Quarterly Review* 15 (1976), pp. 481–6.
43. Robert B. Shaw, 'Philip Larkin: A Stateside View', *Poetry Nation* 6 (1976), pp. 100–9.
44. Martin Scofield, 'The Poetry of Philip Larkin', *The Massachusetts Review* 17.2 (Summer 1976), pp. 370–89.
45. C. B. Cox, 'Philip Larkin: Anti-Heroic Poet', *Studies in the Literary Imagination* 9 (1976), pp. 155–68.
46. John P. McIntyre S.J., 'Radical Imperfection: The Poetry of Philip Larkin', *The Month* (September 1976), pp. 313–17.
47. James Atlas, 'On Philip Larkin', *The American Poetry Review* 6.4 (July–August 1977), pp. 18–19.
48. Bernard Bergonzi, 'Davie, Larkin, and the State of England', *Contemporary Literature* 18.3 (1977), pp. 343–60.

49. David Lodge, 'Philip Larkin', in *The Modes of Modern Writing Metaphor, Metonymy, and the Typology of Modern Literature* (London: Arnold, 1977), pp. 212-20. For a less-focused piece on Larkin in post-war contexts, see Michael Ward, 'We All Hate Home: English Poetry since World War II', *Contemporary Literature* 18.3 (Summer 1977), pp. 305-18.
50. Richard Swigg, 'Descending to the Commonplace', *PN Review* 4.2 (1977), pp. 3-13.
51. John Press, 'The Poetry of Philip Larkin', *Southern Review* 13 (1977), pp. 131-46. See also John Wain, *Professing Poetry* (New York: Viking, 1977), pp. 113-33.
52. Seamus Heaney, 'Now and in England', *Critical Inquiry* 3 (1977), pp. 471-89. Despite its provocative title, Theodore Weiss's 1977 article on Larkin is actually a somewhat astonished report about Larkin's high regard for John Betjeman; see 'The Blight of Modernism and Philip Larkin's Antidote', *The American Poetry Review* 6.1 (January-February 1977), pp. 39-41.
53. Roger Bowen, 'Death, Failure, and Survival in the Poetry of Philip Larkin', *Dalhousie Review* 58 (1978), pp. 79-84.
54. Kenneth Moon, 'Cosmic Perspective: A Use of Imagery in the Poetry of Philip Larkin', *Poetry Australia* 68 (October 1978), pp. 59-63.
55. Norma Procopiow, 'Hands across the Sea: The British and American Poetries of Philip Larkin and Frank O'Hara', *Illinois Quarterly* 40.4 (1978), pp. 49-61.
56. Bruce K. Martin, *Philip Larkin* (Boston: Twayne, 1978), pp. 13-30.
57. Martin, *Philip Larkin*, pp. 31-62.
58. Martin, *Philip Larkin*, pp. 63-90.
59. Martin, *Philip Larkin*, pp. 91-107.
60. Martin, *Philip Larkin*, pp. 108-37.
61. Martin, *Philip Larkin*, pp. 108-48.
62. Keith Cushman, 'Larkin's Landscapes', *Modern British Literature* 4 (1979), pp. 109-19.
63. Cushman, 'Larkin's Landscapes', p. 115.

3   LARKIN TRIUMPHANT: THE 1980s

1. Grevel Lindop, 'Being Different from Yourself: Philip Larkin in the 1970s', in Peter Jones and Michael Schmidt (eds.), *British Poetry since 1970: A Critical Survey* (Manchester: Carcanet, 1980), pp. 46-53.
2. Lindop, 'Being Different from Yourself: Philip Larkin in the 1970s', pp. 52-4.
3. Barbara Everett, 'Philip Larkin: After Symbolism', *Essays in Criticism: A Quarterly Journal of Literary Criticism* 30 (1980), pp. 277-42.
4. Mary Ford, 'Loneliness Clarifies: A Study of the Longer Poems of Philip Larkin', *English Studies in Canada* 6 (1980), pp. 323-32.
5. Simon Petch, *The Art of Philip Larkin* (Sydney: Sydney University Press, 1981).
6. Petch, *The Art of Philip Larkin*, pp. ix-17.
7. Petch, *The Art of Philip Larkin*, pp. 18-61.
8. Petch, *The Art of Philip Larkin*, pp. 62-86.
9. Andrew Motion, *Philip Larkin* (London: Methuen, 1982).
10. Anthony Thwaite (ed.), *Larkin at Sixty* (London: Faber, 1982).
11. Barbara Everett, 'Larkin's Edens', *English: The Journal of the English Association* 31.139 (1982), pp. 41-53.
12. Christopher Miller, 'The Egotistical Banal, or Against Larkitudinising', *Agenda* 21.3 (1983), pp. 69-103.
13. A.T. Tolley, 'Philip Larkin's Unpublished Book: "In the Grip of Light"', *Agenda* 22.2 (1984), pp. 76-86.
14. Michael Saladyga, 'Philip Larkin and Survival Poetry', *The American Poetry Review*, 14.3 (May/June 1985), pp. 10-16.
15. John Reibetanz, 'Lyric Poetry as Self-Possession: Philip Larkin', *University of Toronto Quarterly*, 54.3 (Spring 1985), pp. 266-84.

16. Guido Latré, 'Locking Earth to the Sky': A Structuralist Approach to Philip Larkin's Poetry, European University Studies 14 (Frankfurt; Berne; New York: Peter Lang, 1985).
17. Latré, 'Locking Earth to the Sky', p. 439.
18. Latré, 'Locking Earth to the Sky', pp. 441–2.
19. Andrew Motion, Philip Larkin: A Writer's Life (London: Faber & Faber, 1993), p. 521.
20. Donald Hall, 'Philip Larkin 1922-1985', The New Criterion 4.6 (1986), pp. 165–8.
21. Robert Richman, 'The "Collected" Philip Larkin', The New Criterion 7.8 (1989), pp. 5–14.
22. X.J. Kennedy, 'Larkin's Voice', The New Criterion 4.6 (1986), pp. 16–17; rpt. in Dale Salwak (ed.), Philip Larkin: The Man and His Work (Iowa City: University of Iowa Press, 1989), pp. 162–4.
23. David Young, 'Larkin: An Appreciation', Field: Contemporary Poetry and Poetics 34 (1986), pp. 103–13.
24. John Wain, 'The Importance of Philip Larkin', American Scholar 55 (1986), pp. 349–64.
25. Philip Hobsbaum, 'Larkin's England', Poetry Review 76.1-2 (1986), pp. 23–5.
26. John Woolley, 'Larkin: Romance, Fiction and Myth', English: The Journal of the English Association 35.153 (1986), pp. 237–67.
27. Guido Latré, 'Realist or Romantic? Philip Larkin's Modes of Writing', in Linguistics and the Study of Literature, ed. Theo D'haen (Amsterdam: Rodopi, 1986), pp. 27–41.
28. Roger Elliott, 'The Bard as Moping Owl', Cambridge Quarterly 15 (1986), pp. 207–15 [210].
29. Mike Tierce, 'Philip Larkin's "Cut-Price Crowd": The Poet and the Average Reader', South Atlantic Review 51.4 (1986): 95–110.
30. Terry Whalen, Philip Larkin and English Poetry (Vancouver, BC: University of British Columbia Press, 1986), pp. 1–9 TO 1–31.
31. Whalen, Philip Larkin and English Poetry, pp. 32–55.
32. Whalen, Philip Larkin and English Poetry, pp. 56–76.
33. Whalen, Philip Larkin and English Poetry, pp. 77–114.
34. Whalen, Philip Larkin and English Poetry, pp. 109 and 111.
35. Whalen, Philip Larkin and English Poetry, pp. 115–39.
36. Andrew Swarbrick, The Whitsun Weddings and the Less Deceived by Philip Larkin (London: Macmillan, 1986).
37. William H. Pritchard, 'Philip Larkin', Raritan: A Quarterly Review 6.4 (1987), pp. 62–80.
38. Angela Ball, 'Reading Larkin: Something Almost Being Said', Hawaii Review 21 (1987), pp. 94–103.
39. Salem K. Hassan, Philip Larkin and His Contemporaries: An Air of Authenticity. Introduction by Philip Hobsbaum (Basingstoke: Macmillan, 1988), pp. 1–21.
40. Hassan, Philip Larkin and His Contemporaries, pp. 22–43.
41. Hassan, Philip Larkin and His Contemporaries, pp. 44–126.
42. Hassan, Philip Larkin and His Contemporaries, p. 189.
43. Hassan, Philip Larkin and His Contemporaries, pp. 129–90.
44. George Watson, 'Larkin Ascending', American Scholar 57.3 (1988), pp. 453–60.
45. Barry Spurr, 'Alienation and Affirmation in the Poetry of Philip Larkin', Sydney Studies in English 14.1 (1988), pp. 52–71.
46. G. Singh, 'The Poetry of Philip Larkin', Aligarh Critical Miscellany 1.1 (1988), pp 101–19.
47. Singh, 'The Poetry of Philip Larkin', pp. 102–3.
48. John Goodby, '"The Importance of Being Elsewhere," or "No Man Is an Ireland": Self, Selves and Social Consensus in the Poetry of Philip Larkin', Critical Survey 1.2 (1989), pp. 131–8.
49. Laurence Lerner, 'Larkin's Strategies', Critical Survey 1.2 (1989), pp. 113–21.
50. M.W. Rowe, 'The Transcendental Larkin', English: The Journal of the English Association 38.161 (1989), pp. 143–52.
51. Peter MacDonald Smith, 'The Postmodernist Larkin', English 38 (1989), pp. 153–61.
52. Peter MacDonald Smith, 'The Postmodernist Larkin', pp. 154–5.

53. Hugh Underhill, 'Poetry of Departures: Larkin and the Power of Choosing', *Critical Survey* 1.2 (1989), pp. 183–93.
54. J.R. Watson, 'Clichés and Common Speech in Philip Larkin's Poetry', *Critical Survey* 1.2 (1989), pp. 149–56.
55. John Skinner, 'Philip Larkin by Philip Larkin', *ARIEL: A Review of International English Literature* 20.1 (1989), pp. 77–95.
56. Andrew Gibson, 'Larkin and Ordinariness' in Linda Cookson and Bryan Loughrey (eds.), *Philip Larkin: The Poems* (London: Longman, 1989), pp. 9–18.
57. Cedric Watts, 'Larkin and Jazz', in Linda Cookson and Bryan Loughrey (eds.), *Philip Larkin: The Poems* (London: Longman, 1989), pp. 20–7.
58. Michael Gearin-Tosh, 'Deprivation and Love in Larkin's Poetry', in Linda Cookson and Bryan Loughrey (eds.), *Philip Larkin: The Poems* (London: Longman, 1989), pp. 29–37; John Saunders, 'Beauty and Truth in Three Poems from *The Whitsun Weddings*', in Linda Cookson and Bryan Loughrey (eds.), *Philip Larkin: The Poems* (London: Longman, 1989), pp. 39–48.
59. Peter Hollindale, 'The Long Perspectives', in Linda Cookson and Bryan Loughrey (eds.), *Philip Larkin: The Poems* (London: Longman, 1989), pp. 50–60.
60. Alan Gardiner, 'Larkin's England', in Linda Cookson and Bryan Loughrey (eds.), *Philip Larkin: The Poems* (London: Longman, 1989), pp. 62–70.
61. Harvey Hallsmith, 'The "I" in Larkin', in Linda Cookson and Bryan Loughrey (eds.), *Philip Larkin: The Poems* (London: Longman, 1989), pp. 72–79.
62. Roger Day, '"That Vast Moth-Eaten Musical Brocade": Larkin and Religion', in Linda Cookson and Bryan Loughrey (eds.), *Philip Larkin: The Poems* (London: Longman, 1989), pp. 81–92.
63. Ronald Draper, 'The Positive Larkin', in Linda Cookson and Bryan Loughrey (eds.), *Philip Larkin: The Poems* (London: Longman, 1989), pp. 94–104.
64. Graham Holderness, 'Philip Larkin: The Limitations of Experience', in Linda Cookson and Bryan Loughrey (eds.), *Philip Larkin: The Poems* (London: Longman, 1989), pp. 106–14.
65. William H. Pritchard, 'Larkin's Presence', in Dale Salwak (ed.), *Philip Larkin: The Man and His Work* (Iowa City: University of Iowa Press, 1989), pp. 71–89; David Lodge, 'Philip Larkin: The Metonymic Muse', in Dale Salwak (ed.), *Philip Larkin: The Man and His Work* (Iowa City: University of Iowa Press, 1989), pp. 118–28.
66. J.R. Watson, 'Philip Larkin: Voices and Values', in Dale Salwak (ed.), *Philip Larkin: His Life's Work* (Iowa City: University of Iowa Press, 1989), pp. 90–111.
67. John H. Augustine, 'Tentative Initiation in the Poetry', in Dale Salwak (ed.), *Philip Larkin: The Man and His Work* (Iowa City: University of Iowa Press, 1989), pp. 112–17.
68. Barbara Everett, 'Art in Larkin', in Dale Salwak (ed.), *Philip Larkin: The Man and His Work* (Iowa City: University of Iowa Press, 1989), pp. 129–39.
69. Bruce K. Martin, 'Larkin's Humanity Viewed from Abroad,' in Dale Salwak (ed.), *Philip Larkin: The Man and His Work* (Iowa City: University of Iowa Press, 1989), pp. 140–9.
70. Hilary Kilmarnock, 'A Personal Memoir', in Dale Salwak (ed.), *Philip Larkin: The Man and His Work* (Iowa City: University of Iowa Press, 1989), pp. 153–7; John Bayley, 'Philip Larkin's Inner World', in Dale Salwak (ed.), *Philip Larkin: The Man and His Work* (Iowa City: University of Iowa Press, 1989), pp. 158–61; X. J. Kennedy, 'Larkin's Voice', in Dale Salwak (ed.), *Philip Larkin: The Man and His Work* (Iowa City: University of Iowa Press, 1989), pp. 162–4; Donald Hall, 'Philip Larkin, 1922-85', in Dale Salwak (ed.), *Philip Larkin: The Man and His Work* (Iowa City: University of Iowa Press, 1989), pp. 165–8.
71. Janice Rossen, *Philip Larkin: His Life's Work* (Iowa City: University of Iowa Press, 1989), pp. xv–24.
72. Rossen, *Philip Larkin: His Life's Work*, pp. 25–48.
73. Rossen, *Philip Larkin: His Life's Work*, pp. 49–65.
74. Rossen, *Philip Larkin: His Life's Work*, pp. 66–93.
75. Rossen, *Philip Larkin: His Life's Work*, pp. 92–3.
76. Rossen, *Philip Larkin: His Life's Work*, pp. 94–143.

4 LARKIN UNDER SIEGE: THE 1990s

1. Tom Paulin, 'Into the Heart of Englishness', in Stephen Regan (ed.) *Philip Larkin* New Casebook Series (New York: St. Martin's, 1997), pp. 160–77.
2. Robert Faggen, 'Review of *Collected Poems*', *Harvard Book Review* no. 15/16 (1990), p. 10.
3. Patrick Garland, 'Review of *Collected Poems*', *Review of English Studies* 41.161 (1990), pp. 141–3.
4. James Richardson, 'Reading Larkin', *Poetry* 155.6 (1990), pp. 408–14.
5. Katha Pollitt, 'Philip Larkin', *Grand Street* 9.3 (1990), pp. 250–60.
6. Peter Filkins, 'The Collected Larkin: "But Why Put It into Words?"', *The Iowa Review* 20.1 (1990), pp. 166–81.
7. Tim Trengove-Jones, 'Larkin's Stammer', *Essays in Criticism: A Quarterly Journal of Literary Criticism* 40.4 (1990), pp. 322–38.
8. William Harmon, 'Larkin's Memory', *Sewanee Review* 98.2 (1990), pp. 206–21.
9. Stephen Watson, 'Darkness Encroaching: Philip Larkin and the Situation of Poetry', *Encounter* 74.3 (1990), pp. 30–7.
10. Watson, 'Darkness Encroaching: Philip Larkin and the Situation of Poetry' p. 31.
11. David Punter, *York Notes on Selected Poems [by] Philip Larkin* (London: Longman, 1991).
12. Graham Handley, *Brodie's Notes on Philip Larkin's Selected Poems*. (London: Macmillan, 1991.)
13. A.T. Tolley, *My Proper Ground: A Study of the Work of Philip Larkin and Its Development* (Ottawa, ON: Carleton University Press, 1991), p. 72.
14. Tolley, *My Proper Ground: A Study of the Work of Philip Larkin and Its Development*, pp. 129, 132.
15. Hans Osterwalder, *British Poetry between The Movement and Modernism* (Heidelberg : C. Winter, 1991), pp. 62–98.
16. G.J. Finch, 'Larkin, Nature, and Romanticism', *Critical Survey* 3.1 (1991), pp. 53–60. On Romantic elements in Larkin, see also John Bayley, 'Housman and Larkin: Romantic into Parnassian?', *Essays in Criticism: A Quarterly Journal of Literary Criticism* 41.2 (1991), pp. 147–59. For a dissenting view about Larkin's supposed attraction to Symbolism, see Claude Rawson, 'Larkin's Desolate Attics', *Raritan: A Quarterly Review* 11.2 (1991), pp. 25–47.
17. Peter MacDonald Smith, '"Pretending to Be Me": Larkin versus "Larkin"', in Philip Shaw and Peter Stockwell (eds.) *Subjectivity and Literature from the Romantics to the Present Day* (London: Pinter, 1991), pp. 93–100.
18. James Booth, 'A Room Without a View: Larkin's Empty Attic', *Bête Noire* 12–12 (1991), pp. 320–9.
19. Peter Snowdon, 'Larkin's Conceit', *Critical Survey* 3.1 (1991), pp. 61–70.
20. Snowdon, 'Larkin's Conceit', pp. 66–7.
21. James Booth, *Philip Larkin: Writer* (New York: Harvester Wheatsheaf, 1992).
22. Stephen Regan, *Philip Larkin: The Critics Debate* (New York: Macmillan, 1992).
23. Stephen Regan, *Philip Larkin: The Critics Debate*, pp. 13–33.
24. Regan, *Philip Larkin: The Critics Debate*, pp. 33–50.
25. Regan, *Philip Larkin: The Critics Debate*, p. 77.
26. Regan, *Philip Larkin: The Critics Debate*, pp. 132, 138.
27. Barbara Richardson, 'Philip Larkin's Early Influences', *Northwest Review* 30.1 (1992), pp. 133–40.
28. Rowland Molony, 'Philip Larkin and Personal Space', *English Review* 3.1 (1992), pp. 2–4. Tim Trengove-Jones, 'Larkin and Europe', *English Studies* in Africa 35.2 (1992), pp. 53–75.
29. Jonathan Raban, 'Mr. Misery Guts', *The Independent*, 17 October 1992. www.independent.co.uk/arts-entertainment/books-mr-miseryguts-philip-larkins-letters-show-all-the-grim-humour-that-was-a-hallmark-of-his-great-1558190.html
30. Tom Paulin, 'The Larkin Letters', *Times Literary Supplement* (6 November 1992), p. 15.
31. Andrew Motion, *Philip Larkin: A Writer's Life* (London: Faber & Faber, 1993).

32. Motion, *Philip Larkin: A Writer's Life*, pp. 342–3.
33. Motion, *Philip Larkin: A Writer's Life*, pp. 444–5.
34. Peter Ackroyd, 'Poet Hands on Misery to Man', *The Times*, 1 April 1993, p. 35.
35. Alan Bennett, 'Alas, Deceived! Review of *Philip Larkin: A Writer's Life*', *London Review of Books* 15.6 (1993), pp. 3, 5–9.
36. Christopher Carduff, 'Just let me put this bastard on the skids': Review of *Philip Larkin: A Writer's Life*', *New Criterion* 12.1 (1993), pp. 83–7.
37. Dana Gioia, 'The Still, Sad Music of Philip Larkin: Review of *Philip Larkin: A Writer's Life*', *Book World* (15 August 1996), pp. 1, 9.
38. Andrew Hamilton, 'Review of *Philip Larkin: A Writer's Life*', *Times Literary Supplement* (2 April 1993), pp. 3–4.
39. Penelope Fitzgerald, '"Really, One Should Burn Everything": Review of *Selected Letters of Philip Larkin, 1940–1985*', *The New Criterion*, March 1993, pp. 68–9.
40. Edward Hirsch, 'Sour Majesty', *The Wilson Quarterly*, 17.3 (1993), pp. 112–21.
41. Clive James, 'Getting Larkin's Number: Review of *Philip Larkin: A Writer's Life*', *Independent Sunday Review*, 4 April 1993 (www.clivejames.com/books/even/larkin).
42. Jonathan Raban, 'The Idea of Elsewhere: Review of *Philip Larkin: A Writer's Life*', *The New Republic*, 19 July 1993, pp. 30–6.
43. Stuart Wright, 'Larkin's Outgoing Mail: Review of *Selected Letters of Philip Larkin, 1940-1985*', *Sewanee Review* 101.3 (1993), pp. 427–33.
44. Neil Covey, 'Larkin, Distance, and Observation', *Modern Language Studies* 23.3 (1993), pp. 11–25.
45. T. J. Ross, 'On Philip Larkin', *The Literary Review* 38.2 (1995), pp. 119–27.
46. Paul Volsik, '"The Essential Nexus": Philip Larkin and the Reader', *Q/W/E/R/T/Y: Arts, Littératures & Civilisations du Monde Anglophone* 3 (1993), pp. 436–7.
47. Joseph Epstein, 'Mr. Larkin Gets a Life', *Commentary* 97.4 (1994), pp 39–45.
48. John McCormick, 'Philip Larkin: An American View', *The Sewanee Review* 102.1 (1994), pp. 132–43.
49. Gary Kissick, 'They Turn on Larkin', *The Antioch Review* 52.1 (1994), pp. 64–70.
50. Joseph Bristow, 'The Obscenity of Philip Larkin', *Critical Inquiry* 21.1 (1994), pp. 156–81.
51. Nigel Alderman, '"The Life with a Hole in It": Philip Larkin and the Condition of England', *Textual Practice* 18.2 (1994), pp. 279–301.
52. Steve Clark, '"Get Out as Early as You Can": Larkin's Sexual Politics', 1994; reprinted in Stephen Regan (ed. and intro.) *Philip Larkin* (New York: St. Martin's, 1997), pp. 94–134.
53. Andrew Swarbrick, *Out of Reach: The Poetry of Philip Larkin*, (New York: St. Martin's, 1995).
54. Swarbrick, *Out of Reach: The Poetry of Philip Larkin*, pp. 1–16.
55. Swarbrick, *Out of Reach: The Poetry of Philip Larkin*, pp. 17–42.
56. Swarbrick, *Out of Reach: The Poetry of Philip Larkin*, pp. 43–121.
57. Swarbrick, *Out of Reach: The Poetry of Philip Larkin*, pp. 122–74.
58. Terry Whalen, '"Strangeness Made Sense": Philip Larkin in Ireland', *Antigonish Review* 107 (1996), pp. 157–69.
59. Salem K. Hassan, 'Women in Philip Larkin', *English Studies: A Journal of English Language and Literature* 77.2 (1996), pp. 142–54.
60. Warren Hope, *Philip Larkin*. (London: Greenwich Exchange, 1997.)
61. Laurence Lerner *Philip Larkin*, (Plymouth, England: Northcote House, with British Council, 1997).
62. A.T. Tolley, *Larkin at Work: A Study of Larkin's Mode of Composition as Seen in His Workbooks* (Hull: Hull University Press, 1998), p. 181.
63. Stephen Regan (ed.), *Philip Larkin* (New York, St. Martin's Press, 1997).
64. Michael Baron (ed.), *Larkin with Poetry* (Leicester: English Association, University of Leicester, 1997).

65. James Booth, 'Philip Larkin: Lyricism, Englishness and Postcoloniality', in *Larkin with Poetry* (Leicester: English Association, University of Leicester, 1997), pp. 9–30.
66. Marion Lomax, 'Larkin with Women', in *Larkin with Poetry* (Leicester: English Association, University of Leicester, 1997), pp. 31–45.
67. Stephen Regan, 'Larkin's Reputation', in *Larkin with Poetry* (Leicester: English Association, University of Leicester, 1997), pp. 47–69.
68. Andrew Swarbrick, 'Larkin in the Sixth Form', in *Larkin with Poetry* (Leicester: English Association, University of Leicester, 1997), pp. 71–6.
69. James Booth, 'Why Larkin's Poetry Gives Offence', *English* 46 (1997), pp. 1–19.
70. Gary Day, '"Never Such Language Again": The Poetry of Philip Larkin'. In Gary Day and Brian Docherty (eds.), *British Poetry from the 1950s to the 1990s: Politics and Art* (London, England & New York, NY: Macmillan & St. Martin's, 1997), pp. 33–47.
71. David C. Ward, '"Love Again": Larkin and Obscenity', *Sewanee Review* 105.2 (1997), pp. 227–43.
72. William Kerrigan, 'Larkin and the Difficult Subject', *Essays in Criticism* 48.4 (1998), pp. 291–307.
73. Janice Rossen, 'Philip Larkin and *Lucky Jim*', *Journal of Modern Literature* 22.1 (1998), pp. 147–64.
74. Antony Rowland, '"All is Not Dead": Philip Larkin, Humanism and Class', *Critical Survey* 10.2 (1998), pp. 1–14.
75. Dale Salwak, 'Sketches from Life: Philip Larkin-An American View', *Biography: An Interdisciplinary Quarterly* 21.2 (1998), pp. 195–205.
76. Martin Scofield, 'Refining the life: Philip Larkin's Poetry Reconsidered', *English Studies* 79.1 (1998), pp. 33–47.
77. B.J. Leggett, *Larkin's Blues: Jazz, Popular Music, and Poetry* (Baton Rouge; London: Louisiana State University Press, 1999), pp. 1–43.
78. Leggett, *Larkin's Blues: Jazz, Popular Music, and Poetry*, pp. 44–206.

5 LARKIN TRIUMPHANT ONCE MORE: THE 2000s

1. Barbara Everett, 'Larkin's Money', in James Booth (ed. and intro.) *New Larkins for Old: Critical Essays* (Basingstoke: Macmillan; New York: St. Martin's, 2000), pp. 11–28.
2. Edna Longley, 'Larkin, Decadence and the Lyric Poem', in James Booth (ed. and intro.) *New Larkins for Old: Critical Essays* (Basingstoke: Macmillan; New York: St. Martin's, 2000), pp. 29–50.
3. John Carey, 'The Two Philip Larkins', in James Booth (ed. and intro.) *New Larkins for Old: Critical Essays* (Basingstoke: Macmillan; New York: St. Martin's, 2000), pp. 51–65.
4. Carey, 'The Two Philip Larkins', p. 65.
5. George H. Gilpin, 'Patricia Avis and Philip Larkin', in James Booth (ed. and intro.) *New Larkins for Old: Critical Essays* (Basingstoke: Macmillan; New York: St. Martin's, 2000), pp. 66–78.
6. M.W. Rowe, 'Unreal Girls: Lesbian Fantasy in Early Larkin', in James Booth (ed. and intro.) *New Larkins for Old: Critical Essays* (Basingstoke: Macmillan; New York: St. Martin's, 2000), pp. 79–96.
7. Liz Hedgecock, 'New Worlds for Old: Mythology and Exile in the Novels of Philip Larkin', in James Booth (ed. and intro.) *New Larkins for Old: Critical Essays* (Basingstoke: Macmillan; New York: St. Martin's, 2000), pp. 97–106.
8. Tom Whalen, 'Philip Larkin and Lady Chatterley's Lover', in James Booth (ed. and intro.) *New Larkins for Old: Critical Essays* (Basingstoke: Macmillan; New York: St. Martin's, 2000), pp. 107–20.
9. Stephen Regan, 'In the Grip of Light: Larkin's Poetry of the 1940s', in James Booth (ed. and intro.) *New Larkins for Old: Critical Essays* (Basingstoke: Macmillan; New York: St. Martin's, 2000), pp. 121–9.

10. Raphaël Ingelbien, 'The Uses of Symbolism: Larkin and Eliot', in James Booth (ed. and intro.) *New Larkins for Old: Critical Essays* (Basingstoke: Macmillan; New York: St. Martin's, 2000), pp. 130–43.
11. John Osborne, 'Postmodernism and Postcolonialism in the Poetry of Philip Larkin', in James Booth (ed. and intro.) *New Larkins for Old: Critical Essays* (Basingstoke: Macmillan; New York: St. Martin's, 2000), pp. 144–65.
12. Steve Clark, '"The Lost Displays"; Larkin and Empire', in James Booth (ed. and intro.) *New Larkins for Old: Critical Essays* (Basingstoke: Macmillan; New York: St. Martin's, 2000), pp. 166–81.
13. Ian Almond, 'Larkin and the Mundane: Mystic without a Mystery', in James Booth (ed. and intro.) *New Larkins for Old: Critical Essays* (Basingstoke: Macmillan; New York: St. Martin's, 2000), pp. 182–9.
14. James Booth, 'From Here to Bogland: Larkin, Heaney and the Poetry of Place', in James Booth (ed. and intro.) *New Larkins for Old: Critical Essays* (Basingstoke: Macmillan; New York: St. Martin's, 2000), pp. 190–212.
15. V. Penelope Pelizzon, 'Native Carnival: Philip Larkin's Puppet-Theatre of Ritual', in James Booth (ed. and intro.) *New Larkins for Old: Critical Essays* (Basingstoke: Macmillan; New York: St. Martin's, 2000), pp. 213–23.
16. István Rácz, 'Larkin from an East European Perspective', in James Booth (ed. and intro.) *New Larkins for Old: Critical Essays* (Basingstoke: Macmillan; New York: St. Martin's, 2000), pp. 224–30.
17. Alex R. Falzon *Negative Indicative: Philip Larkin in the Forties: A Study in Transformation* (Pisa: ETS, 2000), pp. 1–80.
18. Falzon *Negative Indicative*, pp. 81–130.
19. Stan Smith, 'Something for Nothing: Late Larkins and Early', *English: The Journal of the English Association* 49.195 (2000), pp. 255–75.
20. Peter Groves, '"What Music Lies in the Cold Print": Larkin's Experimental Metric', *Style* 35.4 (2001), pp. 703–23.
21. Roger Craik, 'Animals and Birds in Philip Larkin's Poetry', *Papers on Language and Literature* 38.4 (2002), pp. 395–412.
22. Raphaël Ingelbien, "Neither Here Nor There: Larkin and His Misreaders' in *Misreading England: Poetry and Nationhood since the Second World War* (Amsterdam, Rodopi, 2002), pp. 189–228.
23. Andrew McKeown, 'Ambiguity and Religion in Philip Larkin's Poems', *Imaginaires: Revue du Centre de Recherche sur l'Imaginaire dans les Littératures de Langue Anglaise* 8 (2002), pp. 173–83.
24. Raphaël Ingelbien, 'From Hardy to Yeats? Larkin's Poetry of Ageing', *Essays in Criticism: A Quarterly Journal of Literary Criticism* 53.3 (2003), pp. 262–77.
25. Victoria Longino, 'The Alien Moment: Philip Larkin and Gender', *Hungarian Journal of English and American Studies* 9.2 (2003), pp. 91–104.
26. Longino, 'The Alien Moment', pp. 100–01.
27. John Osborne, 'Larkin, Modernism and Jazz', *Hungarian Journal of English and American Studies* 9.2 (2003), pp. 7–27.
28. Stephen Cooper, *Philip Larkin: Subversive Writer* (Brighton; Portland, OR: Sussex Academic Press, 2004), pp. 1–5.
29. Cooper, *Philip Larkin: Subversive Writer*, pp. 6–121.
30. Cooper, *Philip Larkin: Subversive Writer*, pp. 122–82.
31. Cooper, *Philip Larkin: Subversive Writer*, p. 182.
32. James Booth, *Philip Larkin: The Poet's Plight* (Basingstoke; New York: Palgrave Macmillan, 2005).
33. Booth, *Philip Larkin: The Poet's Plight*, pp. 1–20.
34. Booth, *Philip Larkin: The Poet's Plight*, pp. 21–111.
35. Booth, *Philip Larkin: The Poet's Plight*, p. 111.

36. Booth, *Philip Larkin: The Poet's Plight*, pp. 112–43.
37. Booth, *Philip Larkin: The Poet's Plight*, pp. 144–203.
38. Dan Jacobson, 'Philip Larkin's "Element"', *New Criterion* 23.6 (2005), pp. 14–20.
39. Richard Bradford, *First Boredom, Then Fear: The Life of Philip Larkin* (London: Owen, 2005).
40. Bradford, *First Boredom, Then Fear*, pp. 128, 137, 149, 152–3.
41. Bradford, *First Boredom, Then Fear*, pp. 157, 160, 200.
42. Bradford, *First Boredom, Then Fear*, pp. 201, 203–4, 213.
43. Bradford, *First Boredom, Then Fear*, p. 228.
44. Andrew McKeown and Charles Holdefer (eds.), *Philip Larkin and the Poetics of Resistance* (Paris: L'Harmattan, 2006).
45. Raphaël Ingelbien, 'An Enormous No!: Larkin's Resistance to Translation', in Andrew McKeown and Charles Holdefer (eds.), *Philip Larkin and the Poetics of Resistance* (Paris: L'Harmattan, 2006), pp. 19–36.
46. Jacques Nassif, '"Out of Reach": Philip Larkin's "Here"', in Andrew McKeown and Charles Holdefer (eds.), *Philip Larkin and the Poetics of Resistance* (Paris: L'Harmattan, 2006), pp. 37–54.
47. Jean-Charles Perquin, '"Why Put It into Words?": Philip Larkin's Perilous Poetics of Resistance', in Andrew McKeown and Charles Holdefer (eds.), *Philip Larkin and the Poetics of Resistance* (Paris: L'Harmattan, 2006), pp. 55–66.
48. Charles Holdefer, 'Camping with Larkin', in Andrew McKeown and Charles Holdefer (eds.), *Philip Larkin and the Poetics of Resistance* (Paris: L'Harmattan, 2006), pp. 67–80.
49. István Rácz, 'Are Days Where We Live?', in Andrew McKeown and Charles Holdefer (eds.), *Philip Larkin and the Poetics of Resistance* (Paris: L'Harmattan, 2006), pp. 81–92.
50. Martine Semblatt, 'Classical Prosody in Philip Larkin's Poetry', in Andrew McKeown and Charles Holdefer (eds.), *Philip Larkin and the Poetics of Resistance* (Paris: L'Harmattan, 2006), pp. 93–106.
51. Helen Goethals, 'Philip Larkin and the Poetics of Resistance in the Second World War', in Andrew McKeown and Charles Holdefer (eds.), *Philip Larkin and the Poetics of Resistance* (Paris: L'Harmattan, 2006), pp. 109–22.
52. Stephen Cooper, 'Resisting Tradition: The Decentred Perspectives of Larkin, Auden, and MacNeice', in Andrew McKeown and Charles Holdefer (eds.), *Philip Larkin and the Poetics of Resistance* (Paris: L'Harmattan, 2006), pp. 123–47.
53. David Ten Eyck, '"Alien Territory": Resistance and the Poet's Social Function in the Work of Philip Larkin', in Andrew McKeown and Charles Holdefer (eds.), *Philip Larkin and the Poetics of Resistance* (Paris: L'Harmattan, 2006), pp. 149–63. Adrian Grafe, 'Larkin's Impulse to Preserve', in Andrew McKeown and Charles Holdefer (eds.), *Philip Larkin and the Poetics of Resistance* (Paris: L'Harmattan, 2006), pp. 170–1.
54. Grafe, 'Larkin's Impulse to Preserve', pp. 179–88.
55. James Booth, 'Resistance and Affinity: Philip Larkin and T. S. Eliot', in Andrew McKeown and Charles Holdefer (eds.), *Philip Larkin and the Poetics of Resistance* (Paris: L'Harmattan, 2006), pp. 189–209.
56. Tijana Stojković, *Unnoticed in the Casual Light of Day: Philip Larkin and the Plain Style* (London; New York: Routledge, 2006), pp. 1–75.
57. Stojković, *Unnoticed in the Casual Light of Day*, p. 128.
58. Stojković, *Unnoticed in the Casual Light of Day*, pp. 128–215.
59. Sisir Kumar Chatterjee, *Philip Larkin: Poetry That Builds Bridges* (New Delhi: Atlantic, 2006), pp. 1–30.
60. Chatterjee, *Poetry That Builds Bridges*, p. 322.
61. B. G. Tandon, *Philip Larkin: A Critical Discussion of Selected Poems*. New Delhi: Spectrum, 2006. Unfortunately, a 2007 book by another Indian scholar, K. Rajamouly (*The Poetry of Philip Larkin: A Critical Study* [New Delhi: Prestige Books, 2007]) is far less effective than either the Chatterjee or Tandon volumes, which is why I have chosen not to discuss it.

62. Nicholas Marsh, *Philip Larkin: The Poems*, Analysing Texts Series (New York: Palgrave Macmillan, 2007), pp. 1–35.
63. Marsh, *Philip Larkin: The Poems*, pp. 36–111.
64. Marsh, *Philip Larkin: The Poems*, pp. 112–216. Also worth mentioning is a 2007 study guide prepared by Steve Eddy and issued as part of the 'York Notes' series. Titled *High Windows: Philip Larkin* (London: York Press, 2007), this book discussed many poems rather briefly and was formatted in ways designed to seem visually appealing but could also seem inefficient in its use of space.
65. Terry Castle, 'The Lesbianism of Philip Larkin', *Daedalus: Journal of the American Academy of Arts and Sciences* 136:2 (2007), pp. 88–102.
66. Stephen Regan, 'Philip Larkin: A Late Modern Poet'. In Neil Corcoran (ed.) *The Cambridge Companion to Twentieth-Century English Poetry* (Cambridge: Cambridge University Press, 2007), pp. 147–58.
67. Robert Lance Snyder, '"Elbowing Vacancy": Philip Larkin's Non-Places', *Papers on Language & Literature* 43.2 (2007), pp. 115–45.
68. A. Banerjee, 'Larkin Reconsidered', *Sewanee Review* 116.3 (2008), pp. 428–41; see esp. pp. 438–9.
69. John Osborne, *Larkin, Ideology and Critical Violence: A Case of Wrongful Conviction* (New York: Palgrave Macmillan, 2008).
70. Osborne, *Larkin, Ideology and Critical Violence*, pp. 25–6.
71. Richard Palmer, *Such Deliberate Disguises: The Art of Philip Larkin* (London; New York: Continuum, 2008), pp. xiii–xxii.
72. Palmer, *Such Deliberate Disguises*, pp. 3–67.
73. Sunnil Kumar Sarker, *A Companion to Philip Larkin* (New Delhi: Atlantic Publishers & Distributers, 2009), vol. 2, pp. 400–36.
74. Sarker, *A Companion to Philip Larkin*, vol. 2, pp. 437–93.
75. Sarker, *A Companion to Philip Larkin*, vol. 2, pp. 494–9.

6 NEWER APPROACHES TO LARKIN: THE 2010s

1. Gillian Steinberg, *Philip Larkin and His Audience* (Basingstoke: Palgrave Macmillan, 2010).
2. Steinberg, *Philip Larkin and His Audience*, p. xii.
3. Steinberg, *Philip Larkin and His Audience*, pp. 1–31.
4. Steinberg, *Philip Larkin and His Audience*, pp. 32–63.
5. Steinberg, *Philip Larkin and His Audience*, pp. 64–120.
6. Steinberg, *Philip Larkin and His Audience*, pp. 121–47.
7. Steinberg, *Philip Larkin and His Audience*, p. 147.
8. Sam Perry, '"Only in Dreams": Philip Larkin and Surrealism', *English* 59:224 (2010), pp. 95–119.
9. Daniel Weston, 'A Sustained Movement: Philip Larkin's Poetics of Consensus' *Textual Practice* 24.2 (2010), pp. 313–30.
10. M. W. Rowe, *Philip Larkin: Art and Self: Five Studies*. New York: Palgrave Macmillan, 2011, pp. 1–5.
11. Rowe, *Philip Larkin: Art and Self: Five Studies*, pp. 6–47.
12. Rowe, *Philip Larkin: Art and Self: Five Studies*, pp. 48–87.
13. Rowe, *Philip Larkin: Art and Self: Five Studies*, pp. 88–123.
14. Rowe, *Philip Larkin: Art and Self: Five Studies*, pp. 124–61.
15. Rowe, *Philip Larkin: Art and Self: Five Studies*, pp. 162–204.
16. Rowe, *Philip Larkin: Art and Self: Five Studies*, p. 199.
17. Peter Holbrook, 'Endless Mournings on Endless Faces: Shakespeare and Philip Larkin', *Shakespeare Survey* 64 (2011), pp. 328–39.
18. Holbrook, 'Endless Mournings on Endless Faces: Shakespeare and Philip Larkin', p. 338.

19. S. J. Perry, '"So unreal": The Unhomely Moment in the Poetry of Philip Larkin', *English Studies* 92.4 (2011), pp. 432–48.
20. Carol Atherton, 'Passing It On: Teaching and Learning Larkin" *Use of English* 62.2 (2011), pp. 99–108.
21. Francis O'Gorman, 'Larkin Hearing', *Literary Imagination* 14.1 (2012), pp. 35–45.
22. Graham MacPhee, 'Anticipating the Neoliberal Nation: Philip Larkin and the Displacement of Englishness' in *Literature of an independent England: Revisions of England, Englishness and English Literature.* (eds.) Claire Westall and Michael Gardiner (New York: Palgrave Macmillan, 2013), pp. 130–44.
23. Adam Piette, 'Childhood Wiped Out: Larkin, His Father, and the Bombing of Coventry', *English* 62.238 (2013), pp. 230–47.
24. John Osborne, *Radical Larkin: Seven Types of Technical Mastery* (New York: Palgrave Macmillan, 2014), pp. 1–20.
25. Osborne, *Radical Larkin: Seven Types of Technical Mastery*, pp. 21–47.
26. Osborne, *Radical Larkin: Seven Types of Technical Mastery*, pp. 48–81.
27. Osborne, *Radical Larkin: Seven Types of Technical Mastery*, pp. 81–112.
28. Osborne, *Radical Larkin: Seven Types of Technical Mastery*, p. 108.
29. Osborne, *Radical Larkin: Seven Types of Technical Mastery*, pp. 112–51.
30. Osborne, *Radical Larkin: Seven Types of Technical Mastery*, p. 132.
31. Osborne, *Radical Larkin: Seven Types of Technical Mastery*, pp. 151–77.
32. Osborne, *Radical Larkin: Seven Types of Technical Mastery*, pp. 178–201.
33. Osborne, *Radical Larkin: Seven Types of Technical Mastery*, pp. 211–12.
34. Osborne, *Radical Larkin: Seven Types of Technical Mastery*, pp. 220–7.
35. Osborne, *Radical Larkin: Seven Types of Technical Mastery*, pp. 227–37.
36. James Booth, *Philip Larkin: Life, Art and Love* (London: Bloomsbury, 2014).
37. Booth, *Philip Larkin: Life, Art and Love*, pp. 176, 300–1.
38. Booth, *Philip Larkin: Life, Art and Love*, pp. 313, 318.
39. Booth, *Philip Larkin: Life, Art and Love*, pp. 327–9, 332–4, 336–45.
40. Booth, *Philip Larkin: Life, Art and Love*, p. 374.
41. Peter Krahé, 'Philip Larkin, Solitary Man: From Splendid Isolation to Remorse and Fear', *Zeitschrift für Anglistik und Amerikanistik* 62:2 (2014), pp. 113–29.
42. Piers Pennington, 'Lines, Crossings, and Crossroads in Philip Larkin', English 63.243 (2014), pp. 276–95.
43. Ryan Hibbett, 'Philip Larkin, British Culture, and Four-letter Words', *Cambridge Quarterly* 43.2 (2014), pp. 125–6.
44. Hibbett, 'Philip Larkin, British Culture, and Four-letter Words', pp. 120–37.
45. Isván D. Racz, *Philip Larkin's Poetics: Theory and Practice of an English Post-war Poet* (Leiden: Brill Rodopi, 2016), pp. 1–32.
46. Racz, *Philip Larkin's Poetics: Theory and Practice of an English Post-war Poet*, pp. 32–52.
47. Racz, *Philip Larkin's Poetics: Theory and Practice of an English Post-war Poet*, pp. 53–66.
48. Racz, *Philip Larkin's Poetics: Theory and Practice of an English Post-war Poet*, pp. 67–82.
49. Racz, *Philip Larkin's Poetics: Theory and Practice of an English Post-war Poet*, pp. 84–5.
50. Racz, *Philip Larkin's Poetics: Theory and Practice of an English Post-war Poet*, pp. 85–114.
51. Racz, *Philip Larkin's Poetics: Theory and Practice of an English Post-war Poet*, pp. 115–214.

CONCLUSION

1. The first film, *Down Cemetery Road*, featured Larkin being interviewed by John Betjeman and was first broadcast as part of the BBC *Monitor* series in 1964. The second, part of LWT's *South Bank Show* series, was first broadcast in 1982. *Return to Larkinland* was first broadcast by the BBC in 2015.
2. Archie Burnett (ed.), *The Complete Poems of Philip Larkin* (London: Faber & Faber, 2012).

3. *The Cambridge Edition of the Works of Ben Jonson*, (eds.) Ian Donaldson, et al. 7 vols. (Cambridge: Cambridge University Press, 2012).
4. See R. Neil Scott, *Flannery O'Connor: An Annotated Reference Guide to Criticism* (Milledgeville: Timberlane, 2002) and, for example, John R. Roberts, *John Donne: An Annotated Bibliography of Modern Criticism: 1912-1967* (Columbia: University of Missouri Press, 1973) and Roberts's subsequent volumes.
5. R. Neil Scott and Irwin H. Streight, *Flannery O'Connor: The Contemporary Reviews* (Cambridge: Cambridge University Press, 2009).

Select Bibliography

LARKIN'S WORKS
Larkin, Philip. *All What Jazz: A Record Diary*. 2nd edn. London: Faber & Faber, 1985.
Larkin, Philip. *The Complete Poems of Philip Larkin*, ed. Archie Burnett. London: Faber and Faber, 2012.
Larkin, Philip. *Early Poems and Juvenilia*, ed. A. T. Tolley. London: Faber and Faber, 2005.
Larkin, Philip. *Further Requirements: Broadcasts, Statements, and Book Reviews 1952-1985*, ed. Anthony Thwaite. 2nd edn. London: Faber & Faber, 2002.
Larkin, Philip. 1947. *A Girl in Winter*. London: Faber & Faber, 1975.
Larkin, Philip. *High Windows*. London: Faber and Faber, 1974.
Larkin, Philip. *Jill*. 1946. London: Faber and Faber, 1975.
Larkin, Philip. *Larkin's Jazz: Essays and Reviews 1940-84*, ed. Richard Palmer and John White. London: Continuum, 2001.
Larkin, Philip. *The Less Deceived*. 1955. Hull: Marvell Press, 1955.
Larkin, Philip. *The North Ship*. London: Fortune, 1945.
Larkin, Philip. *Philip Larkin: Collected Poems*, ed. Anthony Thwaite. 1988. Rev. edn. London: Faber and Faber, 1990.
Larkin, Philip. *Philip Larkin: Collected Poems*, ed. Anthony Thwaite. Shorter edn. London: Faber & Faber, 2003.
Larkin, Philip. *Required Writing: Miscellaneous Pieces 1955-82*. London: Faber & Faber, 1983.
Larkin, Philip. *Trouble at Willow Gables and Other Fictions*, ed. James Booth. London: Faber & Faber, 2002.
Larkin, Philip. *The Whitsun Weddings*. London: Faber & Faber, 1964.
Larkin, Philip. *XX Poems*. Belfast: privately printed, 1951.

BIOGRAPHIES
Booth, James. *Philip Larkin: Life, Art and Love*. New York: Bloomsbury, 2014.
Bradford, Richard. *First Boredom, Then Fear: The Life of Philip Larkin*. London: Owen, 2005.
Bradford, Richard. *The Odd Couple: The Curious Friendship between Kingsley Amis and Philip Larkin*. London: Robson Press, 2012.
Brennan, Maeve. *The Philip Larkin I Knew*. Manchester, England: Manchester University Press, 2002.
Hartley, Jean. *Philip Larkin, The Marvell Press, and Me*. Manchester, England: Carcanet, 1989.
Motion, Andrew. *Philip Larkin: A Writer's Life*. London: Faber & Faber, 1993.

CORRESPONDENCE
Larkin, Philip. *Letters to Monica*, ed. Anthony Thwaite. London: Faber & Faber, 2010.
Larkin, Philip. *Selected Letters of Philip Larkin: 1940–1985*, ed. Anthony Thwaite. London: Faber & Faber, 1992.

BIBLIOGRAPHIES
Bloomfield, B. C. *Philip Larkin: A Bibliography, 1933-94*. London: Faber & Faber, 2002.

STUDENT HANDBOOKS
Brownjohn, Alan. *Philip Larkin*. London: Longman, 1975.
Cookson, Linda and Bryan Loughrey (eds.). *Critical Essays on Philip Larkin: The Poems*. London: Longman, 1989.
Gilroy, John. *Reading Philip Larkin: Selected Poems*. Tirril: HEB: Humanities-Ebooks, 2009.
Handley, Graham. *Brodie's Notes on Philip Larkin's Selected Poems*. London: Macmillan, 1991.
Hope, Warren. *Philip Larkin*. London: Greenwich Exchange, 1997.
Jones, Alison. *A Student's Guide to High Windows and the Poetry of Philip Larkin*. Oxford: Twin Serpents, 2009.
Lerner, Laurence. *Philip Larkin*. Plymouth, England: Northcote House, 1997.
Marsh, Nicholas. *Philip Larkin: The Poems*. Basingstoke: Macmillan, 2007.
Punter, David. *Philip Larkin: The Whitsun Weddings and Selected Poems*. London: Longman, 2003.
Punter, David. *York Notes on Selected Poems [by] Philip Larkin*. London: Longman, 1991.
Tandon, B. G. *Philip Larkin: A Critical Discussion of Selected Poems*. New Delhi: Spectrum, 2006.
Swarbrick, Andrew. *The Whitsun Weddings and The Less Deceived*. London: Macmillan, 1986.

1 LARKIN ARRIVES: THE 1950s AND 1960s
Cox, C.B. 'Philip Larkin'. *Critical Quarterly* 1 (1959): 14–17.
Gardner, Philip. 'The Wintry Drum: The Poetry of Philip Larkin'. *Dalhousie Review* 48 (1968): 88–99.
Jones, Alun R. 'The Poetry of Philip Larkin: A Note on Transatlantic Culture'. *Western Humanities Review* 16 (1962): 143–52.
Wain, John. 'Engagement or Withdrawal? Some Notes on the Work of Philip Larkin'. *Critical Quarterly* 6 (1964): 167–78.

2 LARKIN RISES: THE 1970s
Atlas, James. 'On Philip Larkin'. *The American Poetry Review* 6.4 (1977): 18–19.
Bedient, Calvin. *Eight Contemporary Poets: Charles Tomlinson, Donald Davie, R.S. Thomas, Philip Larkin, Ted Hughes, Thomas Kinsella, Stevie Smith, W.S. Graham*. London: Oxford University Press, 1974.
Bowen, Roger. 'Death, Failure, and Survival in the Poetry of Philip Larkin'. *Dalhousie Review* 58 (1978): 79–94.
Cox, C.B. 'Philip Larkin, Anti-Heroic Poet'. *Studies in the Literary Imagination* 9.1 (1976): 155–68.
Martin, Bruce. *Philip Larkin*. Twayne's English Author Series. Boston: Twayne, 1978.
Moon, Kenneth. 'Comic Perspective: A Use of Imagery in the Poetry of Philip Larkin'. *Poetry Australia* 68 (1978): 59–63.
Peschmann, Hermann. 'Philip Larkin: Laureate of the Common Man'. *English: The Journal of the English Association* 24 (1975): 49–58.
Press, John. 'The Poetry of Philip Larkin'. *Southern Review* 13 (1977): 131–46.

Press, John. 'W.B. Yeats, Thomas Hardy and Philip Larkin'. *Aligarh Journal of English Studies* 3 (1978): 153–65.
Scofield, Martin. 'The Poetry of Philip Larkin'. *Massachusetts Review: A Quarterly of Literature, the Arts and Public Affairs* 17.2 (1976): 370–89.
Timms, David. *Philip Larkin*. Edinburgh: Oliver and Boyd, 1973.
Weatherhead, A. Kingsley. 'Philip Larkin of England'. *English Literary History* 38:4 (1971): 616–30.

3 LARKIN TRIUMPHANT: THE 1980s

Bayley, John. 'On Philip Larkin'. *The New York Review of Books* 32 (1986): 21–2.
Beeton, Ridley. 'The Early Philip Larkin: A Manuscript Exploration'. *University of Cape Town Studies in English* 15 (1986): 35–65.
Blessington, Francis C. '"An Old-Type Natural Fouled-Up Guy": The Conflicting Voice in Philip Larkin'. In *The Motive for Metaphor: Essays on Modern Poetry*, ed. Francis C. Blessington and Guy L. Rotella, pp. 93-107. Boston, MA: Northeastern University Press, 1983.
Chambers, Harry. *'An enormous yes': In Memoriam Philip Larkin, 1922-1985*. Calstock, England: Peterloo Poets, 1986.
Chambers, Harry. 'Meeting Philip Larkin'. In *Larkin at Sixty*, ed. Anthony Thwaite, pp. 61–4. London, England: Faber, 1982.
Everett, Barbara. 'Philip Larkin: After Symbolism'. *Essays in Criticism: A Quarterly Journal of Literary Criticism* 30 (1980): 277–42.
Ford, Mary. 'Loneliness Clarifies: A Study of the Longer Poems of Philip Larkin'. *English Studies in Canada* 6 (1980): 323–32.
Goodby, John. '"The Importance of Being Elsewhere," or "No Man Is an Ireland": Self, Selves and Social Consensus in the Poetry of Philip Larkin'. *Critical Survey* 1.2 (1989): 131–8.
Hall, Donald. 'Philip Larkin 1922–1985'. *The New Criterion* 4.6 (1986): 10–12.
Hamburger, Michael. 'Philip Larkin: A Retrospect'. *PN Review* 14.4 (1987): 71–80.
Holt, Hazel. 'Philip Larkin and Barbara Pym: Two Quiet People'. In *Philip Larkin: The Man and His Work*, ed. Dale Salwak, pp. 59–68. Iowa City, IA: University of Iowa Press, 1989.
Jones, Willie. 'The Proper End of Life: Philip Larkin (1922-1985)'. *Language and Culture* 14 (1988): 25–65.
Lindop, Grevel. 'Being Different from Yourself: Philip Larkin in the 1970s'. In *British Poetry since 1970: A Critical Survey*, ed. Peter Jones and Michael Schmidt, pp. 46-54. New York: Persea, 1980.
Phillips, Robert. 'Philip Larkin: The Art of Poetry No. 30'. *Paris Review* 84 (1982): Electronic Publication.
Ponsford, Michael. 'Death, Dying and the Contemporary Sensibility of Philip Larkin'. *University of Windsor Review* 20.2 (1987): 13–25.
Pritchard, William H. 'Philip Larkin'. *Raritan: A Quarterly Review* 6.4 (1987): 62–80.
Reibetanz, John. 'Lyric Poetry as Self-Possession: Philip Larkin'. *University of Toronto Quarterly: A Canadian Journal of the Humanities* 54.3 (1985): 265–83.
Reibetanz, John. 'Philip Larkin: The Particular Vision of *The Whitsun Weddings*'. *Modern Language Quarterly: A Journal of Literary History* 43.2 (1982): 156–73.
Richman, Robert. 'The "Collected" Philip Larkin'. *The New Criterion* 7.8 (1989): 5–14.
Rossen, Janice. 'Philip Larkin Abroad'. In *Philip Larkin: The Man and His Work*, ed. Dale Salwak, pp. 48–53. Iowa City, IA: University of Iowa Press, 1989.

Rossen, Janice. *Philip Larkin: His Life's Work*. Iowa City, IA: University of Iowa Press, 1989.
Salwak, Dale, ed. *Philip Larkin: The Man and His Work*. Iowa City, IA: University of Iowa Press, 1989.
Singh, G. 'The Poetry of Philip Larkin'. *Aligarh Critical Miscellany* 1.1 (1988): 101–19.
Skinner, John. 'Philip Larkin by Philip Larkin'. *ARIEL: A Review of International English Literature* 20.1 (1989): 77–95.
Spurr, Barry. 'Alienation and Affirmation in the Poetry of Philip Larkin'. *Sydney Studies in English* 14.1 (1988): 52–71.
Thomas, Jane E., ed. 'Philip Larkin: Seven Verbal Snapshots'. Interviews by Maeve Brennan, Donald Campbell, Janet Duffin, Jean Hartley, Anthony Hedges, Peter Sheldon, Sue Wilsea. *Bête Noire* 5 (1988): 87–92.
Watson, J. R. 'Philip Larkin: Voices and Values'. In *Philip Larkin: The Man and His Work*, ed. Dale Salwak, pp. 90–111. Iowa City, IA: University of Iowa Press, 1989.
Watson, Stephen. 'Philip Larkin and the Situation of Poetry'. *Contrast: South African Literary Journal Cape Town, South Africa* 17.3 (1989): 12–31.
Whalen, Terry. *Philip Larkin and English Poetry*. Vancouver, BC: University of British Columbia Press, 1986.
Whalen, Terry. 'Philip Larkin: Detachment or Impersonality?' *The Critical Review* 23 (1981): 20–33.

4 LARKIN UNDER SIEGE: THE 1990s

Aisenberg, Katy. *Ravishing Images: Ekphrasis in the Poetry and Prose of William Wordsworth, W.H. Auden, and Philip Larkin*. In Series *American University Studies IV: English Language and Literature*. New York: Peter Lang, 1995.
Alderman, Nigel. '"The Life with a Hole in It": Philip Larkin and the Condition of England'. *Textual Practice* 18.2 (1994): 279–301.
Auberlen, Eckhard. 'The Theme of Death in the Poetry of Philip Larkin and Charles Tomlinson'. *Arbeiten aus Anglistik und Amerikanistik* 16.2 (1991): 175–203.
Banerjee, Amitava. 'Philip Larkin: Critic'. *Kobe College Studies* 42.3 (1996): 13–26.
Banerjee, Amitava. 'Philip Larkin: The Hunted Man behind the Haunting Poems'. *Kobe College Studies* 43.3 (1997): 1–16.
Bell, Vereen. '"Was It Bondage, Sir?": The Life of Philip Larkin'. *The Southern Review* 30.2 (1994): 358–63.
Booth, James. 'Philip Larkin: Lyricism, Englishness and Postcoloniality'. In *Philip Larkin*, ed. Stephen Regan, pp. 187–210. New York: St. Martin's, 1997.
Booth, James. *Philip Larkin: Writer*. New York: Harvester Wheatsheaf, 1992.
Bristow, Joseph. 'The Obscenity of Philip Larkin'. *Critical Inquiry* 21.1 (1994): 156–81.
Cauldwell, Richard. 'Openings, Rhythm and Relationships: Philip Larkin Reads Mr Bleaney'. *Language and Literature: Journal of the Poetics and Linguistics Association* 8.1 (1999): 35–48.
Craik, Roger. 'Changing Places: Philip Larkin as Train Traveler'. *University of Dayton Review* 24.1 (1996): 63–81.
Day, Gary. '"Never Such Language Again": The Poetry of Philip Larkin'. In *British Poetry from the 1950s to the 1990s: Politics and Art*, ed. Gary Day and Brian Docherty, pp. 33–47. London, England & New York: Macmillan & St. Martin's, 1997.
Everett, Barbara. 'Philip Larkin: After Symbolism'. In *Philip Larkin*, ed. Stephen Regan, pp. 55-70. New York: St. Martin's, 1997.
Everett, Barbara. 'The Treasurer's Son: Money, Worth, and the Inner Life in Philip Larkin'. *TLS: The Times Literary Supplement* 4929 (1997): 3–6.

Hassan, Salem K. 'Women in Philip Larkin'. *English Studies: A Journal of English Language and Literature* 77.2 (1996): 142–54.

Ingelbien, Raphael. '"England and Nowhere": Contestations of Englishness in Philip Larkin and Graham Swift'. *English: The Journal of the English Association* 48.190 (1999): 33–48.

Latane, David. 'Full Moon and Philip Larkin'. *English Language Notes* 34.3 (1997): 57–62.

Lerner, Laurence. *Philip Larkin*. Plymouth, England: Northcote House, with British Council, 1997.

Lodge, David. 'Philip Larkin: The Metonymic Muse'. In *Philip Larkin*, ed. Stephen Regan, pp. 71–82. New York: St. Martin's, 1997.

Moeyes, Paul. 'The Return to the Native: Time and Tradition in the Poetry of Philip Larkin'. In *In Black and Gold: Contiguous Traditions in Post-War British and Irish Poetry*, ed. C.C. Barfoot, pp. 95–117. Amsterdam: Rodopi, 1994.

Motion, Andrew. 'Philip Larkin and Symbolism'. In *Philip Larkin*, ed. Stephen Regan, pp. 32–54. New York: St. Martin's, 1997.

Pollitt, Katha. 'Philip Larkin'. *Grand Street* 9.3 (1990): 250–60.

Priestman, Judith. 'Philip Larkin and the Bodleian Library'. *Bodleian Library Record* 14.1 (1991): 30–66.

Punter, David. 'Philip Larkin: Humiliation and Survival'. In *In Black and Gold: Contiguous Traditions in Post-War British and Irish Poetry*, ed. C.C. Barfoot, pp. 119–35. Amsterdam: Rodopi, 1994.

Rácz, István D. 'Agnosticism, Masks and Monologues in Philip Larkin'. *Hungarian Journal of English and American Studies* 1.2 (1995): 93–120.

Rawlings, Peter. 'Philip Larkin and the Provincial Imperative'. *Studies in English Language and Literature* 4.7 (1997): 17–37.

Regan, Stephen, ed. *Philip Larkin*. New York: St. Martin's, 1997.

Ross, T. J. 'Getting to Know Philip Larkin: The Life and Letters'. *Literary Review: An International Journal of Contemporary Writing* 38.2 (1995): 292–94.

Ross, T. J. 'On Philip Larkin'. *Literary Review: An International Journal of Contemporary Writing* 37.1 (1993): 119–27.

Rossen, Janice. 'Philip Larkin and Lucky Jim'. *Journal of Modern Literature* 22.1 (1998): 147–64.

Salwak, Dale. 'Encountering Philip Larkin'. In *A Passion for Books*, ed. Dale Salwak, pp. 87–97. New York: St. Martin's, 1998.

Salwak, Dale. 'Sketches from Life: Philip Larkin – An American View'. *Biography: An Interdisciplinary Quarterly* 21.2 (1998): 195–205.

Smith, Adrian. 'The Coventry Factor: Philip Larkin and John Hewitt'. *Literature and History* 8.1 (1999): 34–55.

Swarbrick, Andrew. *Out of Reach: The Poetry of Philip Larkin*. New York: St. Martin's, 1995.

Tolley, A. T. *My Proper Ground: A Study of the Work of Philip Larkin and Its Development*. Ottawa, ON: Carleton University Press, 1991.

Verdonk, Peter. 'Poems as Text and Discourse: The Poetics of Philip Larkin'. In *Literary Pragmatics*, ed. Roger D. Sell, pp. 94–109. London, England: Routledge, 1991.

Volsik, Paul. '"The Essential Nexus": Philip Larkin and the Reader'. *Q/W/E/R/T/Y: Arts, Littératures & Civilisations du Monde Anglophone* 3 (1993): 155–9.

Watson, Stephen. 'Darkness Encroaching: Philip Larkin and the Situation of Poetry'. *Encounter* 74.3 (1990): 30–7.

Watt, R.J.C. (Ed.). *Philip Larkin: A Concordance to the Poetry of Philip Larkin*. New York: Olms-Weidmann, 1995.

Whalen, Terry. '"Strangeness Made Sense": Philip Larkin in Ireland'. *Antigonish Review* 107 (1996): 157–69.
Zieger, Agatha. 'Two Poets on Love and Work: Stevie Smith and Philip Larkin'. *Webster Review* 16 (1992): 88–98.

5 LARKIN TRIUMPHANT ONCE MORE: THE 2000s

Banville, John. 'Homage to Philip Larkin'. *New York Review of Books* 53.3 (2006): 20–3.
Booth, James. *Philip Larkin: The Poet's Plight*. Basingstoke, England: Palgrave Macmillan, 2005.
Bradford, Richard. *First Boredom, Then Fear: The Life of Philip Larkin*. London, England: Owen, 2005.
Brennan, Maeve. *The Philip Larkin I Knew*. Manchester, England: Manchester University Press, 2002.
Castle, Terry. 'The Lesbianism of Philip Larkin'. *Daedalus: Journal of the American Academy of Arts and Sciences* 136:2 (2007): 88–102.
Everett, Barbara. 'A Lethal Fall: Barbara Everett on Philip Larkin and Philip Marlowe'. *London Review of Books* 28.9 (2006): 13–16.
Gearey, Adam. 'The Poetics of Practical Reason: Joseph Raz and Philip Larkin'. *Law and Literature* 19.3 (2007): 377–99.
Gilpin, George H. 'Patricia Avis and Philip Larkin'. In *New Larkins for Old: Critical Essays*, ed. James Booth, pp. 66–78. Basingstoke, England & New York: Macmillan & St. Martin's, 2000.
Gilroy, John. *Philip Larkin: Selected Poems*. Penrith, England: Humanities Ebooks, 2009.
Harte, Liam. 'Living beyond the Severed Ends: Poetry of Louis MacNeice and Philip Larkin'. *Studies: An Irish Quarterly Review* 89.353 (2000): 45–53.
Hedgecock, Liz. 'New Worlds for Old: Mythology and Exile in the Novels of Philip Larkin'. In *New Larkins for Old: Critical Essays*, ed. James Booth, pp. 97–106. Basingstoke, England & New York: Macmillan & St. Martin's, 2000.
Isenberg, Steven L. 'Lunching on Olympus: My Meals with W. H. Auden, E. M. Forster, Philip Larkin, and William Empson'. *American Scholar* 78.1 (2009): 118–25.
Johnson, Rebecca. 'Trespassing: Philip Larkin and the Legacy of D. H. Lawrence'. *D. H. Lawrence Review* 29.3 (2000): 41–8.
King, Don W. 'Sacramentalism in the Poetry of Philip Larkin'. *Christian Scholar's Review* 39.1 (2009): 57–74.
Longino, Victoria. 'The Alien Moment: Philip Larkin and Gender'. *Hungarian Journal of English and American Studies* 9.2 (2003): 91–104.
McKeown, Andrew. 'The Metaphysical Joke: Church Going with Philip Larkin'. In *Ecstasy and Understanding: Religious Awareness in English Poetry from the Late Victorian to the Modern Period*, ed. Adrian Grafe, pp. 135–44. London, England: Continuum, 2008.
Osborne, John. 'Postmodernism and Postcolonialism in the Poetry of Philip Larkin'. In *New Larkins for Old: Critical Essays*, ed. James Booth, pp. 144–65. Basingstoke, England & New York: Macmillan & St. Martin's, 2000.
Palmer, Richard. 'Philip Larkin & Vincent Van Gogh: Congruences'. *Use of English* 59.1 (2007): 29–46.
Phillips, Robert. 'Philip Larkin: The Art of Poetry'. In *The Paris Review Interviews, Vol. II*, ed. Philip Gourevitch, trans. Maureen Freely, pp. 207–36. New York: Picador, 2007.
Rácz, István D. 'The Experience of Reading and Writing Poetry: Auden and Philip Larkin'. *Hungarian Journal of English and American Studies* 14.1 (2008): 95–103.
Regan, Stephen. 'Philip Larkin: A Late Modern Poet'. In *The Cambridge Companion to Twentieth-Century English Poetry*, ed. Neil Corcoran, pp. 147–58. Cambridge, England: Cambridge University Press, 2007.

Rowland, Antony. 'A Case of Plagiarism? Philip Larkin and Ted Hughes'. *Hungarian Journal of English and American Studies* 9.2 (2003): 53–61.
Soccio, Anna Enrichetta. 'Scenes from Urban Life: Philip Larkin and the City'. *Merope* 17.49–50 (2006): 35–45.
Thomas, Francis-Noel. 'Philip Larkin, Barbara Pym, and the Accident of Literary Fame'. *New England Review: Middlebury Series* 27.2 (2006): 8–26.
Thwaite, Anthony, ed. *Philip Larkin: Further Requirements: Interviews, Broadcasts, Statements and Book Reviews, 1942–85*. Ann Arbor, MI: University of Michigan Press, 2004.
Updike, John. 'Twice Collected: The Well-Cared-for Poems of Philip Larkin'. *New Yorker* 80.20 (2004): 84–8.
Whalen, Terry. "Philip Larkin and *Lady Chatterley's Lover*'. In *New Larkins for Old: Critical Essays*, ed. James Booth, pp. 107–20. Basingstoke, England & New York: Macmillan & St. Martin's, 2000.

6 NEWER APPROACHES TO LARKIN: THE 2010s

Booth, James. *Philip Larkin: Life, Art and Love*. New York: Bloomsbury, 2014.
Francis, Matthew. '"A Difficult Home": Work, Love and Community in the Poetry of W.S. Graham and Philip Larkin'. *English Studies: A Journal of English Language and Literature* 94.5 (2013): 535–61
Hibbett, Ryan. 'Philip Larkin, British Culture, and Four-letter Words'. *Cambridge Quarterly* 43.2 (2014): 120–38.
Hodgkins, Christopher. 'In a Serious House: Church-Going with George Herbert and Philip Larkin'. In *George Herbert's Travels: International Print and Cultural Legacies*, ed. Christopher Hodgkins, pp. 207–23. Newark, DE: University of Delaware Press, 2011.
Krahé, Peter. 'Philip Larkin, Solitary Man: From Splendid Isolation to Remorse and Fear'. *Zeitschrift für Anglistik und Amerikanstik: A Quarterly of Language, Literature and Culture* 62.2 (2014): 113–29.
Marks, Peter. 'Money, "Money", Money: Cultural Transactions between Philip Larkin and Martin Amis". *Sydney Studies in English* 37 (2011): 71–91.
Osborn, Pamela. '"The Priest and the Doctor": Medical Mystique as a Substitute for Religious Authority in the Work of Barbara Pym and Philip Larkin'. *Women: A Cultural Review* 25.4 (2014): 384–94.
Pennington, Piers. 'Lines, Crossings, and Crossroads in Philip Larkin'. *English: The Journal of the English Association* 63.243 (2014): 276–95.
Perry, S.J. '"So Unreal": The Unhomely Moment in the Poetry of Philip Larkin'. *English Studies: A Journal of English Language and Literature* 92.4 (2011): 432–48.
Perry, Sam. '"Only in Dreams": Philip Larkin and Surrealism'. *English: The Journal of the English Association* 59.224 (2010): 95–119.
Rowe, M.W. *Philip Larkin: Art and Self: Five Studies*. New York: Palgrave Macmillan, 2011.
Rowland, Antony. 'A Case for Pastiche? Ted Hughes and Philip Larkin'. *PN Review* 41.4[222] (2015): 52–4.
Steinberg, Gilliam. *Philip Larkin and His Audience*. Basingstoke, England: Palgrave Macmillan, 2010.
Waterman, Rory. *Belonging and Estrangement in the Poetry of Philip Larkin, R.S. Thomas and Charles Causley*. Farnham, England: Ashgate, 2014.
West, Robert. '"Here's the Church, Here's the Steeple": Robert Morgan, Philip Larkin, and the Emptiness of Sacred Space'. *Southern Quarterly: A Journal of the Arts in the South* 47.3 (2010): 91–7.
Wootten, William. '"Gold As on a Coin": Philip Larkin and Vernon Watkins after The North Ship'. *PN Review* 39.4[210] (2013): 73–5.

Index

Ackroyd, Peter, 83, 151
age, 5, 6, 17, 48–9, 56, 68, 78, 100, 136
ageing, 1, 6, 45, 62, 83, 99, 134, 135, 137
Alderman, Nigel, 87, 91, 151, 160
alienation, 13, 40, 42, 46, 51, 59, 67, 71, 77, 111
Allott, Kenneth, 16
allusions, 28, 42, 44, 50, 93, 97, 123, 130, 138
Alvarez, A., 12, 143
America, 10, 11, 13–14, 21–3, 38–9, 41–4, 47, 53, 55, 59, 66, 91–2, 97, 105, 140, 144–7, 151, 153, 156, 158, 160–63 [see also 'United States']
Amis, Kingsley, 2, 4, 8, 31, 44, 52, 61, 66, 74, 78, 92, 131–2, 157, 163
Arnold, Matthew, 29, 146
Atherton, Carol, 124, 157
Atlas, James, 42, 145, 158
Auden, W. H., 8, 16, 28, 30, 36, 51, 71, 73, 76, 78–80, 83, 88, 101, 103, 129, 133–4, 154, 160, 162
audience(s), 5, 11, 27, 42, 56, 85, 94, 107–08, 117, 119
Austen, Jane, 55

Barnes, William, 31
Baron, Michael, 91, 151
Bayley, John, 33–4, 66, 145, 148, 150, 159
beauty, 13, 30, 47, 54, 57–60, 65, 72, 79, 95, 105, 109, 123–4, 133
Bedient, Calvin, 38, 145, 158
Bennett, Alan, 52, 83, 90, 133, 151
Bergonzi, Bernard, 42, 145
Berryman, John, 32
Betjeman, John, 22, 31, 53, 55, 74, 76, 78, 146
Bloomfield, B. C., 52, 158
blues, 29, 31, 64, 92–3, 131

Bogan, Louise, 21–2, 143
Booth, James, 7, 77–9, 91–2, 95, 97–8, 100–07, 131–2, 142, 150–57, 160, 162–3
Bowen, Roger, 43, 146, 158
Bowman, Ruth, 3, 103
Bradford, Richard, 7, 104–5, 142, 154, 157, 162
Brennan, Maeve, 66, 103, 157, 160, 162
Brewer, Derek, 11, 142
Bristow, Joseph, 86–7, 91, 151, 160
Britain, 1, 2, 5, 12, 15, 21, 30, 35, 40, 42–4, 55, 58, 62, 74, 76, 80, 83–4, 86–8, 92–3, 97, 99, 125, 129, 133, 140, 142–4, 146–7, 150–1, 157, 159, 160–63 [see also 'England']
Brooke, Rupert, 43
Browning, Robert, 35, 39, 55
Brownjohn, Alan, 34, 145, 158
Burnett, Archie, 116, 138, 157
Byron, George Gordon, Lord, 63

Carduff, Christopher, 83, 151
Carey, John, 24, 95, 144, 151
Chambers, Harry, 33, 52, 145, 159
Christianity, 16, 96, 134
Clark, Steve, 87, 91, 97, 151, 153
class, 3, 5, 10–11, 21, 68, 79–81, 92, 96, 101, 125, 132–3, 137, 140
Clucas, Humphrey, 35, 145
Cohen, J. M., 24, 144
colloquial language, 9, 14, 23, 32, 35–6, 38, 45, 51, 58–9, 71, 94, 99, 112, 124, 136
community, 58, 80–1, 92, 96, 117, 133, 137
compassion, 13, 21, 25, 27, 36, 40, 42, 45, 52, 57
complexity, 2, 4, 21, 29, 36–7, 46, 49, 51, 57, 65–6, 73, 79, 86, 107, 110, 117–18, 120, 123, 125–7

164

INDEX 165

Conquest, Robert, 4, 52
conservativism, 5, 26, 32, 34, 40–41, 58–9, 65, 74, 79, 81, 92, 97, 104, 125
consolation, 2, 41, 134
Cookson, Linda, 64–5, 148, 158
Cooper, Stephen, 100–02, 106, 153–4
Covey, Neil, 85, 151
Cox, C. B., 13, 41, 143, 145, 158
Craik, Roger, 99, 153, 160
Curtis, Anthony, 66
Cushman, David, 47, 146

Davie, Donald, 9, 15, 30, 142–5, 158
Dawes, Edwin A., 66
Day, Gary, 92, 151, 160
Day, Roger, 65, 114
death, 1, 5–7, 11, 13, 20–21, 23, 26, 29, 39, 43, 45, 48–9, 51, 54, 56–7, 60, 62, 66, 68, 72–3, 75, 78–9, 83, 87–8, 90–93, 98, 104, 106, 108, 109, 111, 113–14, 117–18, 121–3, 129–37
depression, 6, 54, 61, 67
Dickey, James, 41
Dickey, William, 21,143
Dickinson, Emily, 91, 140
disappointment, 1, 5, 26, 29, 47, 57, 72–3, 83, 137
Dodsworth, Martin, 21, 92, 143
doubt, 54, 66–7, 112, 128
Draper, Ronald, 65, 148
Dunn, Douglas, 52

Eliot, T. S., 4, 8, 17, 39, 54, 62, 75, 90, 96–8, 106–7, 118, 123, 126, 129, 131, 153–4
Elliott, Roger, 56, 147
England, 2–6, 11, 15, 17, 21–2, 27–8, 30, 33, 38, 41–2, 47–8, 53, 55, 66–7, 70, 80, 85, 87, 89, 91, 99, 106, 114, 123–4, 128, 136–7, 140–8, 151, 153, 157–63 [*see also* 'Britain']
Enright, D. J., 24, 61, 144
Epstein, Joseph, 86, 151
Everett, Barbara, 49, 52, 66, 79, 90, 94, 119–20, 146, 148, 151, 159–62
existentialism, 131

Faggen, Robert, 71, 150
failure, 26, 42, 67, 72, 88, 123, 131
Falck, Colin, 18–19, 143
Falzon, Alex, R., 98, 153
fate, 30, 52, 60
Faulkner, William, 27, 144
fear, 11, 26, 51, 54, 67, 72–3, 87, 117–18
female, 91, 95–6, 100, 134
Filkins, Peter, 71, 150
Fitzgerald, Penelope, 83–4, 151
foreign matters, 33, 64, 71, 105
form, 11, 17, 19, 21–2, 31, 33, 35, 44–5, 47, 49, 51, 54, 68, 71, 73, 85, 97, 100, 110, 112, 121, 138, 139
Fraser, G. S., 12–14, 143
Frost, Robert, 31, 39, 54, 66, 131, 140
frustration, 67–8, 78

Gardiner, Alan, 65, 148
Gardiner, Michael, 157
Gardner, Philip, 26–7, 33, 144, 158
Garland, Patrick, 71, 150
Gearin-Tosh, Michael, 65, 148
gender, 68, 96, 100–01, 108, 112, 119, 127, 130, 137
Gibson, Andrew, 64, 148
Gilpin, George H., 95–6, 151, 162
Gioia, Dana, 83–4, 151
Goethals, Helen, 106, 154
Goodby, John, 62, 147, 159
Graves, Robert, 25, 27
Groves, Peter, 99, 153
Grubb, Frederick, 24, 33, 144–5
Gunn, Thom, 8, 21, 25–6, 59, 61

Hall, Donald, 54, 66, 147–8, 159
Hallsmith, Harvey, 65, 148
Hamilton, Ian, 18, 83–4, 143, 151
Handley, Graham, 73, 150, 158
Hardy, Thomas, 3, 8, 10, 13, 17, 23–8, 30, 31, 33, 35, 39–44, 49–51, 55, 57, 67, 71, 73, 78–80, 83, 88, 96, 100, 111, 113, 129, 133–7, 140, 144, 153, 159
Harmon, William, 71–2, 150
Hartley, Anthony, 142
Hartley, George, 8–9, 33, 38–9, 145
Hartley, Jean, 157, 160

Hassan, Salem K., 60–1, 89, 147, 151, 161
Heaney, Seamus, 43, 59, 79, 90–1, 97, 127, 140, 146, 153
Hedgecock, Liz, 96, 151, 162
Hibbett, Ryan, 132–3, 157, 163
Hilliard, Stephen S., 39, 145
Hirsch, Edward, 84, 151
history, 10, 18, 33, 43, 51, 63, 79, 103, 108, 116, 140, 159, 161
Hobsbaum, Philip, 17, 18, 55, 143, 147
Holbrook, Peter, 122–3, 156
Holdefer, Charles, 105, 154
Holderness, Graham, 65–6, 90, 148
Hollindale, Peter, 65, 148
Holloway, John, 10, 142
Holt, Hazel, 66, 159
Hope, Francis, 20, 143
Hope, Warren, 89–90, 151, 158
Hopkins, Gerard Manley, 29
Housman, A. E., 10, 20, 31, 39, 71, 76, 150
Hughes, Ted, 8, 31, 33, 52, 59, 66, 140, 158, 163
humour, 38–9, 57, 60, 71, 86, 89, 97, 106, 114, 129, 137, 150

images, 16, 19, 43, 45, 46–7, 59, 77, 132, 134
Ingelbien, Raphaîl, 96, 99–100, 105, 153–4, 161
irony, 11–12, 15, 26, 30, 34, 45, 57, 59, 62, 67, 73–7, 88, 111, 114, 124
Isherwood, Chistopher, 73

Jacobson, Dan, 34, 104, 145, 154
James, Clive, 34, 84–5, 145, 151
James, M. R., 121
Jarrell, Randall, 39, 59, 131
jazz, 2, 5, 29, 44, 64, 66, 68, 75, 87, 92–4, 97, 100, 112–13, 118–19, 124, 131, 138
Jennings, Elizabeth, 24, 59, 144
Johnson, 55, 58, 162
Jones, Alun, 13, 25, 33, 143–4
Jones, David, 136
Jones, Monica, 3, 103
Jones, Peter, 146
Joyce, James, 101

Kell, Richard, 24, 144
Kennedy, X. J., 54, 66, 147, 148
Kerrigan, William, 92, 151
Kipling, Rudyard, 31
Kissick, Gary, 86, 151
Krahé, Peter, 132, 157, 163
Kuby, Lolette, 35–8, 145

language, 1, 11, 16, 20–21, 25, 27, 30, 32–3, 35–7, 40, 42, 46, 59, 62, 64–5, 68, 72, 80, 82, 88, 105, 106–7, 114, 122–3, 129, 132–3
Larkin, Philip
  biography, 7, 70, 82–3, 85–7, 92, 94, 98, 101, 117, 136
  edited by: *Oxford Book of Twentieth Century English Verse*, 5
  literary 'development' of, 10–11, 14, 16, 21, 28, 30–2, 40, 44–6, 74, 80, 89, 94, 96, 100, 108, 114, 120, 122
  poems and poetry by:
    'Afternoons', 19
    'Ambulance, The', 23
    'Ambulances', 78
    'An April Sunday brings the snow', 89, 98
    'An Arundel Tomb', 22, 55, 87, 95, 104, 120, 127, 131
    'Arrival', 130
    'At Grass', 18, 41, 74, 127, 131
    'Aubade', 2, 6, 49, 60, 92–3, 108, 113, 122, 130–31
    'Building, The', 2, 34, 35, 39, 49, 131
    'Card-Players, The', 46, 127
    'Church Going', 2, 10–16, 18, 20, 22, 27, 32, 39, 49, 56–7, 67, 74, 90, 106–07, 120–21, 127–8, 131, 133, 137, 141, 162
    Collected Poems, 6, 70–71, 142, 150, 157
    'Coming', 106, 130
    'Deceptions', 74
    'Dockery and Son', 22, 74, 132
    'Dry Point', 33
    'Explosion, The', 2, 58, 64, 75, 89, 95
    'Faith Healing', 74, 118
    'Going', 26, 98, 106, 112, 130
    'High Windows', 89, 133

INDEX

High Windows, 1, 5, 6, 33–5, 38–42, 47–8, 51, 60–1, 66, 75, 79–83, 88, 90, 95, 100, 109, 113, 122, 132, 142, 145, 156–58
In the Grip of Light, 3, 96, 146, 152
Less Deceived, The, 1, 4, 8–10, 18–20, 22, 26–7, 29, 31–2, 35, 42, 46–8, 50, 59–60, 62, 75, 80, 88, 90, 100, 106, 109, 113, 132, 142, 157–8
'Lines on a Young Lady's Photograph Album', 15, 55
'Money', 94
'Mr. Bleaney', 9, 22, 32, 74, 90, 97, 104
'Myxomatosis', 24
'Naturally the Foundation Will Bear Your Expenses', 33, 64, 75
'Next, Please', 12, 18, 50, 132
North Ship, The, 3, 5, 24, 26, 28, 31, 41–2, 46–7, 50, 60, 67, 80, 88, 101, 109, 132, 142, 157, 163
'Poetry of Departures', 106, 130, 132
'Reasons for Attendance', 74, 130
'Show Saturday', 58, 131
'Sunny Prestatyn', 78, 86, 132
'The Old Fools', 2, 35, 39, 49, 75, 89, 90, 131
'This Be the Verse', 48, 95
'To the Sea', 58
'Verse de Société', 130
'Wedding Wind', 27, 29
'Whitsun Weddings, The', 2, 18–20, 24, 32, 47, 52, 58, 68, 74, 85, 118, 120, 128–9, 141
Whitsun Weddings, The, 1, 8, 16–19, 21–3, 26, 29, 32, 35, 51, 59–60, 62, 74–5, 80, 82, 85, 88, 90, 95, 100, 104, 109, 113, 120, 143, 147–48, 157–9
XX Poems, 3, 142, 157
prose by:
All What Jazz, 5, 142, 157
Girl in Winter, A, 3, 73, 101, 113, 126, 128, 142, 157
Jill, 2–3, 73, 96, 101, 110, 113, 128, 142, 157
Selected Letters, 6, 77–8, 81–3, 85–6, 94, 98, 101–2, 151

Latré, Guido, 53–6, 147
Lawrence, D. H., 19, 27, 58, 81, 88, 96, 103, 129
Leggett, B. J., 92–3, 151
Lerner, Laurence, 62, 90, 147, 151, 158, 161
Lindop, Grevel, 48–9, 146, 159
Lodge, David, 42, 66, 90, 146, 148, 161
loneliness, 1, 51–2, 62, 92, 110
Longino, Victoria, 100, 153, 162
Longley, Edna, 33, 95, 144, 151
Loughrey, Bryan, 64–5, 148, 158
love, 1–4, 6, 10, 13, 19, 21, 25–6, 29, 31–2, 37, 45, 52, 58, 60, 64–6, 71–2, 75, 80, 85, 87, 92, 96, 102–03, 106, 113, 115, 123, 130, 137, 141
Lowell, Robert, 21, 27, 32, 59
Lucie-Smith, Edward, 40, 145

Mackareth, Betty, 103
MacNeice, Louis, 63, 73, 80, 101, 154, 162
MacPhee, Graham, 124, 125, 157
male gender, 91, 95, 96, 100, 101, 125 [*see also* 'men']
Martin, Bruce, 44–6, 66, 146, 148, 158
Martz, Louis, 22, 143
Marvell, Andrew, 22, 142, 157
McCormick, John, 86, 151
McIntyre, John P., 41–2, 145
McKeown, Andrew, 99, 105, 153, 154, 162
McSweeney, Kerry, 39, 145
memory, 17, 22, 38, 53, 106, 114, 118–19
men, 56–7, 68, 78, 100, 110, 121, 129, 139 [*see also* 'male gender']
metaphor, 19, 53, 56, 114
metre, 5, 13, 20, 25, 32–3, 43, 45–6, 50, 71–2, 110, 114, 122
Miller, Christopher, 52, 53, 146
Modernism, 4, 5, 31, 35, 44, 49, 50, 75, 76, 79, 87, 97–8, 100, 104, 106, 110, 113, 117, 126, 129, 131, 134, 136–8 142, 146, 150, 153
Molony, Rowland, 81, 150
monologue, 83
Monteith, Charles, 52
Moon, Kenneth, 43, 146, 158, 161

Moore, Geoffrey, 12, 89, 142
mortality, 54, 57, 60
Motion, Andrew, 7, 51–2, 79, 82–3, 85, 86, 90, 92, 94, 98, 101, 124, 136, 142, 146–7, 150, 151, 157, 161
'Movement, The', 4, 8–12, 14–15, 31, 35, 40, 42–3, 74, 76, 82, 88, 104, 113, 137, 142, 144, 150, 156
Murphy, Richard, 9, 38, 142, 145
mutability, 1, 10, 20, 35, 37, 45, 47, 52, 59–61, 66, 123, 137

Naremore, James, 35, 145
Nassif, Jacques, 105, 154
nationalism, 91, 99, 101, 103
nature, 19, 36–7, 40–1, 43, 45, 47, 51, 58, 60–1, 67–8, 76, 83, 96, 98, 104–5, 108–9, 112, 114, 137–8
Newton, J. M., 23, 24, 33, 144
Nimmo, David C., 39, 145
nostalgia, 22, 33, 63, 65, 118

O'Brien, Flann, 89
O'Connor, Flannery, 139, 158
O'Connor, William Van, 11–12, 142
O'Gorman, Francis, 124, 157
O'Hara, Frank, 43
Osborne, John, 97, 100, 111–12, 117, 125–31, 140, 153, 156–7, 162
Osterwalder, Hans, 76, 150
Owen, Wilfred, 31

Paulin, Tom, 70–1, 82, 90–1, 126–7, 150
Pearson, Norman Holmes, 21, 143
Pelizzon, V. Penelope, 97, 153
Pennington, Piers, 132, 157, 163
Perquin, Jean-Charles, 105, 154
Perry, Sam (S. J.), 119, 123, 156–7, 163
Peschmann, Hermann, 40, 145, 158
pessimism, 23–6, 35, 40, 60, 73
Petch, Simon, 49–51, 146
philosophy, 38, 74, 107
phrasing, 1, 14, 21, 32, 74, 102, 127
Piette, Adam, 125, 157
Plath, Sylvia, 32, 91
political, 12, 32, 34, 40–1, 43, 45, 48, 55, 62, 78–81, 87, 89–93, 97–9, 102–03, 106–07, 112, 116, 119, 121, 127–8, 131, 134, 136, 140

Pollitt, Katha, 71, 150, 161
Pope, Alexander, 55
pornography, 7
postmodernism, 63, 97, 112
Pound, Ezra, 4, 8, 14, 62, 85, 105, 118, 136, 140
Praed, Winthrop Mackworth, 35
Press, John, 15, 42, 143
Pritchard, William H., 39, 59–60, 66, 145, 147–8, 159
Procopiow, Norma, 43–4
psychology, 36–7, 57, 67–8, 113, 116, 118–19
Punter, David, 73, 150, 158, 161
Pym, Barbara, 66, 76, 91, 159, 163

Raban, Jonathan, 82, 84, 150, 151
racism, 7, 81, 83–4, 86, 113, 131
Rácz, István D., 97, 105, 133–5, 153–4, 161–2
reactionary attitudes, 81, 86, 101
readers, 1, 4, 6, 7, 9, 11–12, 14, 19–22, 24, 26–7, 29, 32, 34, 38–9, 41–3, 45, 47–50, 55–7, 59–61, 66, 74–5, 77, 81–2, 85, 87, 89–90, 92–4, 108–9, 110, 113, 115–21, 124–6, 128, 135–9, 141
realism, 15, 19–20, 38, 40, 45, 50, 52–3, 56, 59, 62, 73, 89, 95
Regan, Stephen, 78–81, 90–1, 96, 110, 150–2, 156, 160–2
Reibetanz, Jonathan, 53, 147, 159
relationships, 21, 59, 73, 87, 103, 107, 114, 116, 121, 137
reputation, 6, 11, 15–17, 20, 25, 41, 52–3, 59, 70, 82, 91, 93, 94, 130, 136
rhyme, 5, 20, 36, 45, 50–1, 54, 60, 71–3, 86, 105–6, 110, 112
rhythms, 1, 11, 17, 19, 32, 36, 51, 54, 59, 99, 105, 106, 110
Richardson, James, 71, 81, 150
Richman, Robert, 54, 147, 159
Ricks, Christopher, 23, 29, 33, 143
Rochester, John Wilmot, Earl of, 63
Roethke, Theodore, 21
Romanticism, 4, 8, 10, 35, 38, 45, 50, 72, 76, 79, 88, 98, 100, 106, 114, 150

Roper, Derek, 14, 143
Rosenthal, M. L., 13, 15, 25, 33, 41, 143, 144
Ross, T. J., 85, 151, 161
Rossen, Janice, 66–9, 77–8, 90, 92, 148–9, 151, 159–61
Rossetti, Christina, 31, 91
Rowe, M. W., 62, 96, 120–2, 147, 151, 156, 163

Saladyga, Michael, 53, 146
Salwak, Dale, 66, 92, 147–8, 151, 159–61
Saunders, John, 65, 148
scepticism, 38, 57, 63, 65–6, 69, 79, 96–7, 101–2, 105
Scofield, Martin, 41, 92, 145, 151, 159
Semblatt, Martine, 105, 106, 154
Sergeant, Howard, 11, 142
sex, 66, 72, 81–2, 87–8, 91, 104, 130
sexism, 7, 68, 81, 100
Silkin, Jon, 16, 143
Skinner, John, 64, 148, 160
Smith, Adrian, 161
Smith, Peter Macdonald, 63, 77, 91, 147, 150
Smith, Stan, 90, 98–99, 153
Smith, Stevie, 76, 158, 162
Snowdon, Peter, 77, 150
society, 30, 36, 41, 49, 51–2, 58, 65–8, 73, 77, 79, 81, 88, 91, 96, 98, 101–2, 107, 110, 113, 121, 131–2, 141
sounds, 1, 61, 63, 82, 90, 99, 122, 124
speaker(s), poetic, 12, 15, 24, 29, 31, 33–4, 41, 45, 47, 50, 57, 66–7, 74, 104, 107–8, 117–8, 123, 128, 133
Spender, Stephen, 73
Spurr, Barry, 62, 147, 160
Stafford, William, 22, 143
Steinberg, Gillian, 116–19, 156, 163
Stevens, Wallace, 118
Strang, Patsy, 3, 103
structure, poetic, 10–11, 21, 25, 45, 49, 59, 109–10, 122
style, 3–5, 8, 17, 19, 21–3, 26, 28, 30–3, 35–6, 38–9, 42, 45–6, 55, 58–9, 62, 65, 71–3, 75–6, 78, 83, 89, 94–8, 101–02, 105, 107–8, 112, 114, 120, 131–2, 136–7

Sutton, James, 101
Swarbrick, Andrew, 59, 87–9, 91, 124, 147, 151, 158, 161
symbolism, 36, 40, 48–9, 51, 53, 56, 73, 78, 96, 119–20
Symbolism, 76, 79, 82, 98, 116, 119, 120
syntax, 18, 46, 59, 114, 144

Ten Eyck, David, 106, 154
Tennyson, Alfred, Lord, 51
themes, 1, 5, 8–10, 17, 26, 28–36, 38, 42–3, 45, 49–51, 56–7, 59–60, 71, 73, 78–9, 89–91, 95–6, 108, 110, 114, 120, 134
Thomas, Dylan, 4, 8, 16, 28, 31, 33, 35, 39, 52, 54, 65, 78, 79, 88, 113, 131, 144, 159, 160
Thomas, Edward, 33, 39, 43, 51, 96, 131, 144
Thomas, Francis Noel, 163
Thomas, Jane E., 160
Thomas, R. S., 59, 158
Thwaite, Anthony, 6, 16, 20–1, 28–9, 33, 51–2, 70–1, 76, 142–4, 146, 157, 159, 163
Tierce, Mike, 56
time, 2, 5–7, 10, 13–16, 22–3, 25–6, 28–9, 31–2, 34, 36–8, 40, 42–5, 48, 52–3, 56–8, 60–1, 66, 74–5, 79–81, 91, 99, 103, 105, 111, 114, 118–9, 122, 130, 133–7
Timms, David, 30–3, 38, 144, 159
Tolley, A. T., 53, 73–6, 90, 146, 150–1, 157, 161
Tomlinson, Charles, 10–11, 15, 20, 27, 59, 142–3, 158, 160
tone, 5, 8–12, 16–17, 19, 25–6, 28–32, 36, 41–2, 46–8, 50, 56–7, 59, 61–2, 65–6, 75, 83, 85, 92, 114, 122, 131–2, 137
tradition, 25, 28, 35, 58, 87, 107, 123, 130
Trengove-Jones, Tim, 71, 81–2, 150

Underhill, Hugh, 63, 148
United States, 10, 23, 28, 42, 47, 86 [see also 'America']

voice, 11, 13, 16, 20, 29, 36–8, 46, 48, 57, 59, 66, 74, 95, 108, 124, 129, 133, 136

Volsik, Paul, 85–6, 151, 161

Wain, John, 8, 10, 20–1, 42–3, 55, 61, 142–3, 146–7, 158
Ward, David C., 92, 146, 151
Watson, George, 61, 147
Watson, J. R., 39, 63–6, 145, 160
Watson, Stephen, 72–3, 150, 161
Watts, Cedric, 64, 148
Weatherhead, A. Kingsley, 29–30, 144, 159
Welz, Dieter, 30, 144
Weston, Daniel, 119–20, 156
Whalen, Terry, 56–9, 89, 96, 147, 160, 162–3
Whalen, Tom, 151
White, John, 66, 157
Wilbur, Richard, 27, 41
Wilde, Oscar, 85, 89, 131
Williams, William Carlos, 20, 118

women, 6, 7, 65, 68–9, 77–8, 84, 86–7, 89, 91, 95–6, 100–3, 110, 121–2, 129
Wooley, John, 55
words, 1, 6, 12, 20–2, 27, 29–30, 34, 45–6, 51, 54, 60–1, 64, 66, 77, 98–9, 102, 108, 110, 112, 122, 125, 127, 132
Wordsworth, William, 14, 23, 35, 51, 64, 113, 160
Wright, Stuart, 84, 85, 151

Yeats, W. B., 2–3, 8, 10, 24, 28–9, 31, 33, 40, 42, 44, 47–8, 50, 51, 54–5, 62, 64, 67, 71, 73, 74, 78–80, 82–3, 85, 87–90, 96, 98, 100, 133, 135, 137, 140, 153, 159
Young, David, 54, 147

Zinnes, Harriet, 23, 143

www.ingramcontent.com/pod-product-compliance
Lightning Source LLC
Chambersburg PA
CBHW070332230426
43663CB00011B/2286